# Discovering Oak Island

## Camera-in-Hand

Kevin Seifert

*and* Linda Seifert

*Discovering Oak Island: Camera-in-Hand*

Photoendeavors, LLC
kevinseifertphotography.com

Published 2015, by Torchflame Books
an Imprint of Light Messages

www.lightmessages.com
Durham, NC 27713 USA
SAN: 920-9298

ISBN: 978-1-61153-143-5



This book's authors particularly want to apologize *a priori* for any behavorial changes among Oak Island's residents, animal, plant, or mineral. Shore birds, for example, have no contractual obligation to remain roosting, breeding, or nesting where they have done so historically. One hurricane can change everything dramatically.

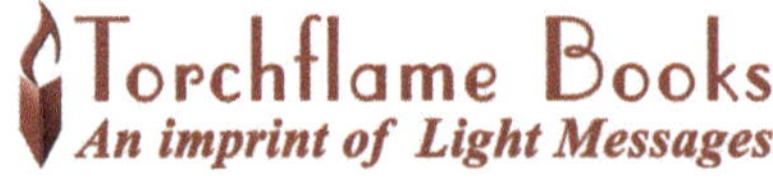

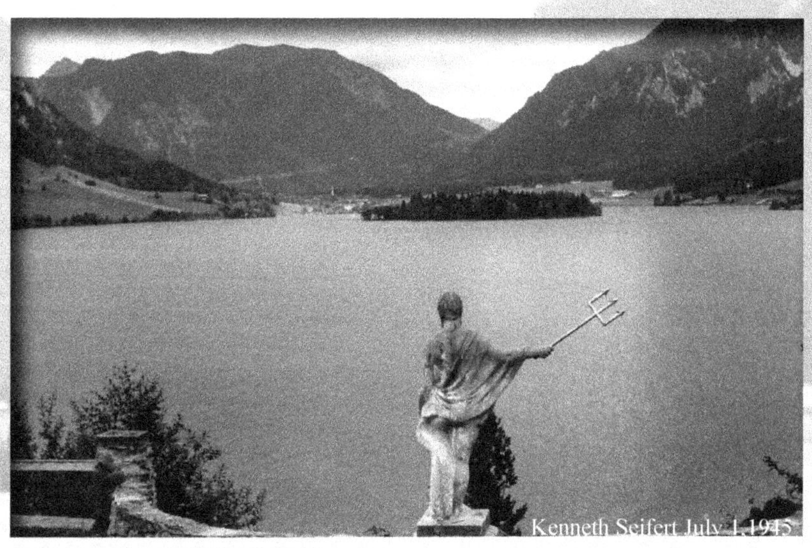

Kenneth Seifert July 4, 1945

In Remembrance of

# Grandpa Kenneth A. Seifert

who was already preserving memories with his camera
between long shifts
as a field hospital surgeon when he followed
Patton's Army across Europe.

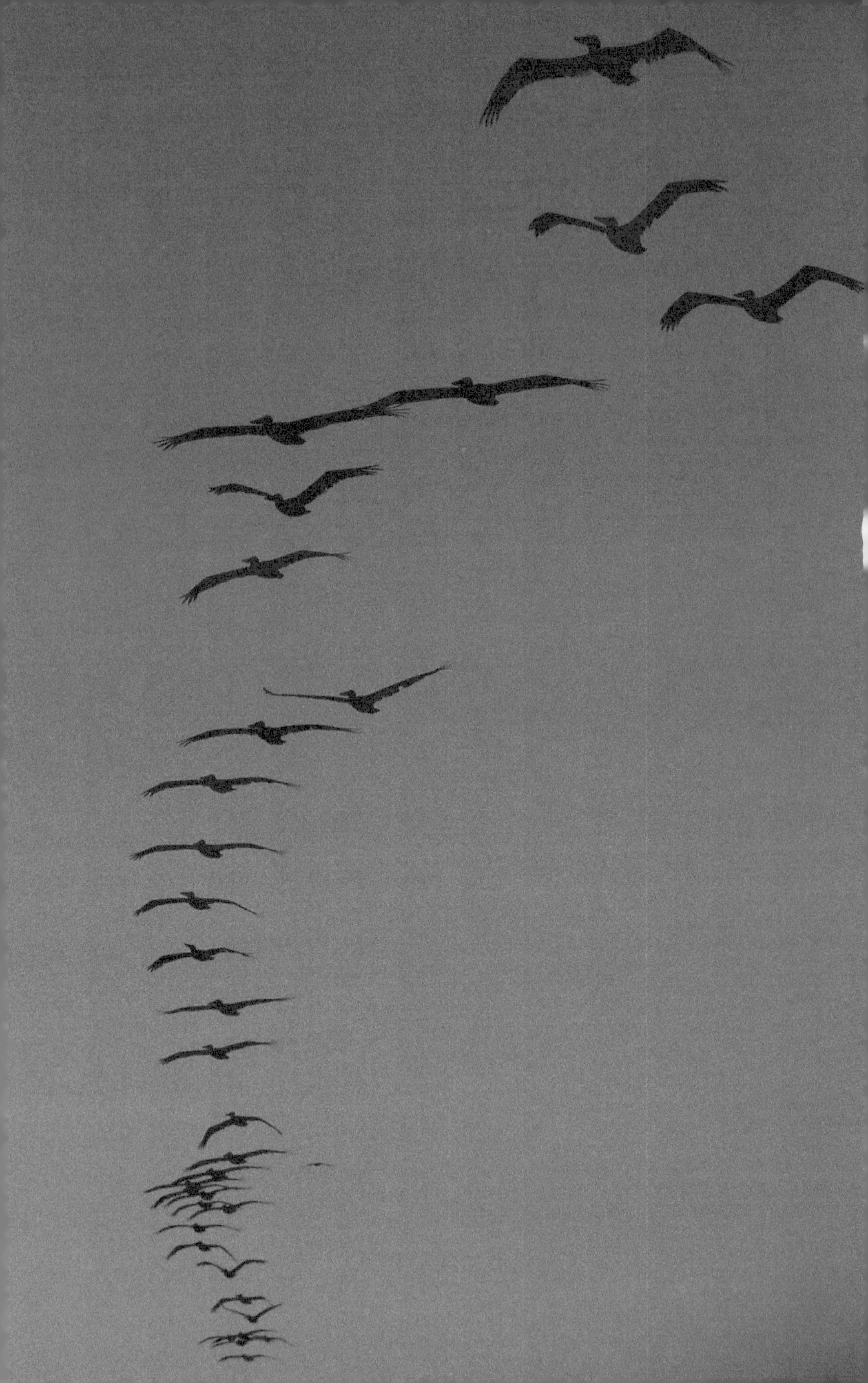

# contents



# focus on insets

# introduction

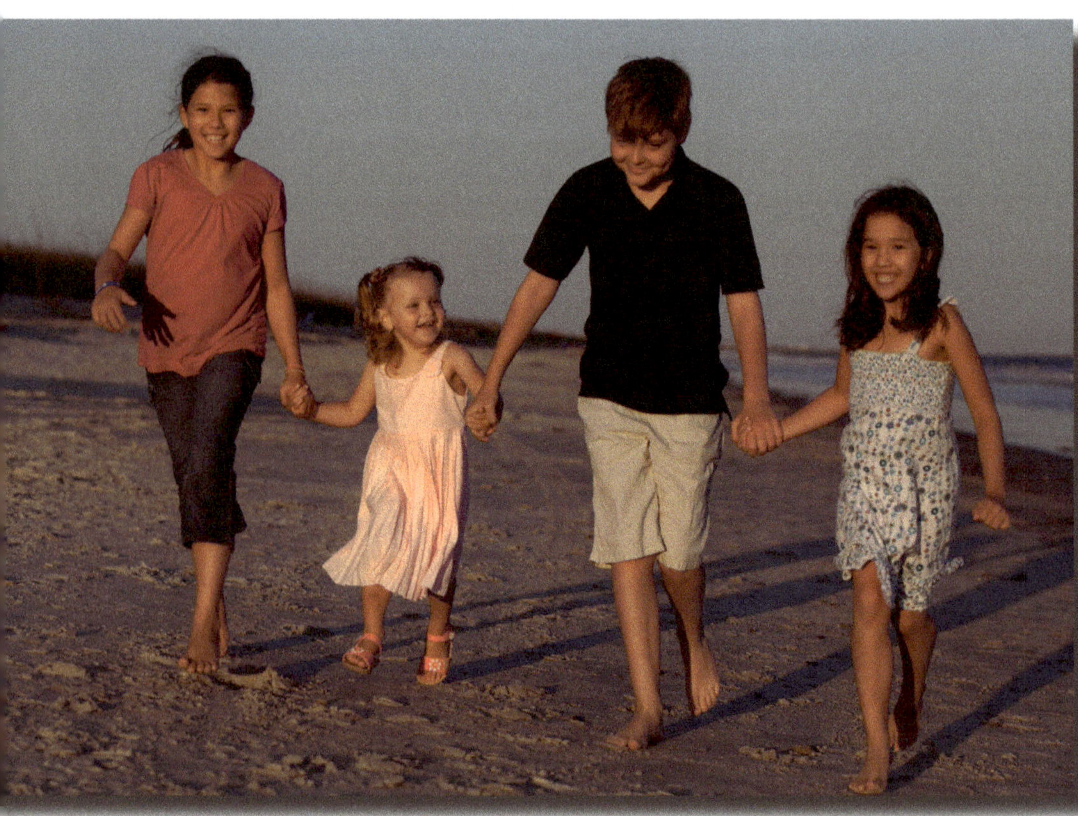

You've opened a guide to photographing Oak Island's special places and experiences. It will introduce you to especially good photo ops on the island. You will learn, as importantly, how to take top-notch pictures when you get to the best spots. This book also serves as a truncated travel guide. Oak Island's best places to be with your camera are very often the most interesting places to experience the island as well.

If you have your camera with you on Oak Island, aka OKI, you can easily get some great shots. Sunsets on Oak Island are world class. If you do the obvious, go to the beach, face west, and click, most evenings you will get a nice photo. The Army Corps of Engineers made taking pictures of boats easy, too. In the 1930s, the Corps created the Intracoastal Waterway. While boating enthusiasts might prefer a channel wider than the Waterway's hundred feet, for a photographer it is priceless. The Intracoastal Waterway is the I-95 for boaters with all of the boats within range of a normal focal length lens. You are unlikely to get bored with either the view or the endless variety of boats before you have caught some framable images.

Thank the Town of Oak Island, residents of Oak Island, and commercial ventures for dotting the waters with piers, docks, bridges, and overlooks. Their weathered wood, lines, shadows, and reflections in the water make it remarkably simple to fill your viewfinder with a classy shot. So you ask, if it is so easy, why this book?

Because, the obvious only scratch the surface. The Point at the west end of the island is a prime example. If you only have a few days on the island, odds are good that you won't get out to this gem. The Point is always wonderful; if you can be picky, it is particularly picturesque at low tide when the sand bars surface. If you are really lucky, low tide will coincide with sunset. Other prime locations abound along Yacht Drive as you travel along the island's north shore. Virtually all street ends are public accesses to views of the Intracoastal Waterway. These pages guide you to some of the best. There are also 60-plus beach accesses on OKI. The vegetation, the sand formations, the access paths, the water patterns, and the vistas vary among them presenting richly varied photo possibilities. You'll learn about some specific accesses and be shown where and how to best shoot them. The middle of Oak Island offers unexpected places to explore with some of the finest that Oak Island provides photographically. Take home a picture of the resident blue heron on 40th Street at Davis Canal, or the fiddler crabs crawling in whole armies at the west end of Oak Island Drive, or the osprey pair nesting in the William "Bill" Smith Park field lights.

The locations of Oak Island photo ops are woven through the narrative of this guide. Many examples featured in the text are on the maps at the end of the book. About half of the suggested places are along seven suggested walks also described in the end pages. Advice from the author, developed from years of experience as a professional photographer, is sprinkled throughout the text.

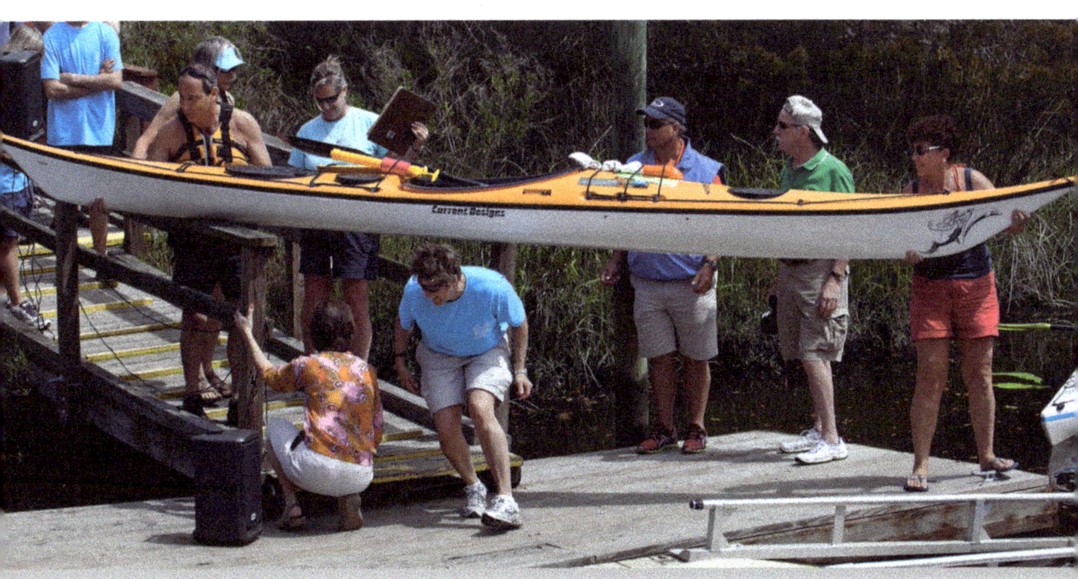

The photo guidance is not intended as a graduate-level course in photography nor is it targeted to the photographer equipped with thousands of dollars worth of equipment. You can do most of what is described with moderately priced equipment or with a basic point-and-shoot. The emphasis is on photo basics. These are complemented by a few technical discussions that are particularly relevant to Oak Island vacation photography. Photographing birds, for instance, or stopping action as you photograph a "wannabe surfer" can be best done with a non-standard focal length lens. You'll learn to do it right if you have the equipment and given some occasional hints on how you might compensate if you don't.

Beyond the photo advice woven into the text, there are "Focus On" insets filled with topical advice. The advice runs the gamut from "Depth-of-Field" to "Direction of Light" to "Panning." In the pages following the body of the book, these insets are whittled down to just ten essentials for taking great Oak Island photos. If you are a serious photographer, the insets will reaffirm what you learned long ago with some Oak Island particulars. If your camera use is generally limited to vacations and family milestones, the "Ten Shot Thoughts" section includes fundamentals required to morph snapshots into fine photos. While expensive equipment is helpful, the greatest difference between going home with disappointing photos and gratifying ones comes from mastering the basics.

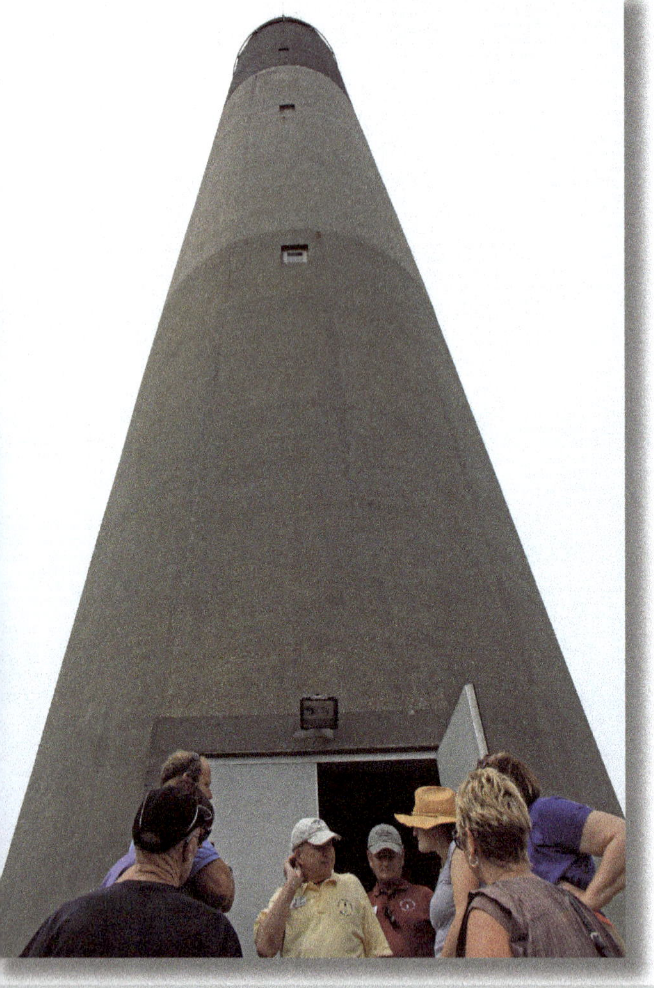

The body of the book is divided into "Air," "Land," and "Sea." You'll find Oak Island's photo possibilities in the sky above, the water below, and on *terra firma.* For most folk, most of the time, photography is land based. The sky and sea play a much larger role on Oak Island than in a typical city, town, or suburb. Stand in the middle of Oak Island's beach and imagine yourself as the core of a sphere. A quarter of the sphere is air: the

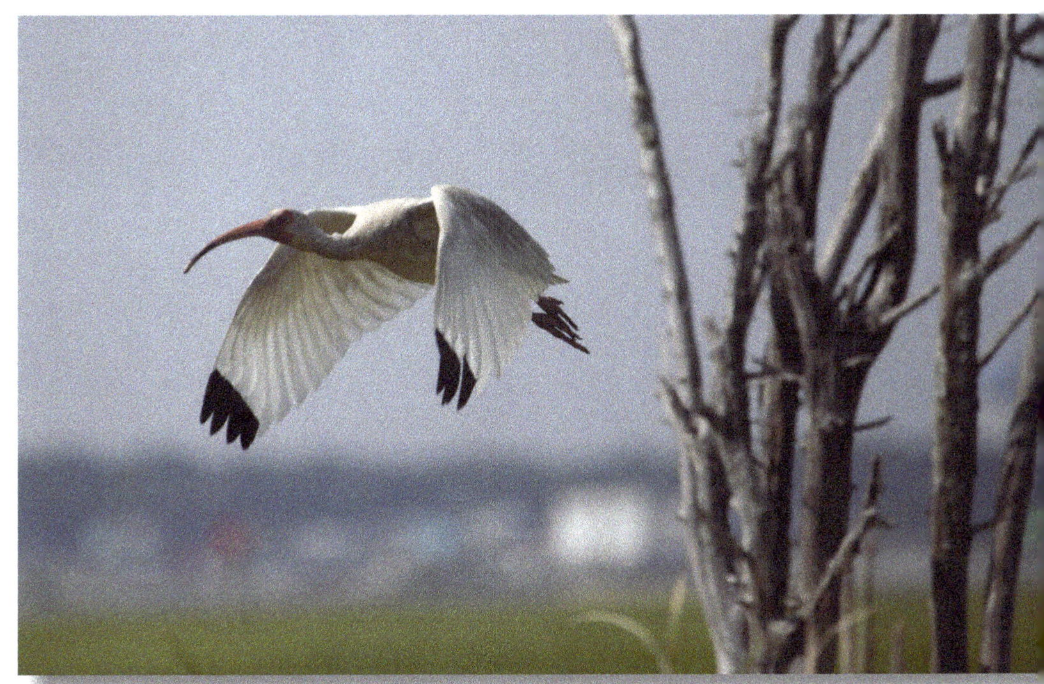

sky above, 180 degrees to your left and right, and the 520 miles south to Grand Bahama Island. That sky is canvas for birds, sails, kites, and leaping dogs. If you turn and face north, the sky is still more prominent than it is most places. Oak Island generally has a 35 foot height restriction on structures with an occasional 41 foot exception. There are no tall dense canopy trees growing near the shore. The palms and windswept oaks that dot the landscape enhance the view rather than obstruct it. Daytime skies, more often than not, are Carolina Blue. On the days they are sprinkled with puffy white clouds, the actuality surpasses an artist's imagination. Sunsets are spectacular. Nighttimes are as inspiring as sunsets and blue-sky days. Because there are seldom lights between you and Grand Bahama, give or take the occasional shrimp boat, and because, beach front home owners turn their lights out as part of the sea turtle protection program in the summer, the night skies are dark. Or, rather, the night skies are dark when there is no stunningly bright and photogenic moon.

While the "Air" sections emphasize nature, landscape, and the stuff of coastal travel photography, the "Land" section is weighted towards preserving vacation memories. Think about capturing your friends or kids running on the beach, your dog sleeping on the sand, your friends joining in on Oak Island events, your favorite vacation beach toys. "Land" also includes some tips on photographing your beach house, OKI oddities, and local activities: golf, disc golf, corn toss, parades and events.

Beyond family and friends, the "Land" section will steer you to good shots of Oak Island vegetation which ranges from old South to Caribbean

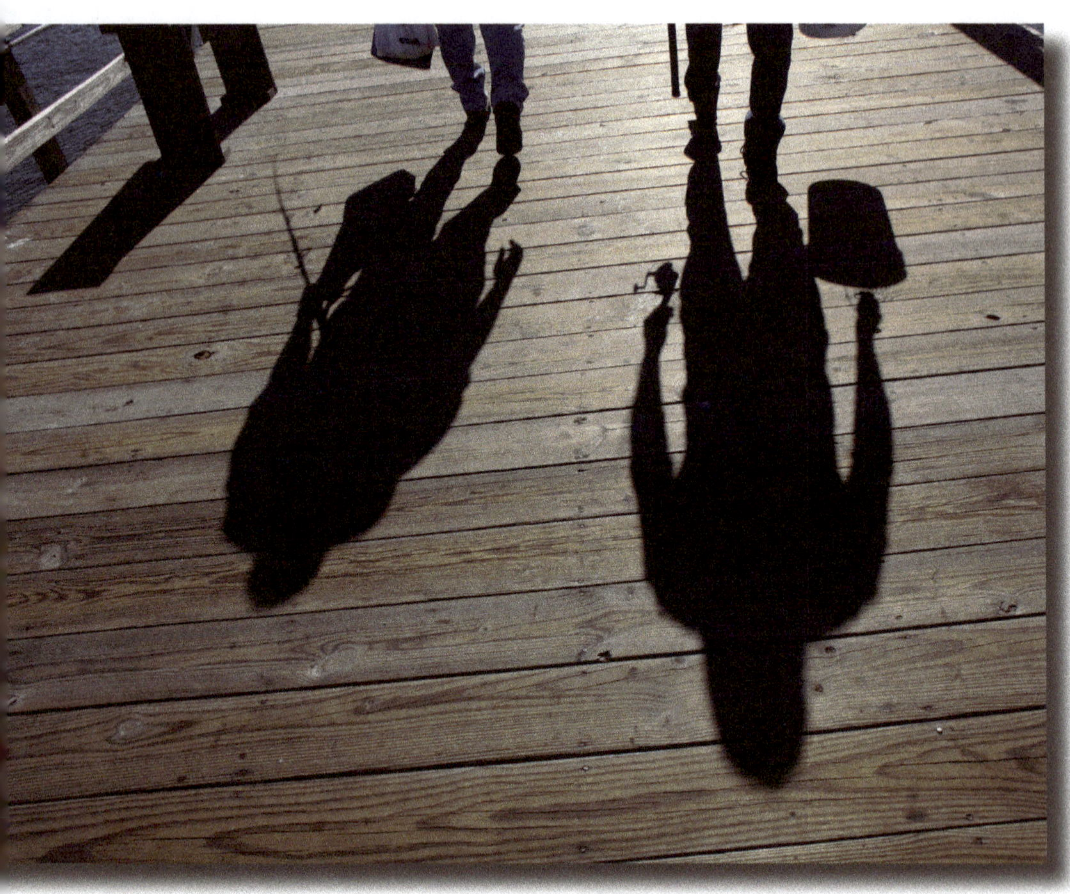

Island, and from high desert to maritime forest, all mixed in with some Northeast transplants. You will also discover the history of Oak Island. It is new; there were only 357 structures on the island when Hurricane Hazel razed it in 1954. It is old; Fort Caswell at the eastern end of the island dates to 1836. In "Land," you will also be introduced to much of what makes Oak Island residents love it. Oak Island is not a cookie-cutter place. On Oak Island a house may be painted purple; an A-Frame can be found next to a neo-Victorian. Oak Island does quirky exceptionally well which inspires really fun photos.

The "Sea" section emphasizes Oak Island's single biggest draw. The devotees to Oak Island, whether permanent residents, second-home owners, or frequent visitors, are very often fishing and/or boating fanatics (although, they only slightly outnumber, the birders). The fishermen come to hook some of the finest near-shore game fish found along the Atlantic seaboard. The bird lovers come to see egrets, herons, cormorants, loons, and ducks joined by the ibises in the spring. "Sea" is also about swimming and surfing; crabs and shrimping; ripples and reflections. The waters of Oak Island include all of its marshlands, Davis Canal, Montgomery Slough and the mouth of the Lockwood Folly River, in addition to the beaches and Intracoastal Waterway. The places on the water to explore, to play, and to frame great pictures are countless.

One place beyond Oak Island is featured, as well. Brunswick Town was the oldest permanent settlement in North Carolina and one of the most important in the New World. Its story encompasses both the Revolutionary War and the Civil War. If you like history, you will love Brunswick Town. If you could care less about history, this state historic site is a wonderful natural park, and a nice stopping place coming in or out of Oak Island from the north.

The final pages include maps with locations of the photographs featured indicated on them, suggested walking routes, some sources of additional information, and ideas for fun stuff to do with your camera. Exploring the island with your camera sure beats the typical day job. Hope you capture wonderful memories through your lens. If though, you sleep on the beach or get sidetracked by family and friends instead, *Camera-in-Hand* includes many of the photos you would have taken if you hadn't been distracted.

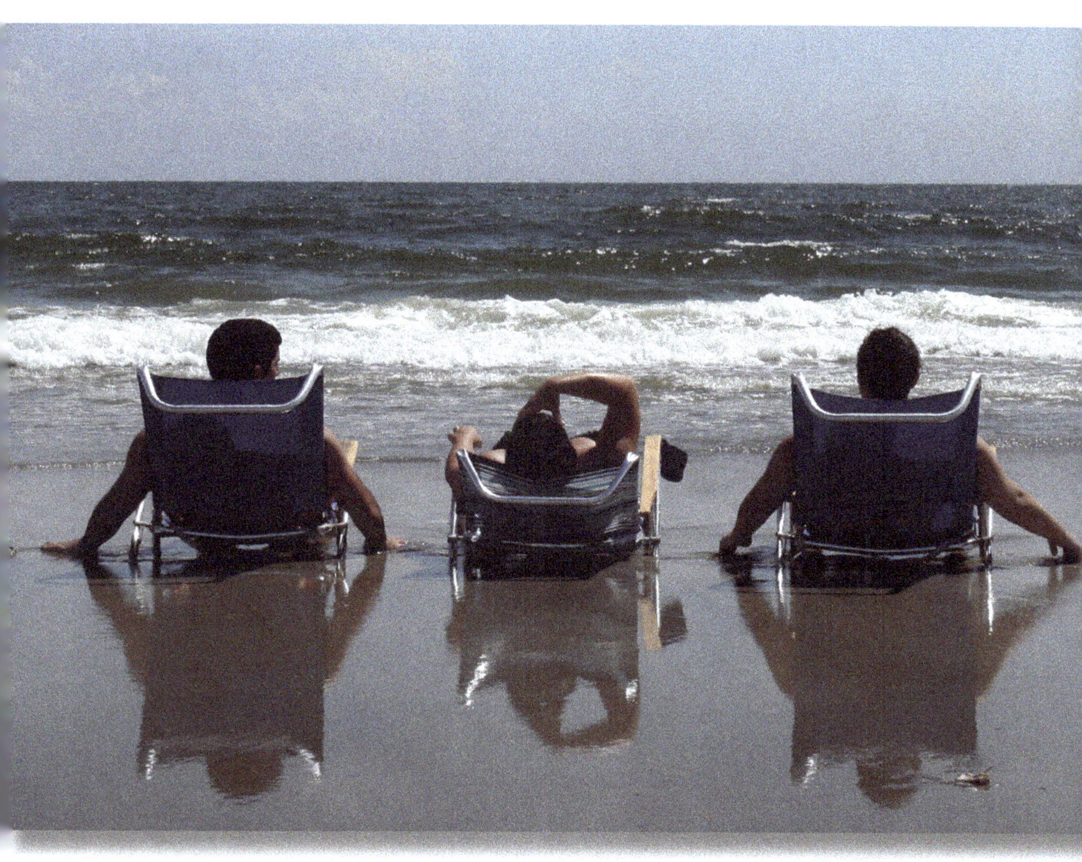

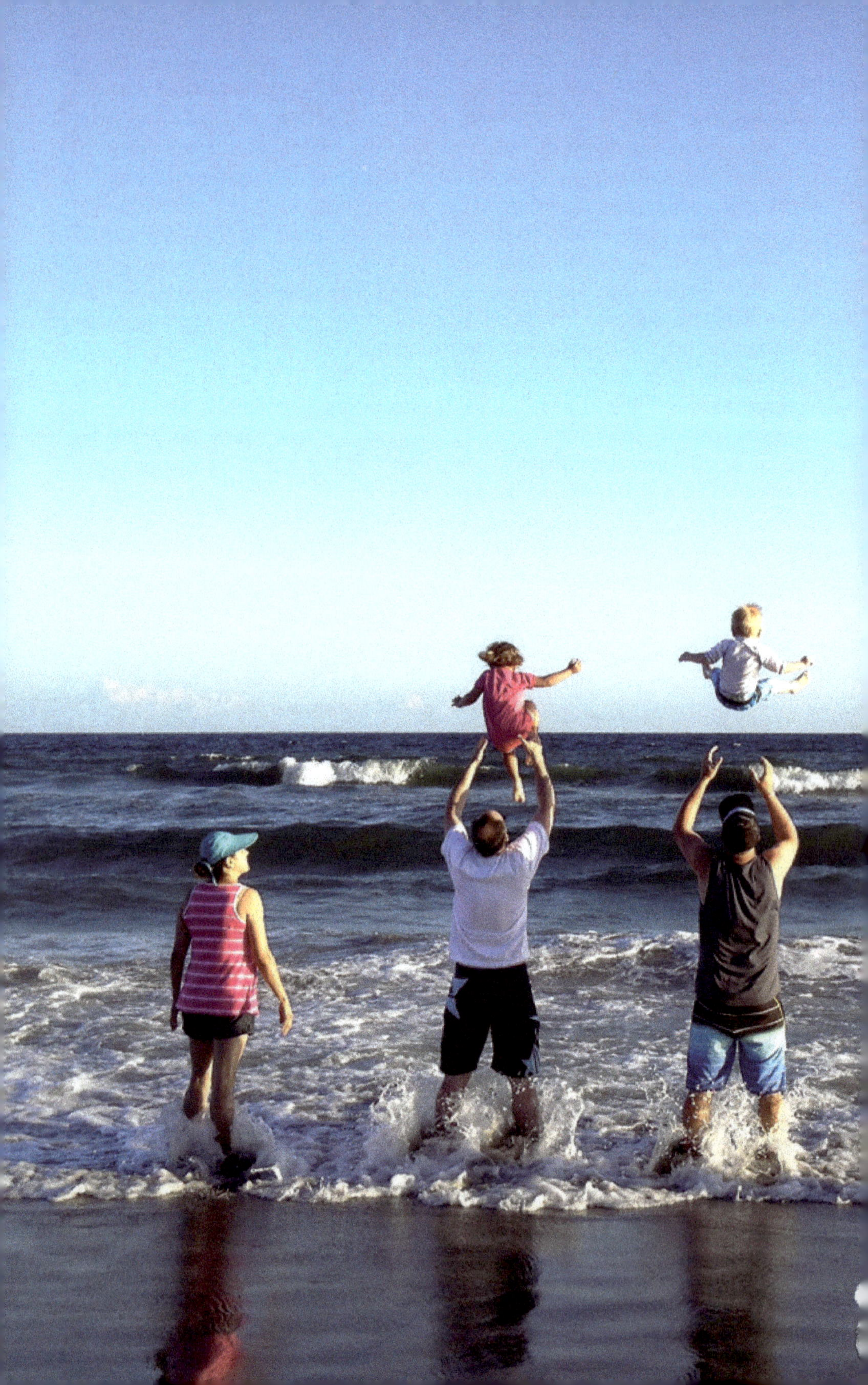

# Air

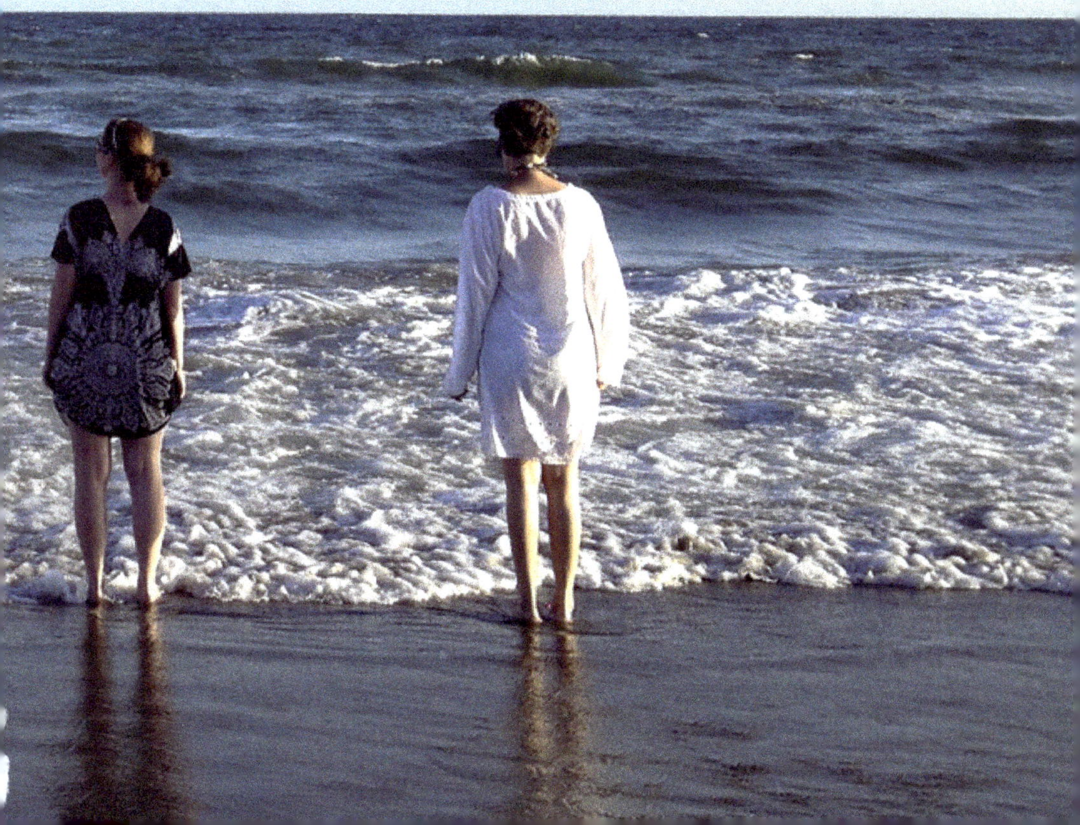

# blue skies

Oak Island days are mostly sunny. For beach lovers this is wonderful; fun-in-the-sun is what beach vacations are all about. For you the photographer, though, it's a challenge. This guide begins with a caution. Imagine arriving at the beach, looking up at an enormous expanse of blue sky, and photographing your loved ones. You focus your camera and find them with squinting eyes and harsh shadows under their noses.

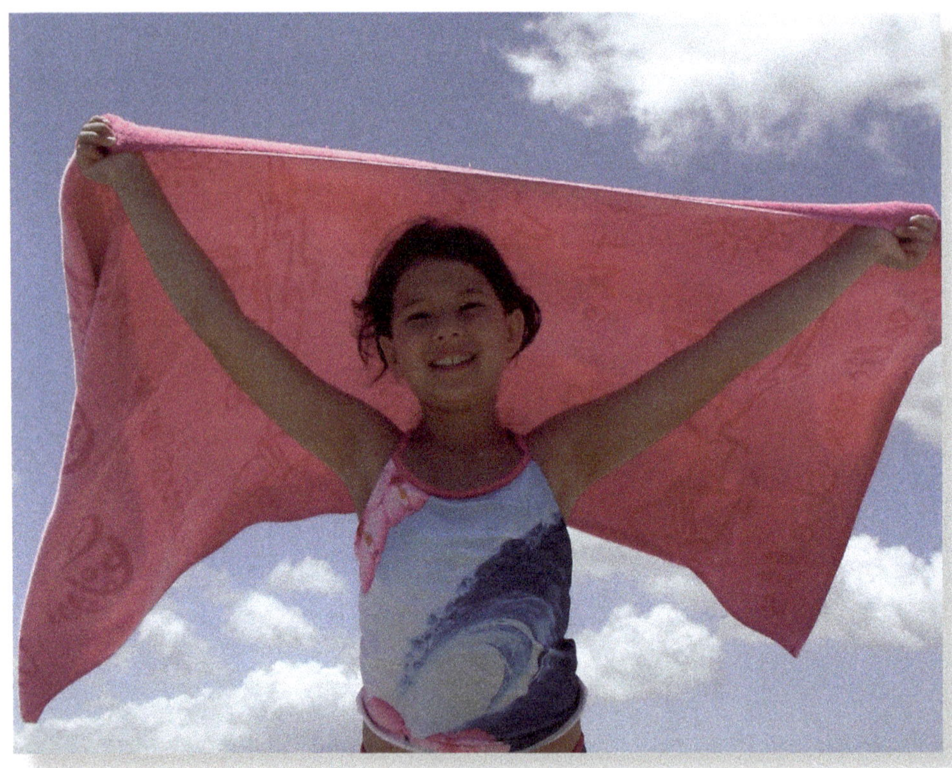

Along with the 215 days of Carolina Blue skies that Oak Island averages are 215 days of glaring midday sun. Your beach going family and friends are not going to be flattered by the light. Instead, they'll want to scrap the pictures they find of themselves in your vacation album. Your landscape shots will tend towards pathetic as well. Harsh midday light ruins more beach vacation shots than anything else. It makes good photographers look bad. I generally favor concentrating on the waves, enjoying friends and family, or napping under an umbrella from 9:00 a.m. to 4:00 p.m. with my camera in its bag, away from the salt spray, melting sun rays, and gritty sand. You've probably come for a little "vacay." A good plan is to enjoy the midday camera free.

Then again, on about half of the blue-sky days, the Oak Island skies are dappled with clouds. A helpful cloud makes all the difference. If you wait patiently for a fluffy white cloud to soften the midday sun, you can sharpen your portrait photography skills. Another option, is to create shade. The photo at the left, shot under shade made by a beach towel, finesses the harshness and unevenness of the midday light. Here, the intense sun hitting the reflective grains of sand works to your advantage. The result approximates the flattering portraits made by studio photographers using a variant of the technique called clamshell lighting. The light from below balances that from above to create a soft shadow free glow.

If the clouds don't cooperate (and you exhaust creative ways to manufacture shade), there are subjects that do photograph nicely when skies are blue. Structures, vegetation, and brightly colored subjects beckon to be photographed. The Oak Island Lighthouse, possibly the island's most photographed icon, looks imposing against a sky spattered with cotton-ball clouds. Even here, though, the color would have been far less vibrant if taken at high noon instead of in the late afternoon as this one was.

Fort Caswell is a rare exception to bright sun being problematic; some of the best Fort Caswell photos require

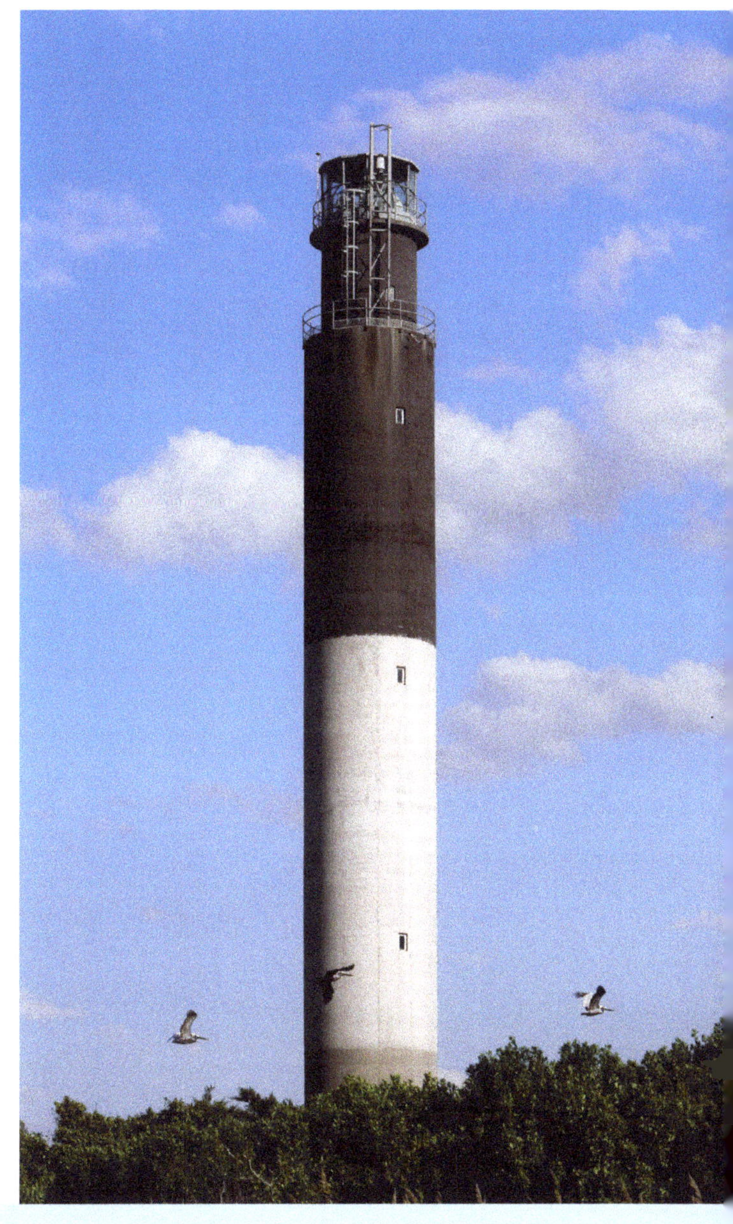

## Focus On: Quality of Light

James Thurber writes, "There are two kinds of light—the glow that illuminates, and the glare that obscures." If you need sunglasses to see decently, that light is too bright to take good people pictures. Beyond intensity, photographers and humankind generally are drawn to color-tinted light rather than pure white light. From the light pink of a spring dawn to the golden glow of an autumn sunset to the soft blue of light shade to the gray of foggy days, soft, diffuse, color tinted light is best for most photography.

Professional photographers mostly use the Golden Hours—the hour after sunrise and the hour before sunset. These hours offer wonderful light quality. Aim for this time frame and your odds of great nature and architectural photos increases.

Pelicans soaring past and structures glow compellingly but people photos are still problematic. Even in the Golden Hours, people will have to squint when looking into the sun. For portraits, the sun being obscured by clouds during the Golden Hours can produce beautiful results as shown in the "On The Beach" portion of the "Land" section.

A commonly used technique is to place the subjects just inside the line of shade near a building or under a structure such as the pier. The quality of light is ideal since there are no harsh shadows and the reflected light from the sand is omnidirectional. The background though is going to be brighter than the subject, so it will appear to be a bit washed out.

As the sun rises or sets, you often see an ethereal glow. Using that light to rim-light the subject can be fantastic. The subject will be backlit but enough reflected light will fill-in the face. The effect will also create a slightly washed out background, softly-glowing hair, and a quiet, serene feel to the photo.

Focusing on light quality can open your eyes to how the camera captures the light we see with the naked eye. Simply taking photos of a single subject under different lighting conditions is an excellent exercise for teaching yourself about good light quality.

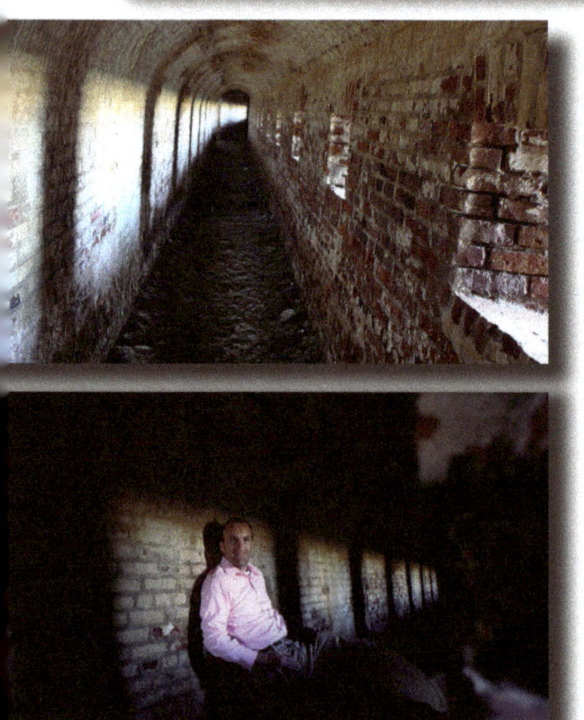

bright sunlight. There are many old tunneled fortifications. Shooting with the sun streaming towards your right shoulder as you look down the tunnel will give you the light you find in the photos to your left. Creating portraits in natural light in a tunnel doesn't sound possible and, of course, it generally isn't. Yet, Fort Caswell's tunnel design offers the opportunity. The light levels will still be low, even with the sunlight beaming; you'll want to find something to brace yourself against or use a tripod. Prefocus on a person or object in the foreground and click.

Fort Caswell gives you a bright sun two-fer. Not only can you effectively use the bright sun for the structures, you can do the same with the vegetation. Try framing the parade ground through the old trees with the three o'clock sun included in the photograph. It's a chance to effectively use backlighting, shooting directly into the sun. If you are ready for a bit more sophistication, use a high f-stop, which was done above to give the sun a star effect. (Even the most basic point-and-shoot model cameras have an aperture priority setting; if yours does, set it to the highest f-stop, smallest aperture, and then try pointing-and-shooting.)

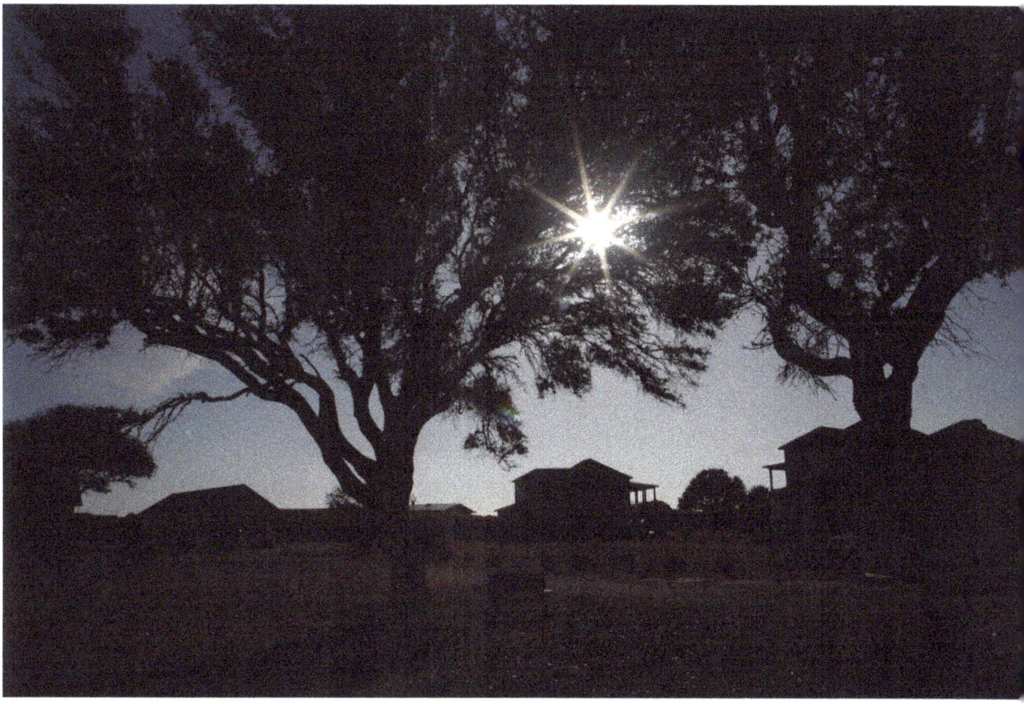

The same techniques can be equally effective with Oak Island's eye-grabbing vegetation sprouting from the dunes. The natural look of the barrier dunes, on the boardwalk-free Oak Island, often makes the shots you take with your back to the ocean as compelling as those you take when you face it.

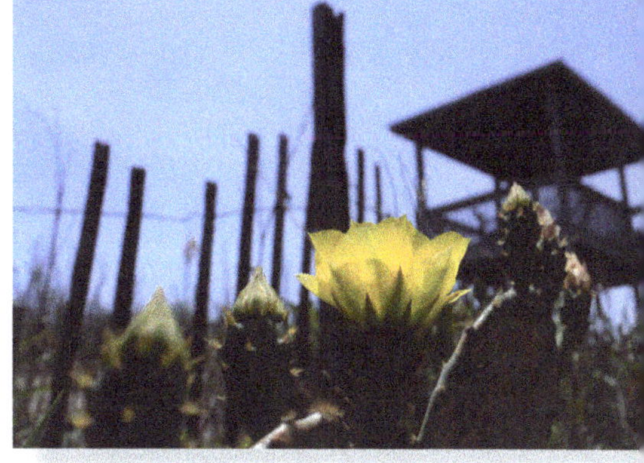

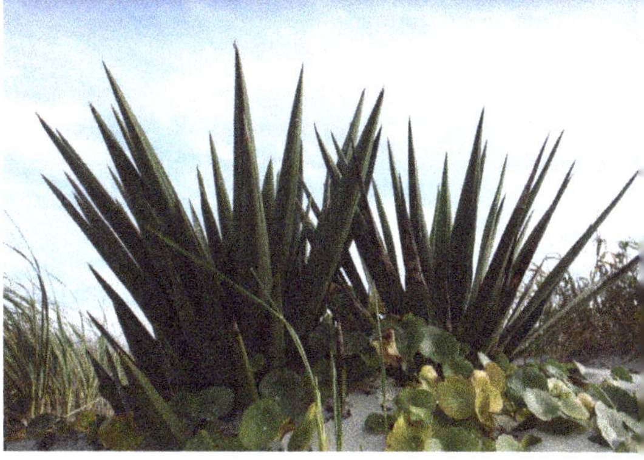

# Sunset

An Oak Island sunset rivals any that you have seen in calendars or travel magazines. Polar opposite to what happens in midday sun, shooting Oak Island sunsets can make even bad photographers look good. The first photo below is the "shoo-in" shot promised in the introduction. Go to the beach; face your camera west; point and shoot.

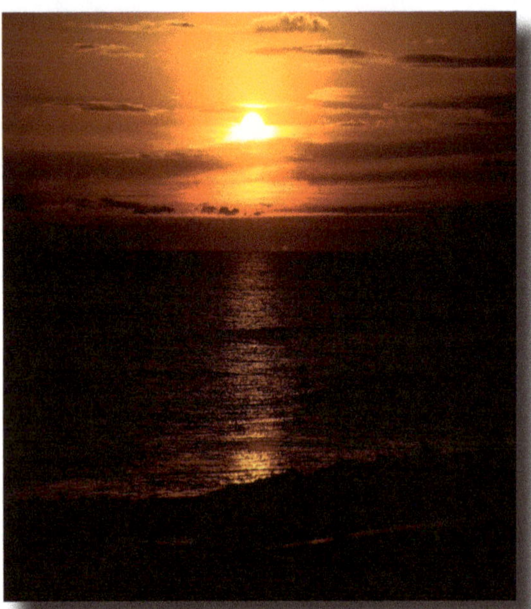

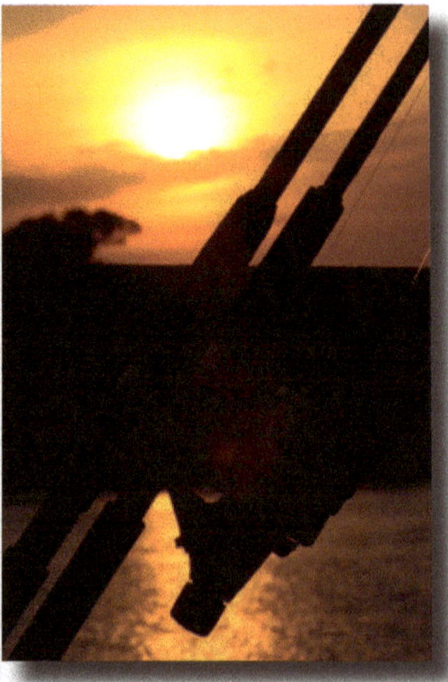

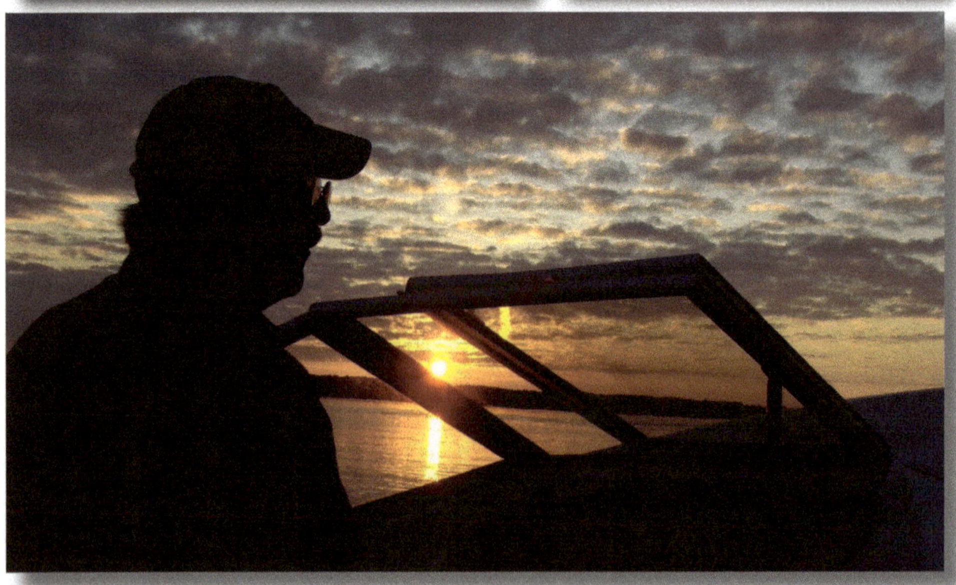

By being creative with the foreground element at sunset you can elevate your photos from good to great. Besides, it is pure camera sport. You'll find wonderful opportunities to take photos that are both high quality and personal. Shoot the setting sun right as it peeks under your beach umbrella. Get a picture of your dog or preschooler catching a ball in the air just ahead for what looks like him catching the setting sun. Click at your boogie boards standing in the sand with the sun setting between them. Get your own bathing suits and beach towels hanging from a clothes line with the sun sinking under the clothes pins. End your day out on a boat with a shot of the sunset coming through its windshield.

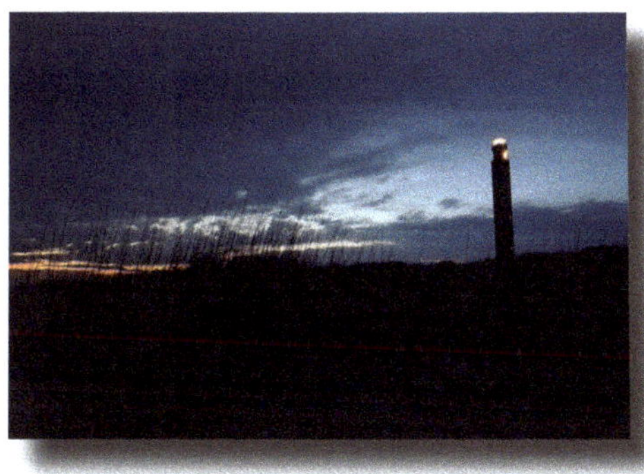

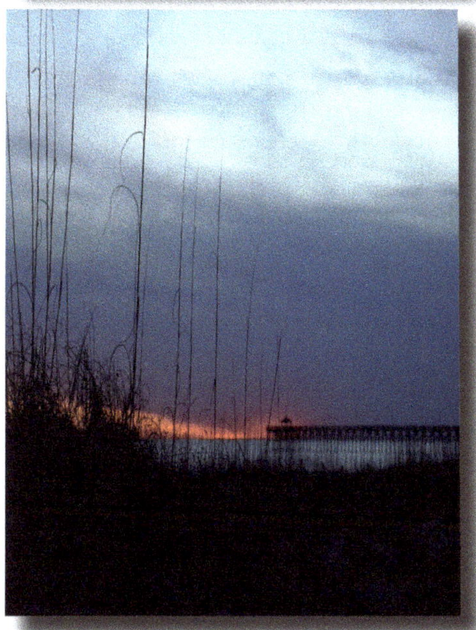

### Focus On: Foreground

Paying attention to the three "grounds" in a two-dimensional photograph is vital. Photographers often call this layering, which is the difference between a common snapshot and the sense of a three-dimensional scene. Artists working on canvas have coped with this issue throughout the ages: how do you create the feel of three-dimensions using a two-dimensional medium?

The foreground is, all too often, where the subject is placed in hobbyist photography. For instance, envision a photo of a family standing in front of a theme park sign. By selecting a foreground as a framing element, you create some sense of depth. Sandwiching your subject between a foreground frame and a distance-defining background heightens the effect. Try taking a family group picture framed through a sea oat covered dune as a foreground with a distant fishing pier as part of the background.

While we usually want our subject to be the focal point, the focus doesn't need to be the foreground element. Try composing your photo with out-of-focus objects in the foreground to frame your subject in the middle ground. Or take a family portrait with the children a few yards in front of the adults and something beachy in the background. The children are the foreground element and in focus, the adults are recognizable but have a flattering soft focus, and the whole image comes together as a beach portrait

To make yourself think about foreground, look through the viewfinder instead of relying on your live LCD display. You will be surprised at what you see when looking through the viewfinder and amazed by what you don't see right before your eyes on the LCD screen.

Capture your beach house in the soft glow of the light created opposite the setting sun on the beach.

Sweeps of sea oats are the most commonly used foreground for sunsets on Oak Island. While I have become jaded about some photo props, sea oats continue to have appeal. Sea oats alone are even better with the Oak Island Pier or a similar iconic beach element incorporated in the distance.

Unlike most places known for their sunsets, there is no typical Oak Island sunset. Many are deep gold striated with deep reds and oranges, but often you will find the OKI skies colored with a palette of pastels associated with the Easter bunny instead. The sky will be awash in soft powder blues, lavenders, and pinks. Once hooked on Oak Island sunsets, you are likely to find yourself ending most days on the beach facing west.

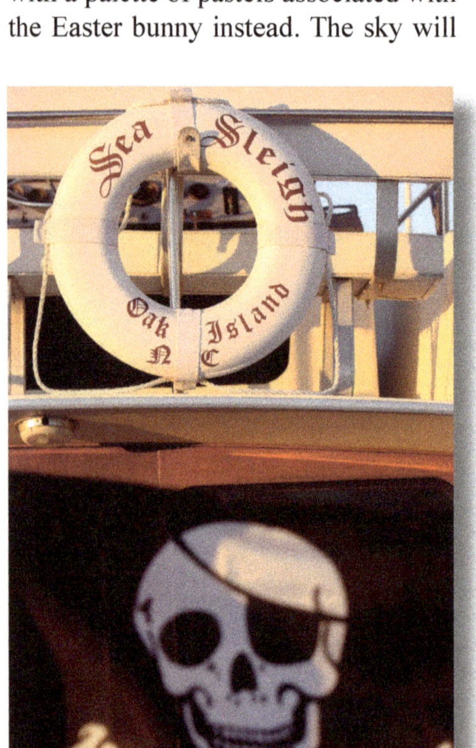


It is all too easy at sunset to be mesmerized by the setting sun itself and be like a horse wearing blinders to what the light is doing to ordinary objects surrounding you. The life preserver at the docks of the Blue Point Marina shown below is a case in point. While always an iconic symbol of being near the sea, it is particularly eye-grabbing during the hour before the sun sets.

Don't write off Oak Island sunsets on a day when storm clouds are hovering. Of course, if clouds are sitting right on the horizon, you don't have a "sunset" shot; however you may have an image that replicates early twilight. If there is a break below the storm clouds, you can get an especially dramatic shot. You can either capture the sun as it sets over an identifiable landmark, such as the island's water tower, or as it leaves its last glow of peach next to the Oak Island Lighthouse

Arguably, the most spectacular sunsets are seen from the Oak Island side of the Intracoastal Waterway towards the west. The best of the best generally occur in the summer. All you need is a spot at one of the street ends that includes some attractive vegetation to frame the shot. On days that include whiffs of clouds, you instantly have a ready made background.

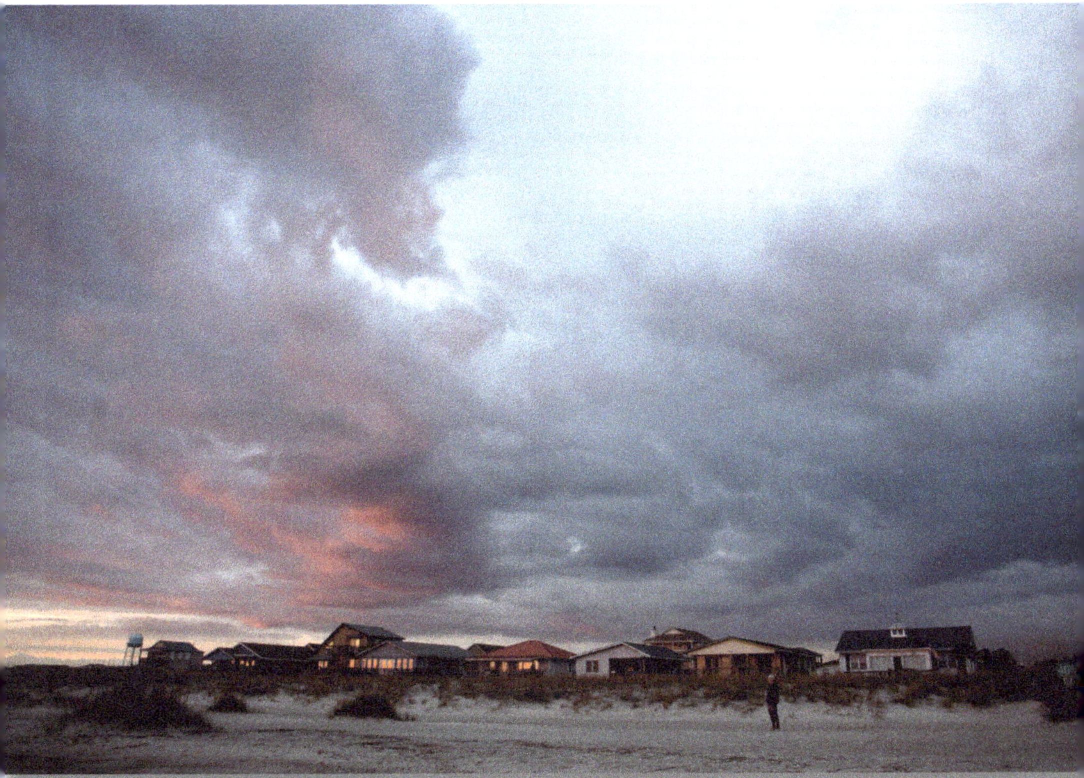

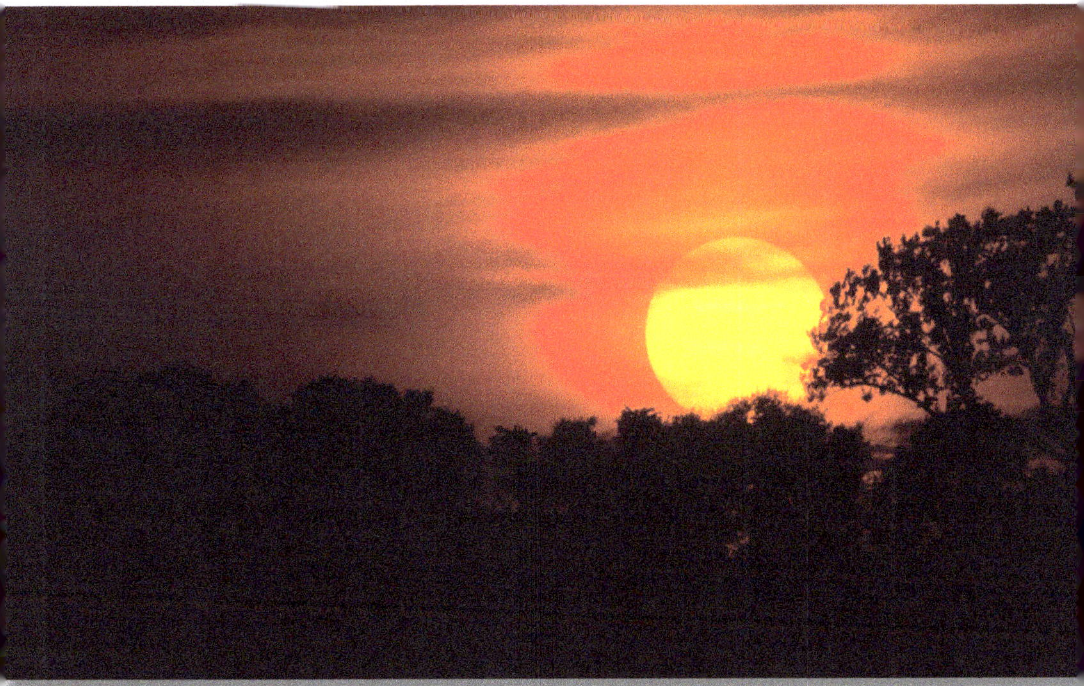

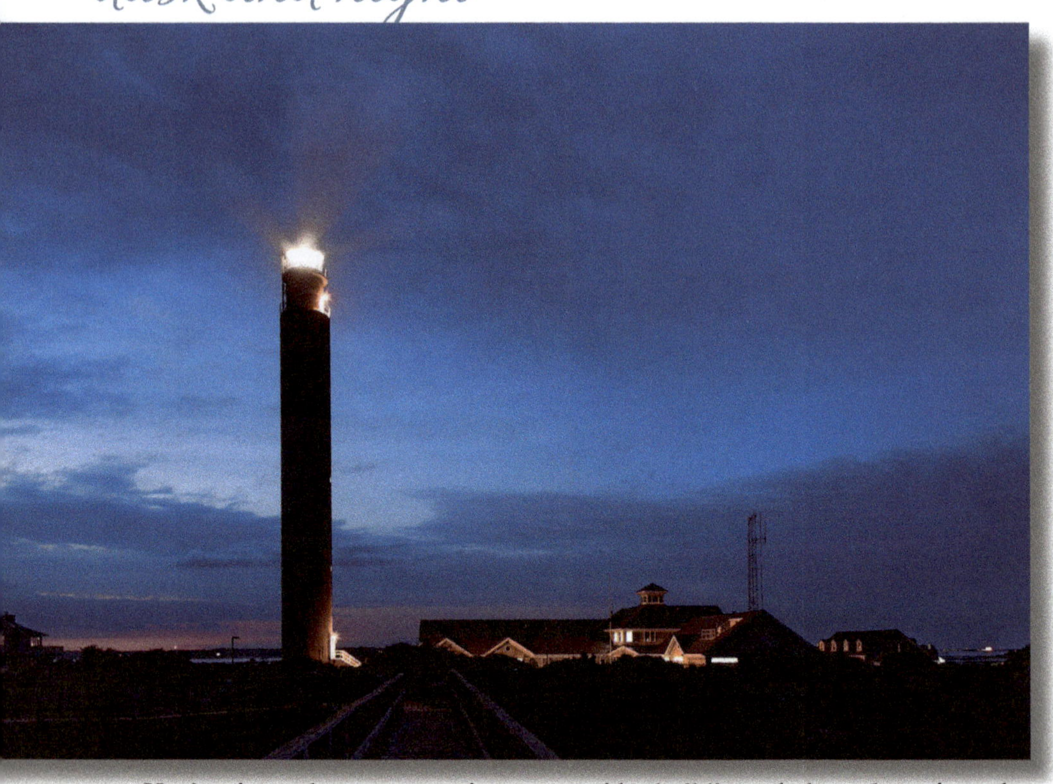

You've just taken a great picture of the sunset and you may start to put your camera away. If you miss the next few minutes, you'll lose one of professional photographers' favorite times of day: dusk. Architecture, in particular, photographs well just after sunset. Here you see the Oak Island Lighthouse, again, this time taken at day's end. The photo, taken in the early dusk, makes the fairly ordinary architecture of the building that abuts the Oak Island landmark appear special, and, of course, the light of the lighthouse only really makes a statement after sundown.

The dark sky though is both your friend and enemy. The golden glow from ordinary interior lighting inside buildings balanced against the soft blue gray sky creates an appealing subtle contrast. However, it is considerably tougher to get a sharply focused shot after dark than it is when shooting in daylight with puffy white clouds. In these examples, the Oak Island Lighthouse picture in the "Blue Skies" subsection was taken at a shutter speed of 1/200 of a second; the "Dusk and Night" one was taken at a little more than 1/30 of a second. Camera shake is not an issue in the first case; it is critical in the second.

Still, after dark photography is worth the extra effort. Picture the many cityscape photos you have seen. There is the "you-name-the-city" skyline with the buildings glowing. You can see the shapes, the materials they are made of, and soft light from their lighted windows. Those memorable photos were taken just after sunset or just before sunrise. The photo of your beach house, the Oak Island bridge, and the pier just after the lights are turned on will photograph memorably as well.

For a great opportunity to try some after dark photography, join Oak Islanders the week encompassing the 4th of July. OKI celebrates the 4th traditionally with lots of flags and the Beach Day fireworks on July 1st. It's fun to gather the light of fireworks on both a small and large scale. Small scale is easy. Just the light of sparklers is sufficient to illuminate your subject's face if the sparklers are close enough to him. You can get a clear shot with a shutter speed of 1/25 of a second as shown here with ordinary ISO and f-stop settings of 400 and f/5.6.

For a rewarding but much more challenging photo shoot, watch the Southport July 4th fireworks from just west of the Oak Island Lighthouse. You'll get what feels like a front row seat for downtown Southport fireworks, without

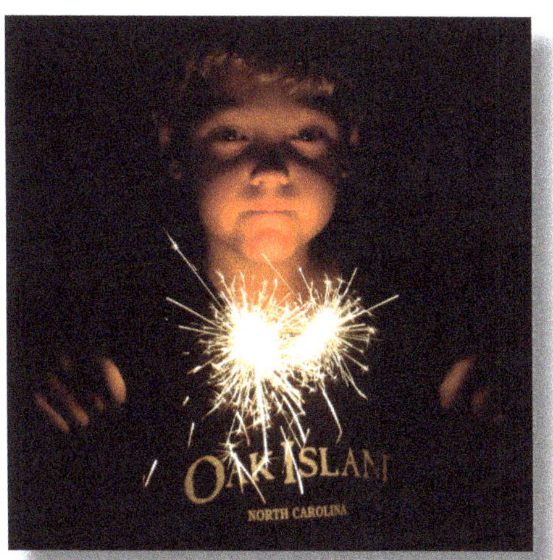


## Focus On: Holding Still

Stability in low light is key. Here is a technique to help eliminate camera shake. Start by placing your right and left legs about a shoulder width apart with your weight on your right leg and your left leg slightly forward of the right one. This will turn your torso about 30 degrees from the direction you plan to focus the camera.

Hold your left elbow against the side of your body with your hand open, your palm up, and your thumb pointed to the left creating a cradle. Position the camera in your left hand with the end of the lens or focus ring cupped by your thumb and index finger. The base of the camera or heaviest part of the lens should rest where your palm and wrist meet.

Nestle your right elbow into the center of your chest, keeping in mind that your torso is twisted a bit. Now you have a stable foundation. Your right hand can relax a little as it merely acts as the shutter release. Looking through the viewfinder will add another point of stability as the camera will balance against your nose or eyebrow. You can note that the right leg combined with the left elbow against the chest creates a monopod-like stability.

Using a tripod is also a good solution if you plan ahead (and want to lug one around). Be aware though, the beach wind will cause tripod shake. You can reduce it by blocking the wind and making sure you remove the camera straps as they will flutter in the breeze. With any lens, you do not need a tripod when using the 1-over-the-focal-length rule. If your focal length is 35mm, you can easily hand hold the camera at a shutter speed of 1/35 of a second.

traveling into Southport proper. The ISO and f-stop used here were equally ordinary at 400 and f/8. The difference is the shutter speed; 15 seconds were needed to expose the event's downtown backdrop properly. More importantly, the sparkle from the firework needs time to travel from the launching spot to its eruption. The above shot is actually 2 or 3 different launches over the 15 second timeframe. You'll need a tripod, cable release and patience to replicate the image

While seemingly simpler than the fireworks, taking good photographs of your friends and family after dark has always been challenging. Photos taken indoors using oodles of studio lighting can, of course, be good. Otherwise, shooting under incandescent light while bouncing the flash off a white ceiling is about the best you can do. Unfortunately, typical indoor shots in vacation albums are taken under fluorescent light with people subjected to overpowering direct flash.

Not using a flash is often key to creating the desired photos of people's activities. All too often folks' behavior changes when strobes or flashes are used, affecting the mood of the image.

Alternative lighting is often available without expensive equipment. The shot on the right was taken with car headlights about 35 feet from the piñata fun. They have added the needed light while maintaining the warmth and spontaneity of the action. Turning a floodlight toward folks gathered around the grill or carousing on the deck could work similarly. Use what you can find.

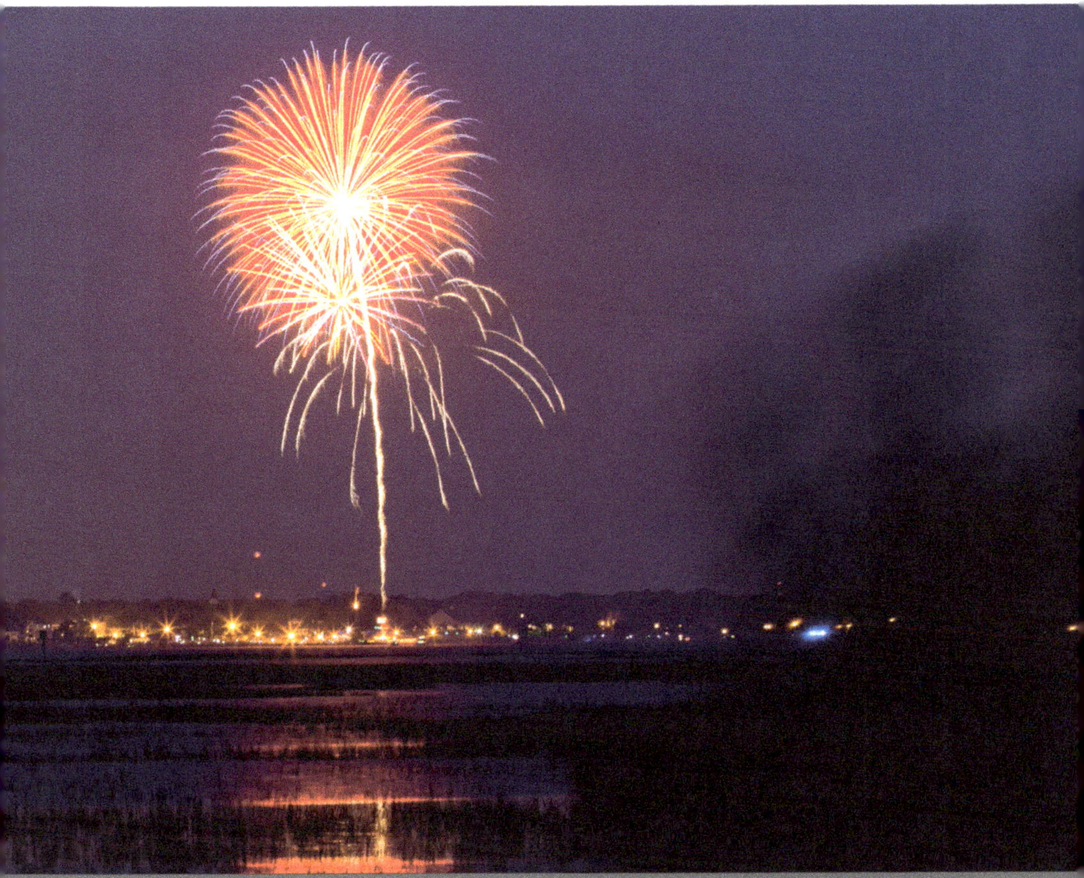

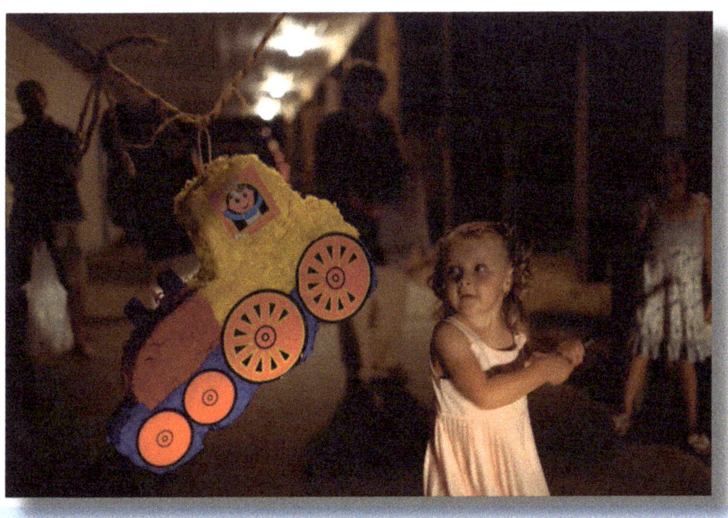

# chance of rain

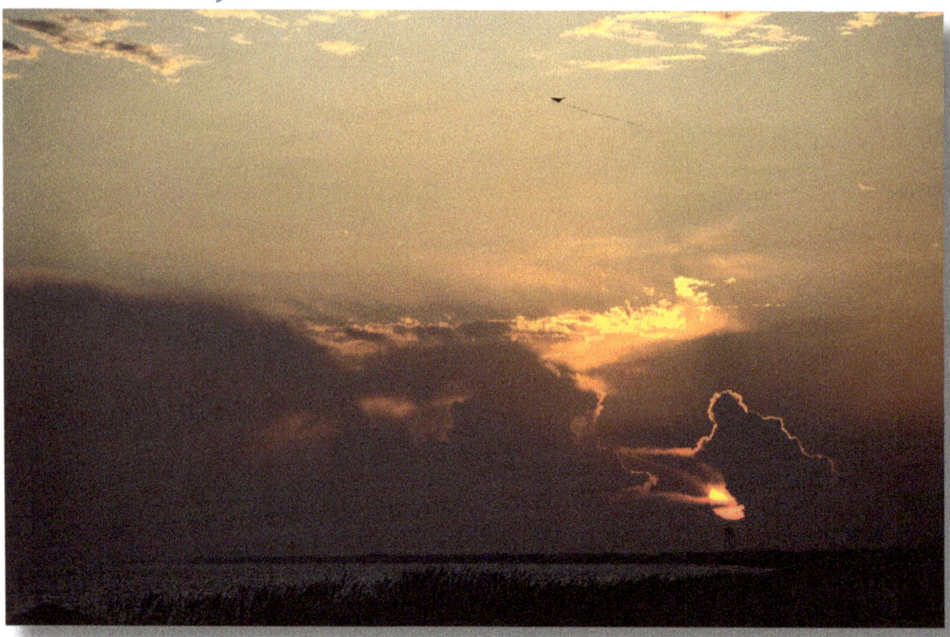

A bit of cloud cover doesn't stop Oak Island fun nor should it. During the summer beach season the water temperature is in the 80s, folks are in their bathing suits, and even the rain is warm. For you as a photographer, the occasional black thunderhead or blowing rain brings new opportunities for dramatic photos. Don't get down on a dreary or overcast day as the soft gray clouds can be used to create subtle images or catch the eye with the contrast of bright bits of color against the colorless gray.

Note, when skies are heavily overcast, you'll usually want to set your ISO to 400 before taking your camera out exploring. The settings to use for dense cloud cover are approximately the same as those used when shooting at dusk.

As a storm front passes through, the waves on Oak Island are frequently really foamy. Visitors sometimes wonder if the foam is due to pollutants. It isn't; the foam is formed through a natural process primarily involving plankton. The frothy foam is a wonderful backdrop for colorful shots. Use your imagination: fluorescent flip flops, kaleidoscopically dressed toddlers, russet colored dogs, a family in bright beach chairs surrounded by foam all work. Don't let your exposure be tricked by the light-colored foam. You will want to set your camera to overexpose by about one f-stop.

The salt spray will stick to and "cloud" the front of your lens creating a soft impressionistic effect that appears more watercolor than photographic. Also, the salt spray itself can create a mist in the air further softening the image. Functioning in heavy salt spray is not ideal for your camera. Whether you consciously choose to shoot in

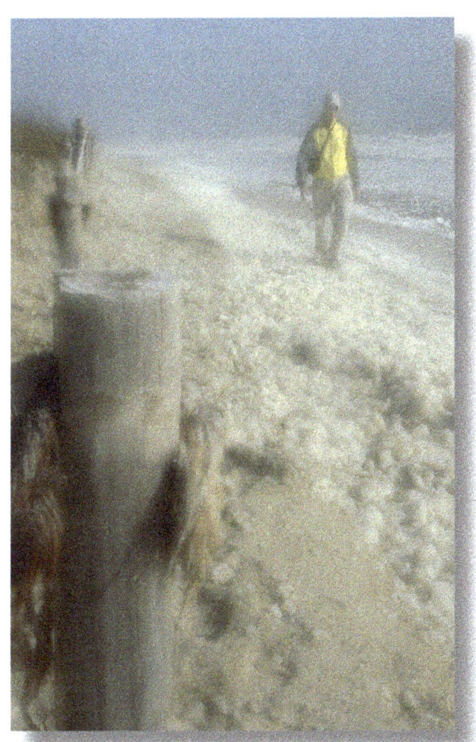

heavy salt spray or realize your images are progressively softening as you view them in your playback screen, do a good cleaning of your camera's parts before you put it away for the night. Having a UV or haze filter on your lens is also recommended as the salt spray will be on the $15 filter instead of your $300 lens.

Just as much as the yellow vest grabs one's eye through the salt spray, the colored belongings of intrepid beach goers pop out from the softness of grayed skies. One day under gray cloud cover some very talented visitors to Oak Island sculpted a piece of sand artistry. "Life's a Beach" was soon swept away by wind and water, but is preserved forever here by camera, a reminder to all those fortunate enough to have seen it.

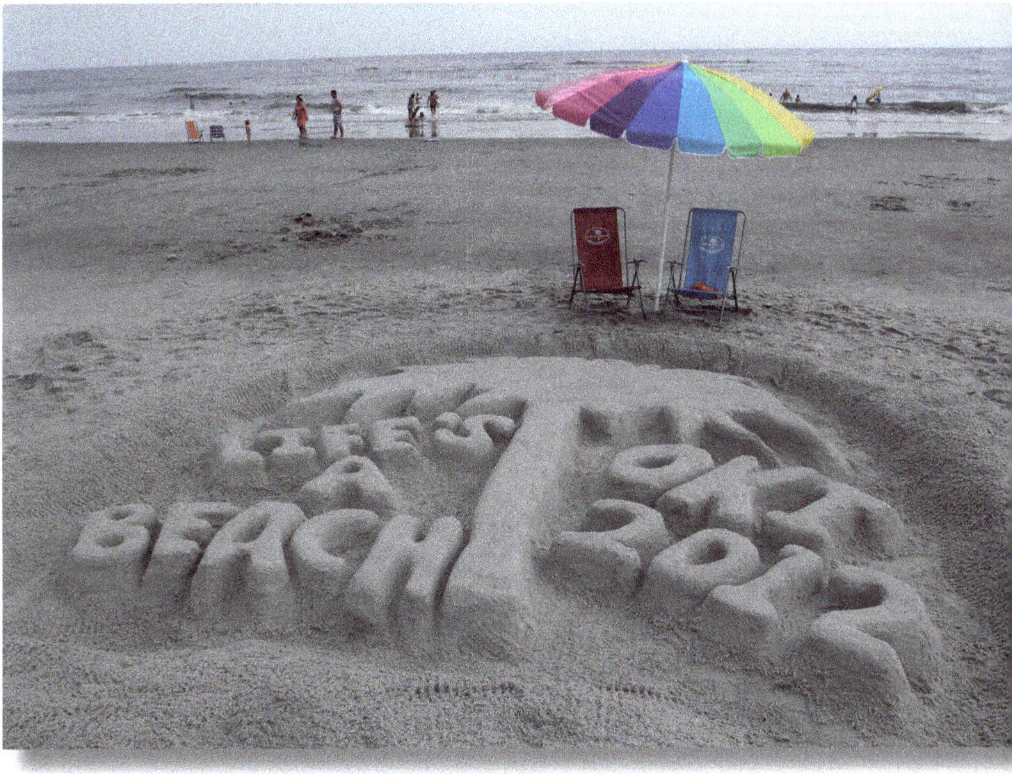

## Focus On: Color and Contrast

The vivid bright colors are part of what makes a beach vacation so liberating. Beach colors are the ones you found in a first childhood Crayon box before being socialized into more muted colors for cars, houses, and clothing. An orange bathing suit against a crisp blue sky is a classic example of using contrasting, aka complementary colors, to create an eye catching image.

While a bit counterintuitive, gray days are arguably the better days to use the bright colors of the beach effectively. While the gray may dampen your spirits a bit, the images you create with your camera can number among your best. Picture the colorful umbrellas on an urban street when it's raining. Beach paraphernalia against a gray sky will be similarly eye-grabbing.

But color is not the only form of contrast. Light and shadow can produce stunning images regardless of color. Stand atop the pier and capture the shadows of people strolling below you. Similarly, shade will produce great contrast to a subject just outside the shade barrier. For instance, a white egret at the edge of the marsh just in front of a shaded area will appear to dramatically "pop" from the black background.

You can also use shadow to create depth during noontime sunshine. The text "drop shadow" was created to mimic depth in two-dimensional artwork. Master photographers use shadow contrast to bring their photos into the third-dimension. Try shooting detailed objects with the shadow falling toward you instead of having the sun at your back.

Combine contrasting color with light-and-shadow to create interesting variations. Colorfully dressed children playing in front of a white wall with their colorless shadows cast upon the wall is a fine example.

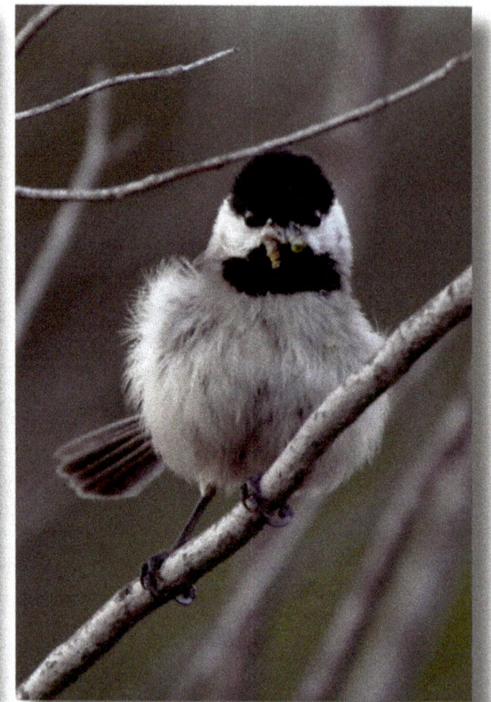

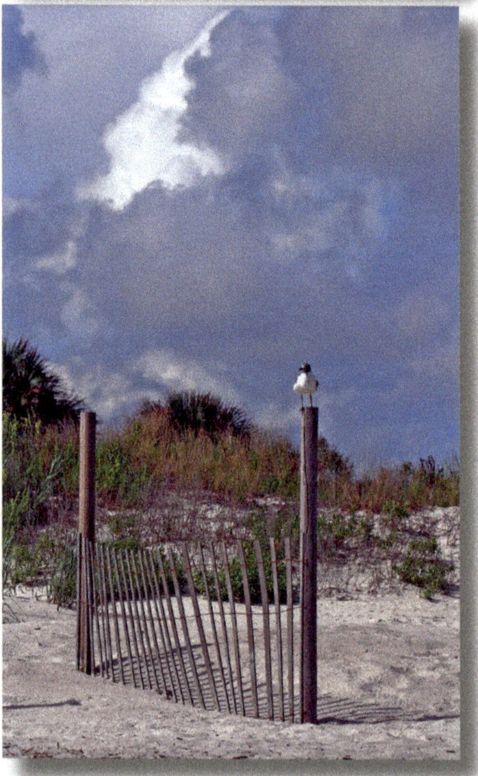

Frequently the subtlety of a gray day or drama of a storm cloud strewn background can transform the commonplace. If you are on Oak Island when the day is chilly and gray, you'll find the little Carolina Chickadees warming themselves by fluffing their feathers. Despite using the same shallow depth-of-field that is typically used for birds on a bright sunny day, the resulting mood created by the photo is decidedly different.

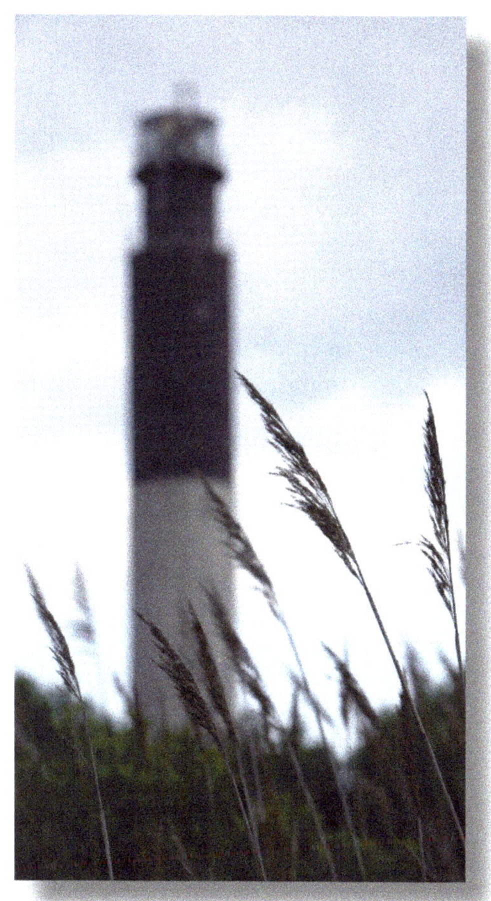

The photos of a single seagull on the post, the lighthouse, and the curly vegetation resemble watercolors while similar photos found in the "Blue Skies" subsection resemble those rendered by a painter with acrylics.

Because of the difference in effect between bright blue and gray days, you may find it gratifying if OKI has some overcast or dreary hours to retake some blue sky shots that seemed promising but didn't quite work. A bit of gray or cloud pattern may be exactly what was missing in your photo artwork.

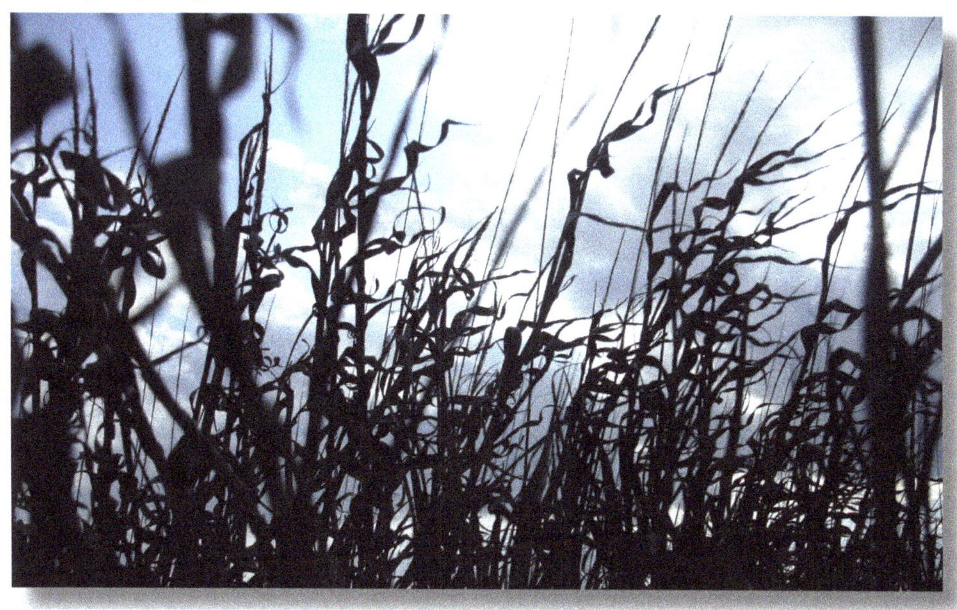

# air toys

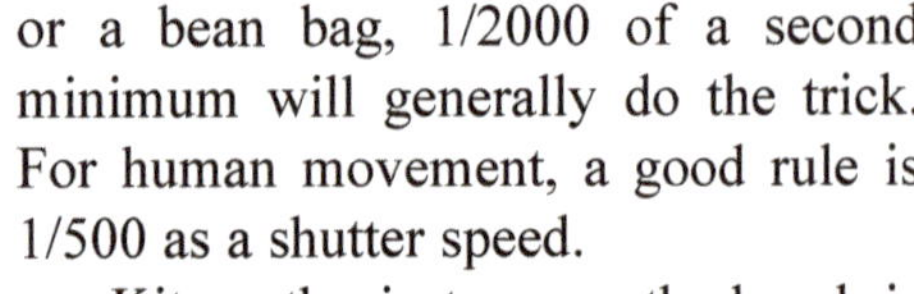

On Oak Island you can compose good photos of kites soaring, Frisbees zipping, bubbles floating, bags cornholing and any other gravity defying OKI offerings against blue skies, at sunset, or after dark. Your biggest challenge will be keeping your subject in sharp focus despite its movement, especially if the object is your subject.

If your subject is moving, you'll need a fast shutter speed to stop it in action. For small objects, like a Frisbee or a bean bag, 1/2000 of a second minimum will generally do the trick. For human movement, a good rule is 1/500 as a shutter speed.

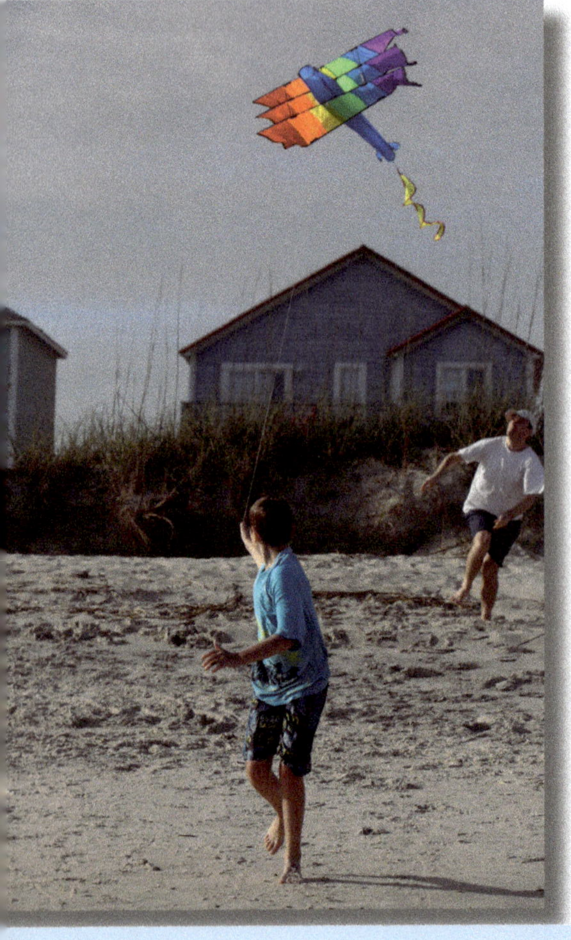

Kite enthusiasts agree the beach is the best place to fly a kite. You need a space free of kite-grabbing trees, the wind at your back, and a good breeze to set your kite soaring. By late afternoon, most days, Oak Island seems to shout "Let's Go Fly a Kite!" Many days you can launch your kite, anchor it to a beach chair, and watch it soar until you pack your gear up for the day.

You can take pictures of strangers' kites flying above Oak Island's shore. Often you will see kites that are pieces of art themselves or you will find kites using more sophisticated aerodynamic principles than those most of us learned in school. Snap away at the more interesting kites, and at worst you will have some nice documentation of an Oak Island vacation day with some chance of creating art.

Flying kites with your family and friends can lead to the quintessential photo of a kite launch. You have the sky as background, the colorful kite and the kite wrangler launching it in the middle ground, and the kite flier in the foreground. For this photo, unlike many others, the elements you would instinctively include are also the elements needed to create a textbook three-dimensional photo. Your focal point will be a person, not the kite in this scenario.

Expanding beyond the launch, try thinking beyond the immediate scene to

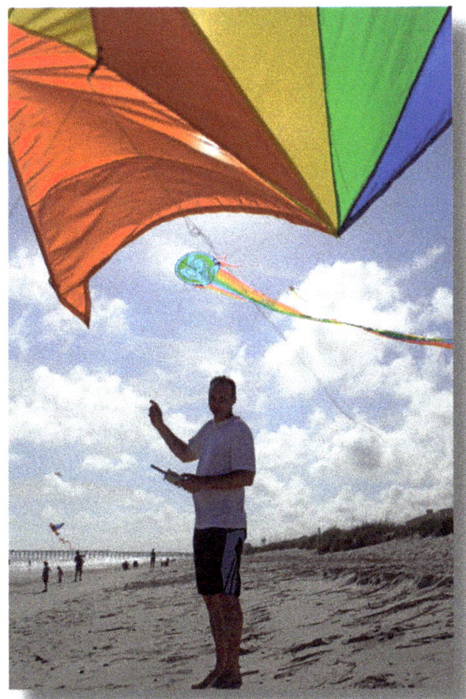

gain some context. You can include the ocean, the dunes, beach umbrellas and/or concurrent beach activities. In the photo above, the subject is in the middle ground framed by a low-flying kite in the foreground, and other kites, the dunes and the pier complete the image as background elements.

For a very different air toy activity than holding a kite soaring in the breeze, Cape Fear Jetport is the place for skydiving. You can watch other brave souls do it or do it yourself. In 2012 sky diving scenes for Iron Man 3 were filmed from just west of the Oak Island Pier. It was a particularly memorable photographic opportunity. While shots of movies in the making are rare, most days skydivers are seen from many different vantage points around the Jetport.

While more mundane, a typical beach experience often includes throw-

## Focus On: Exposure

Your camera focuses light onto a light sensitive media such as a digital camera sensor. A correct exposure is determined by the sensitivity rating of the media (ISO), the amount of light passing through the lens (aperture) and the duration of light (shutter speed).

Mathematically, a scale with a common denominator correlates these three factors. We'll simplify in this book by referring to that scale as "stops of light" or f-stops. Fortunately, this scale has been incorporated in modern cameras and in older cameras via a built-in light meter.

Understanding correct exposure is important because it empowers you to control your camera's settings. A brief explanation will also help you understand what your camera is "thinking" in automatic modes, which most readers will be using. I don't recommend using auto mode ever, but do encourage the use of shutter speed (S or Tv) and aperture modes (A or Av).

Your camera sees (meters) everything as neutral gray. Generally, this will be accurate, but on the beach, you will often be in a high-key situation. High-key is when the majority of the elements in the frame are lighter than neutral gray; therefore, you will want to use exposure compensation to add +1 or +2 stops of light.

Throughout the book I write about the ISO rating and how that affects the quality of the image. The lower the ISO, the better the quality and the larger print you can make. The lower ISO though requires a slower shuttr speed and/or wider aperture than a higher one does which can result in a blurry image due to movement.

Learning how to control light entering your camera using the three settings is the surest way to have your OKI photography going from good to great.

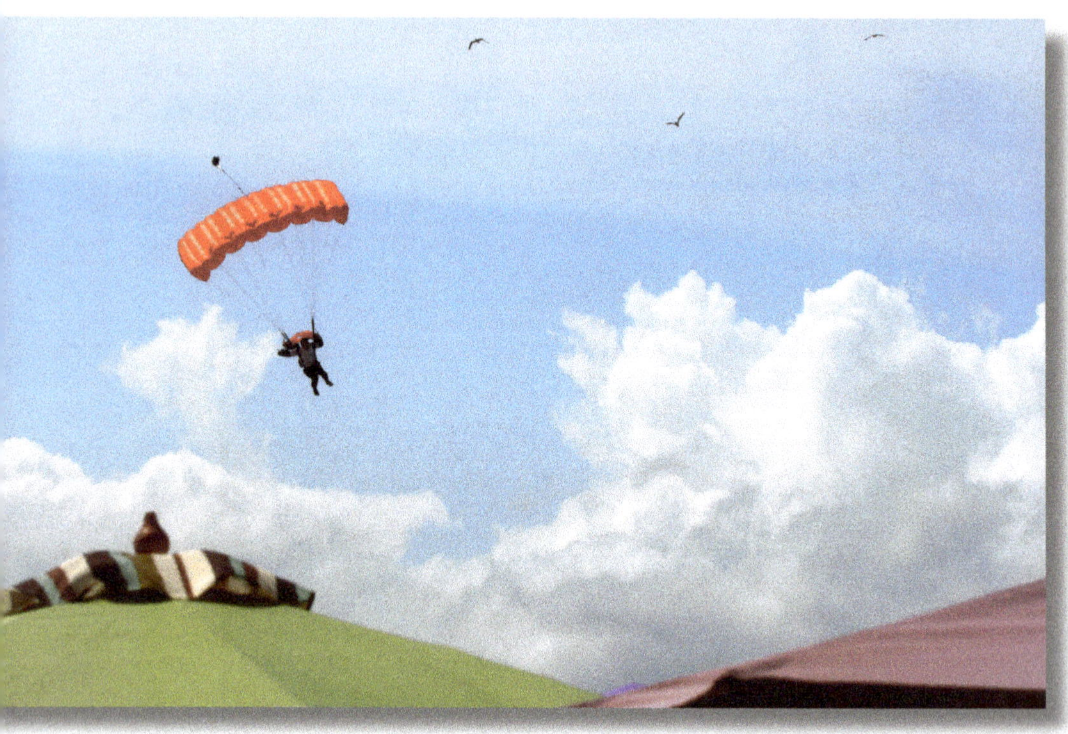

ing something into the air. Two-man beach volleyball is such a long standing part of that tradition that it is now an Olympic event separate from traditional six-man volleyball played indoors. On Oak Island volleyball is much more *ad hoc.* The two volleyball nets are usually up next to the Oak Island Pier where you can photograph others in action, join in on the action, or organize some action yourself.

Frisbees and footballs, the perennial favorites, and bean bags for cornhole, a more recent addition, are Oak Island's most commonly identified flying objects. Practice stop action, panning, and motion blur as your buddies, your family, or perfect strangers throw these objects. You'll want to focus on the receiver or thrower to catch the action. If you can try to anticipate the action, you'll actually be pressing the shutter button early to make up for the camera's shutter-lag. Keep a portion of your eye on the contextual elements to include interesting "grounds" into the frame such as the giant orange octopus on the next page.

You are on vacation and don't need a purpose for taking pictures. Instead, think creatively. Try just tossing interesting objects into the air above the lapping waves and "snap." The totally inexplicable photo on the top of the next page is a sample of what you can do. Is it a sea monster, a giant inflatable dragon or a small plastic object?

Have an accomplice toss the object and practice stopping the action at the object's apex. You may need to toss the same object several times if it is best photographed square in the frame and

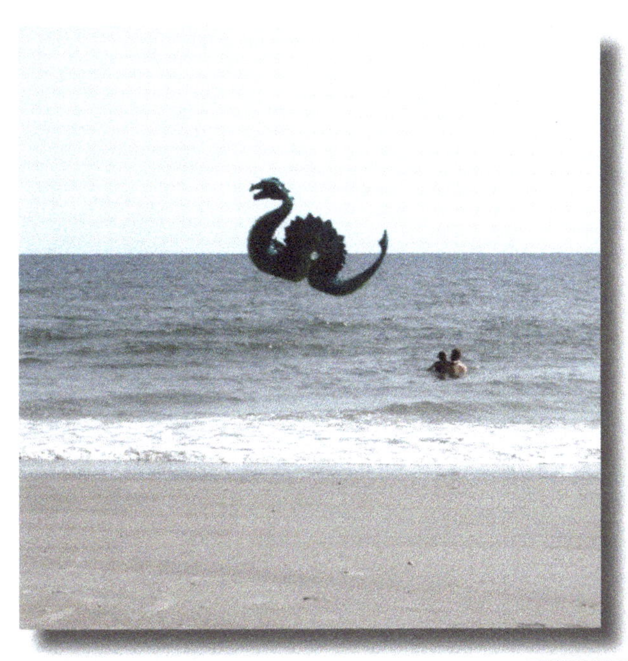

has a right side up. Try it with a beach ball imprinted with Oak Island, your daughter's Dora the Explorer figure, or a small, plastic dragon like this one thrown by my nephew.

Bubbles, toy classics, are as popular today as they were decades ago. Conditions in the summer on Oak Island are often perfect. While there is no photo shown of bubble-blowing on OKI, if you're intrigued see "Learning More" on page 122.

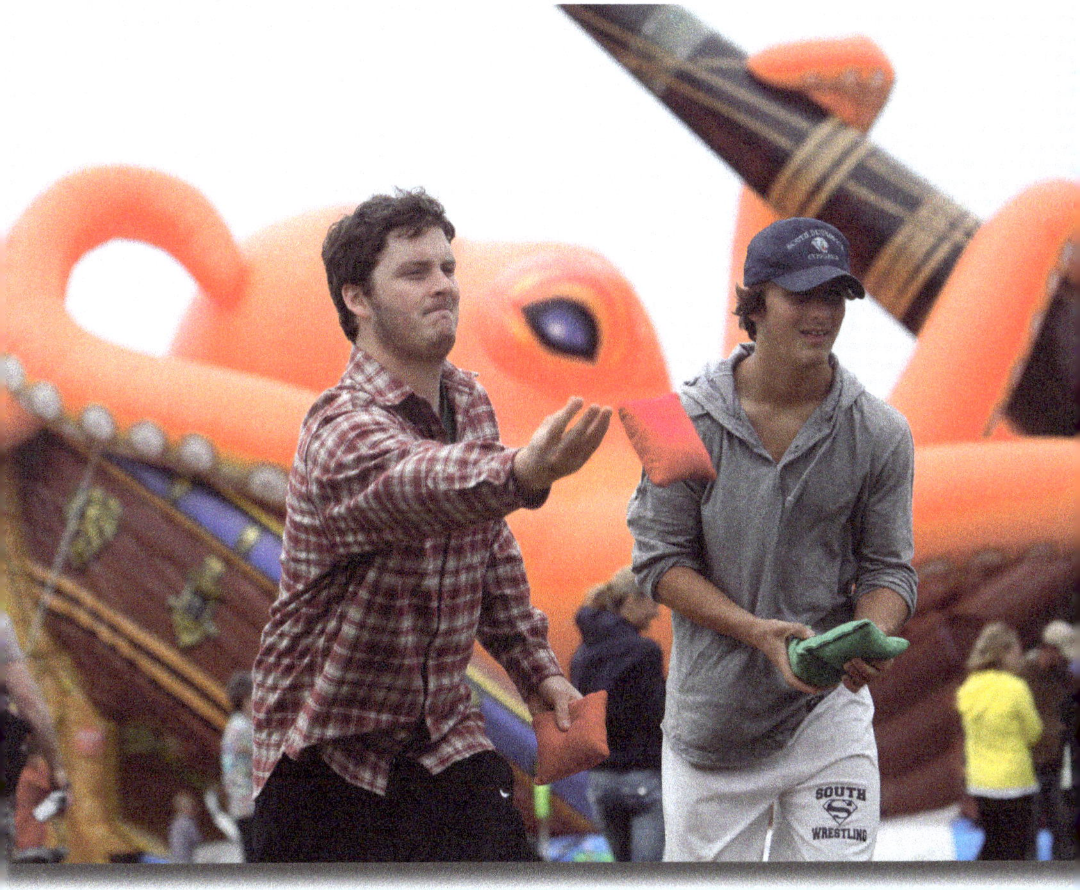

For a photographer, birds divide into two categories. There are those you can photograph with a standard focal length lens and those that require toting a heavy long lens. Fortunately, on Oak Island, you can use standard equipment for the local favorites. Pelicans, seagulls, cormorants, and ospreys are seemingly fearless; they perch on posts, play in sand puddles, slowly soar, flock on the beach or, in the case of Oak Island osprey, roost in unlikely places such as by the parking lots of the Oak Island Golf Course and William "Bill" Smith Park.

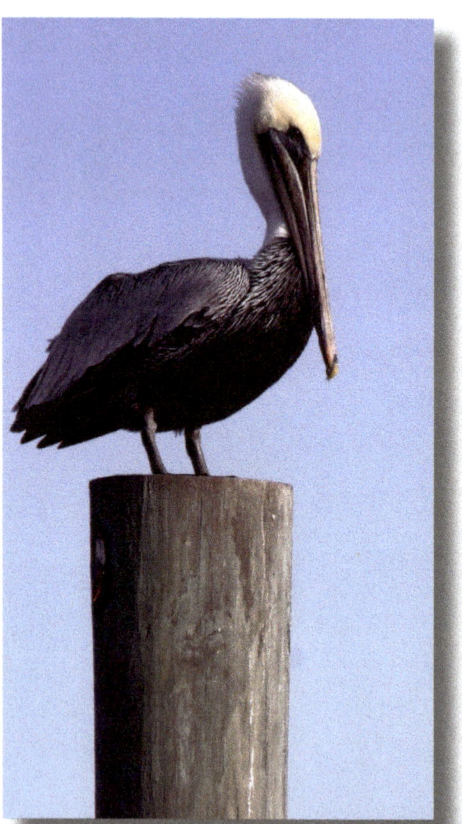

Pelicans can be the most mesmerizing creatures. One day as I stood near the Oak Island Pier a squadron of 57 pelicans flew by. As you would guess, 57 is atypical, but squadrons of 20 or more are quite common. As you look out to the sea or back toward the dunes and watch them fly past, drafting on their leader, click and catch them with your camera. They move slowly and predictably, and often come close. A long lens makes all bird pictures easier, but a typical fixed lens camera, held steady, and then cropped as needed, generally works with passing pelicans. Similarly, photographing pelicans resting on pilings is easy.

As with pelicans, you'll find cormorants standing statue-like on posts or natural outcroppings. If you are patient, you may see one dive and move through

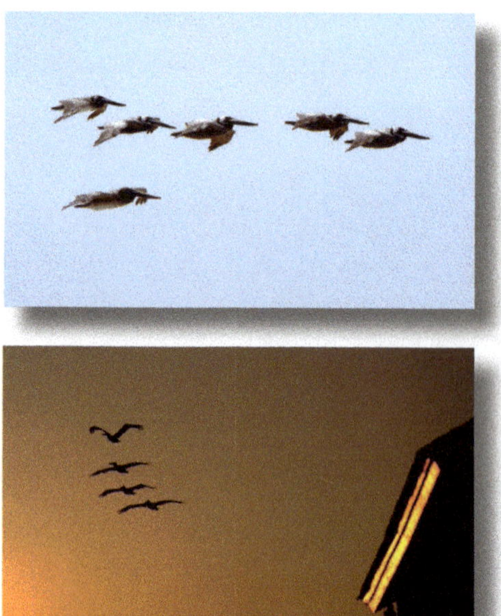

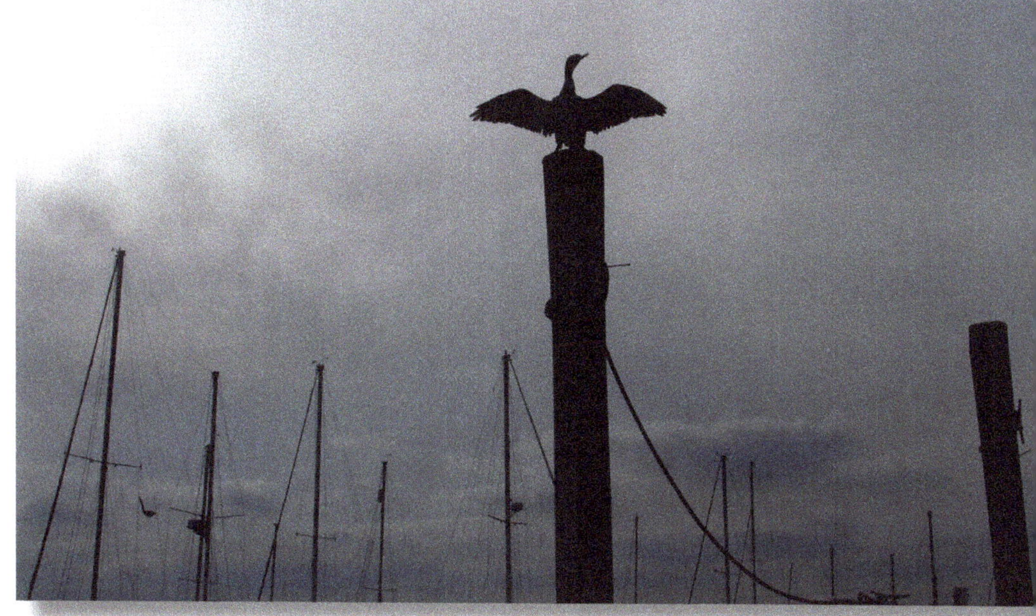

the water to snatch a fish before it resumes its statuesque position, with wings partially spread to dry. The cormorant, shown above, was taken on a hazy, near-overcast day with the partially hidden sun behind the bird causing a silhouette. You'll spot spread-winged cormorants on the pilings of the South Harbor Marina and on private and public boat docks along the interior Oak Island waters.

While you will only encounter an occasional cormorant and mostly sight pelicans as they fly by, you will find seagulls in small groups sprinkled along the length of the OKI shoreline. Loud raucous Laughing Gulls share the beach with the summer beach crowd. In the winter, when most visitors have gone home, the sedate Ringed Billed Gulls replace them. It is easy to photograph them frolicking, resting, or sleeping on the sand. You do have to remember when you are photographing white sea

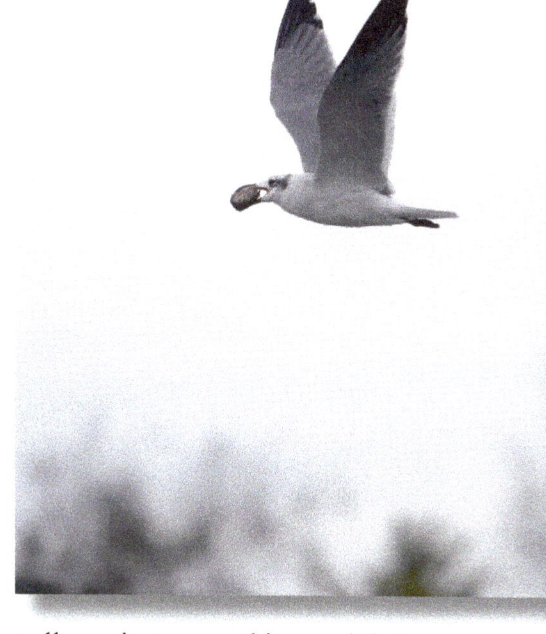

gulls against near white sand that your camera meter will think both are gray, as this is a high-key situation. In order

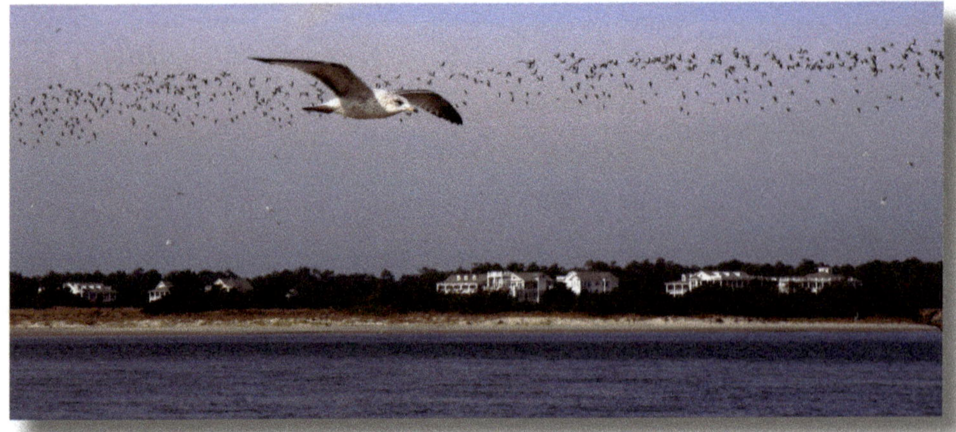

to get a correct exposure, you will need to adjust your exposure compensation by +1 or +2.

Photographing airborne gulls can be more difficult. While a gull hovering in the wind such as the one above is nearly stationary, a fast-moving gull requires you to pan with the bird's movement. By setting your autofocus to continuous you should be able to track the gull.

Because seagulls are so common on beaches, you'll need an unexpected element to make your photo noteworthy. The object in the gull's beak is the eye-grabbing element in the first seagull photo; the background filled with birds serves the purpose in the second.

## Focus On: Focal Length Basics

For those of you that don't do focal length speak, the basics are geeky but simple. Single length camera lenses range in focal length from approximately 8mm to 800mm. The lens that ships with a new camera will usually be 45 to 60mm often referred to as a normal lens or a standard lens. The frame of reference for normalcy is what is seen by the human eye. If you look through the viewfinder, the subject will appear to be at the same distance as if you simply looked at it with the naked eye.

Any lens greater than 60mm is considered a telephoto or long lens. When you look through a telephoto lens, the subject will appear larger and closer to you than it actually is. Most bird photos are taken with a telephoto lens. Stand on the beach and watch a pelican dive for a fish. While your brain and inner core will concentrate on the action of the pelican, if you look at what is actually in your field of vision, it is a whole lot of sky and sea and one small spot of pelican. With a telephoto lens you can capture what your brain finds fascinating and not what your eyes see. If you have a high-resolution, sharp digital image, you can sometimes crop and enlarge an image taken with a normal focus lens to approximate what you can do with a long lens.

Any lens less than 45mm is considered a wide-angle lens. If you look through the viewfinder, the subject will appear smaller or farther away. If you are photographing a large squadron of pelicans flying close by, you will not be able to see the leader and end of the line without moving at least your eyes and perhaps your head. Think of a wide-angle lens as an extension of your peripheral vision. If you are only carrying a normal lens, there is, of course, no simple fix with computer software that is analogous to cropping.

Zoom lenses can be either telephoto or wide-angle and even both. Zoom refers to the ability to change the focal length. Zoom lenses allow us to carry less glass in our arsenal of lenses.

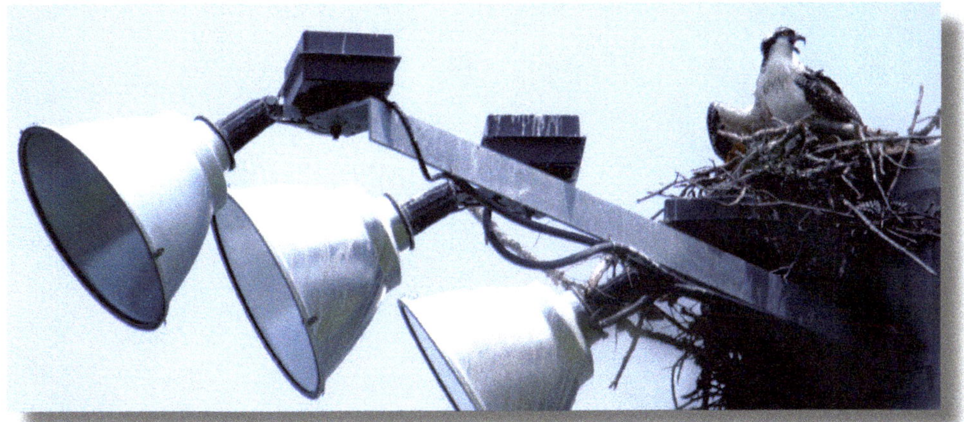

Ospreys, aka Sea Eagles, are regular OKI migrants. They are large impressive birds that roast seemingly fearlessly near bustling human activity. Your best bet to spot one is in the vicinity of one pair's nesting site in the field lights at William "Bill" Smith Park.

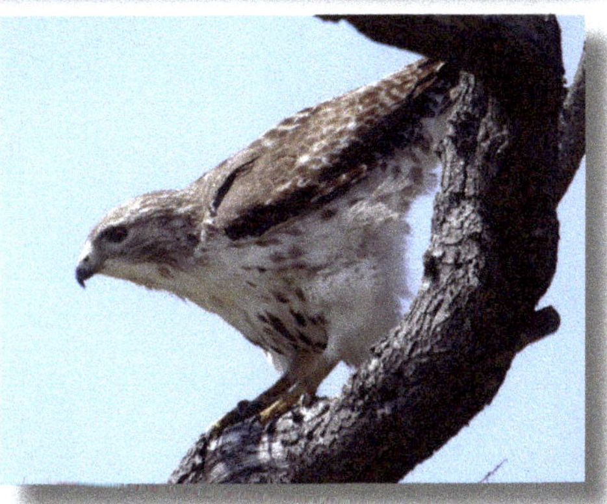

While most of you probably didn't come to Oak Island to see the songbirds, raptors, and woodpeckers that share the island with the shore birds, enthusiastic birders will like OKI. There were 68 bird species counted on Oak Island during a recent Cornell Backyard Bird Count and more than 170 in the 10 mile diameter circle that includes the island during the Audubon Christmas bird count.

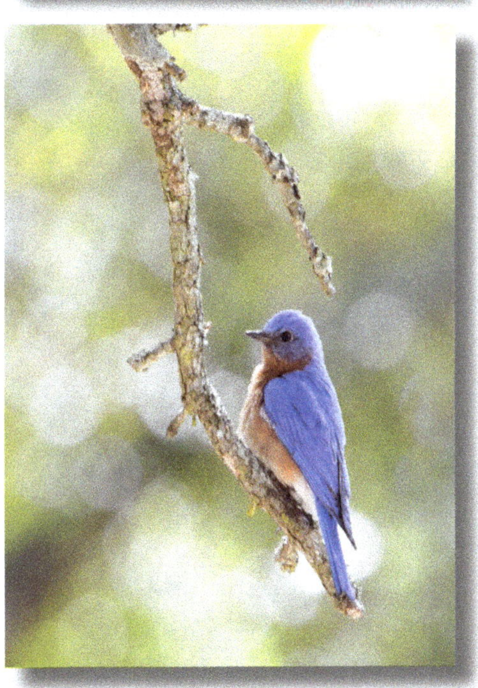

Pine Island at SW 15th Street offers one of the best places to see varieties of birds. The area is strictly residential so please go quietly out of respect for both the human and feathered residents. West Pelican between 2nd and 7th also serves as a particularly good spot with only a couple of houses nestled in what is largely native maritime forest.

# Land

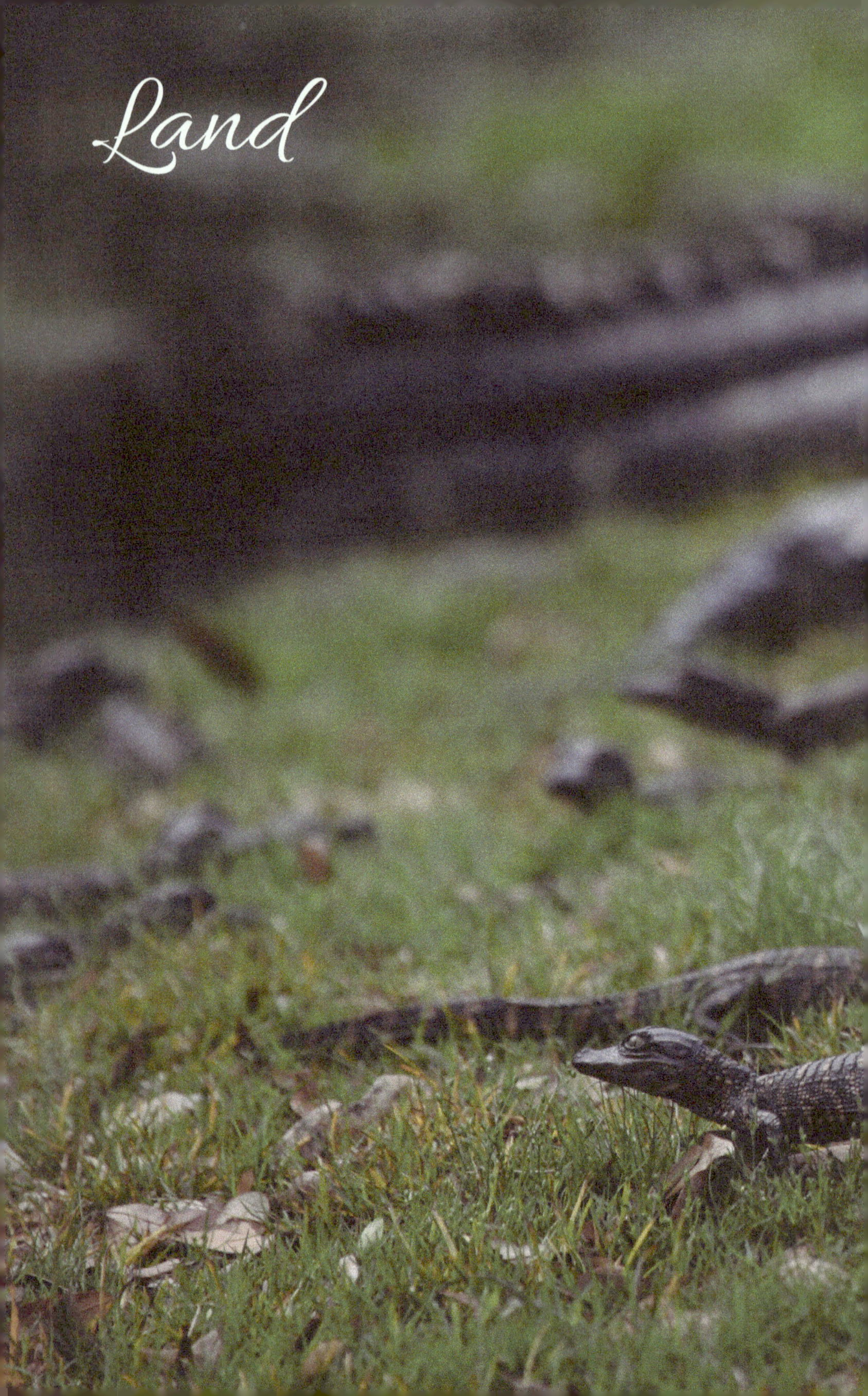

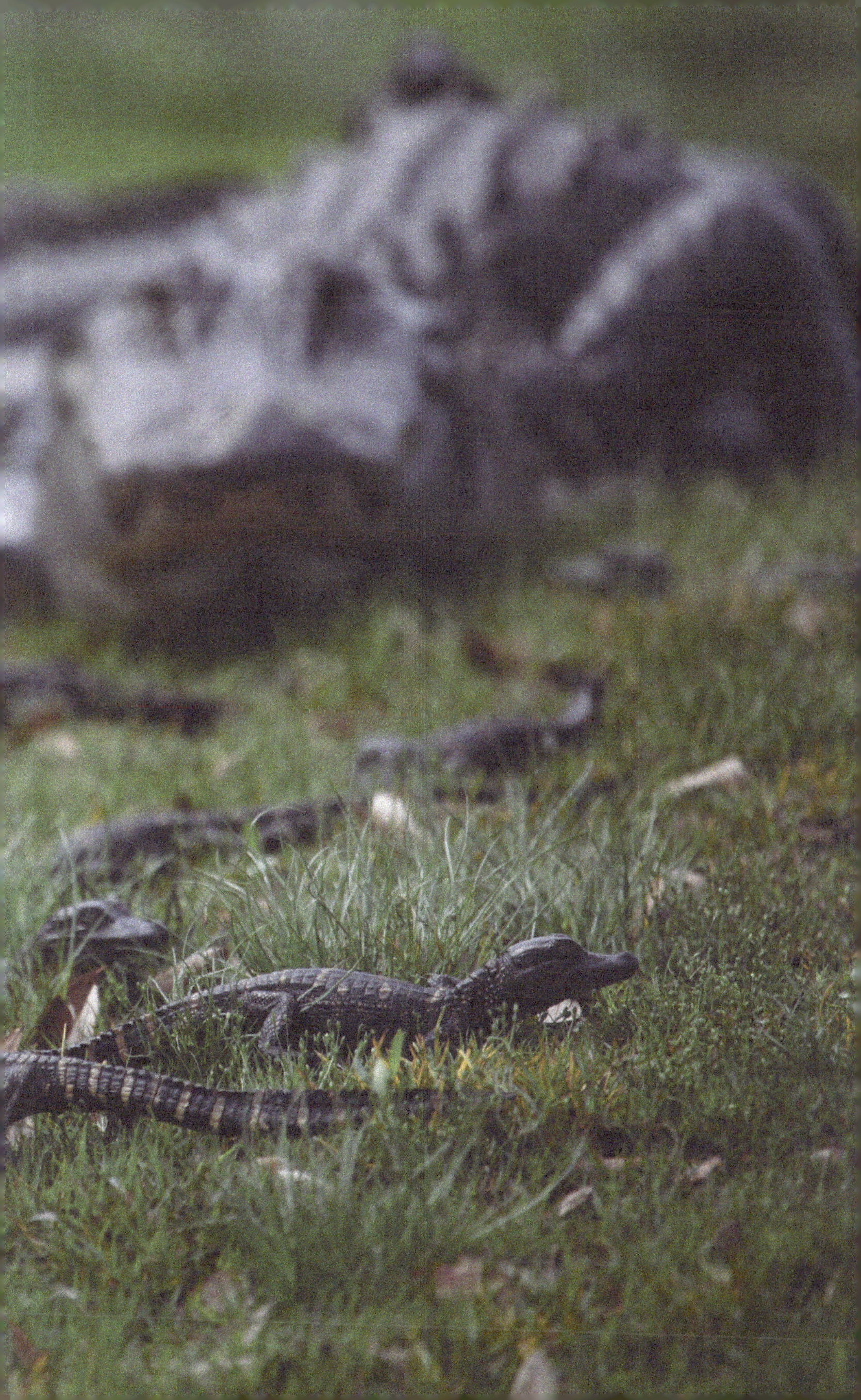

When you first print your Oak Island pictures or see them on a screen, chances are your favorites will be of the places and creatures that make Oak Island special. They'll include the shot you took of the shrimp boat, or 20 pelicans at sunset, or the humongous yacht on the Intracoastal.

In 30 years, your favorite photos are likely to be instead those of your own beach traditions at the age and stage of your life when you shot them. Those will best evoke emotion and spark fond memories. You won't, of course, have those photos unless you take them. Think about taking photos you would use to create a book titled, *A Day on Oak Island with the "Whoevers."* Even family portraits can be active. Sitting for a family portrait seldom

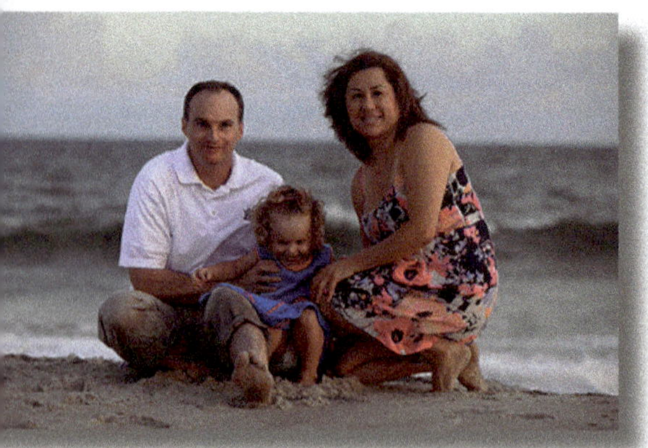

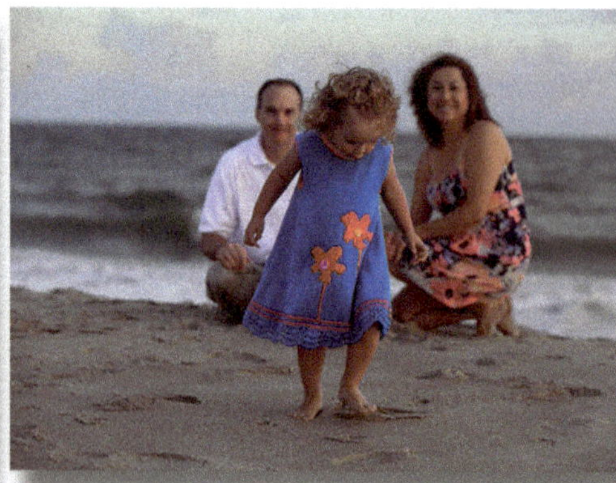

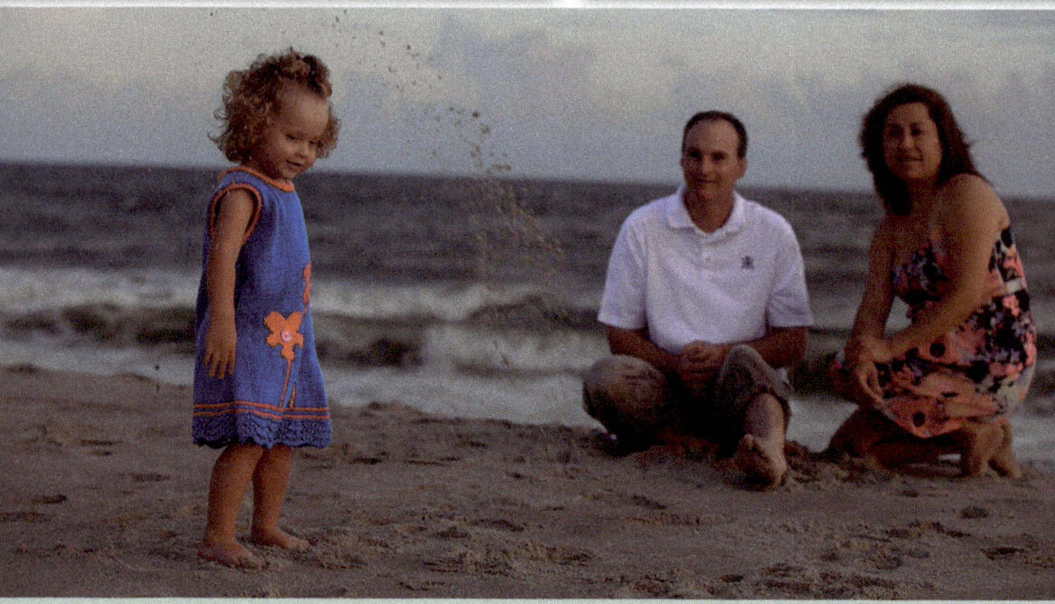

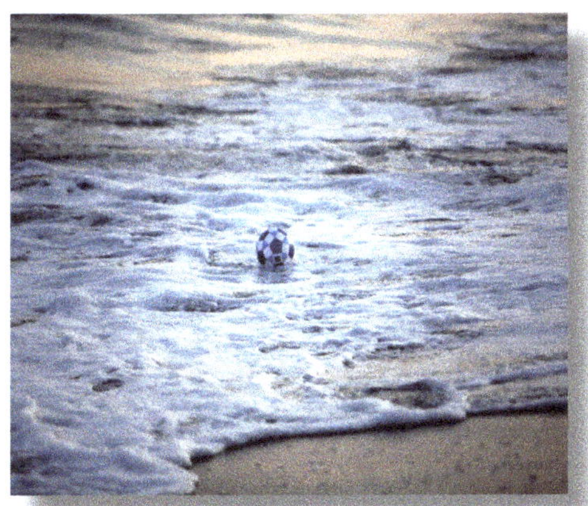

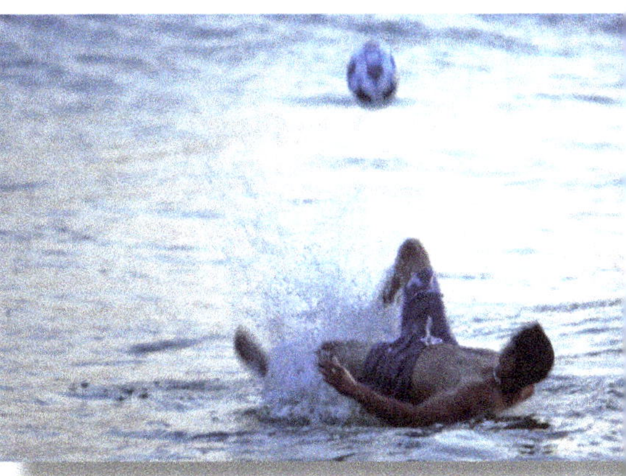

amuses my youngest participants as much as it engrosses me and the older ones. My niece, Yzabella, had the right idea. Making footprints or throwing and watching sand fall is (1) more fun than sitting still, (2) more interesting photographically, and (3) better preserves for posterity how much her parents adore her than a static group shot would.

Unless you own, beg, borrow, or rent a lighting system, the conditions for this sequence are some of the best you can hope to have under natural light. They were taken towards the end of the Golden Hour; there was a soft cloud cover, and the waves were breaking just enough to froth white, providing a bit of reflection from below off their glistening curls.

Beyond group shots, apt photos of spontaneous activities friends and families enjoy on the beach vary a lot between vacationing groups. Most of the time you can collect the memory with your camera by either taking a picture of the people engaged in the activity or by framing a stylized shot that visually capsulizes the activity without the participant(s).

Soccer at the beach is photographed both ways in the example above. That particular soccer ball will surely ignite remembrances of time spent with it on the beach and many other times and places. The ball alone within the waves at sunset is enough to mentally relive the activity; the action shot, though, begged to be taken as well.

I do think pet photos need the pet. I suppose a favorite dog toy without the dog could work, but why do it? The picture you take of your pet on the beach will be particularly poignant in 30 years. Your pet most certainly will have been long gone, making your *Day on Oak Island* photo priceless.

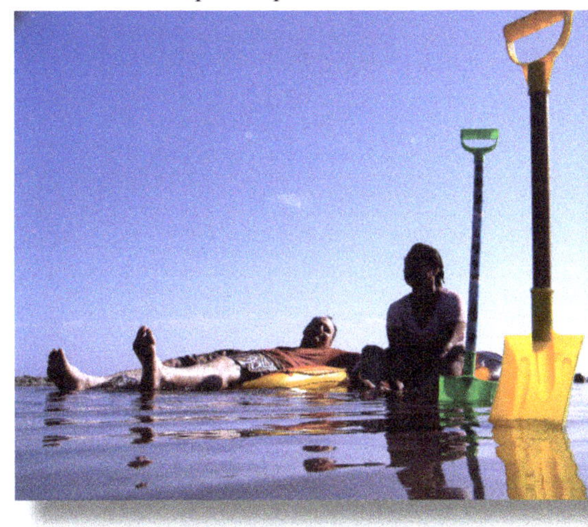

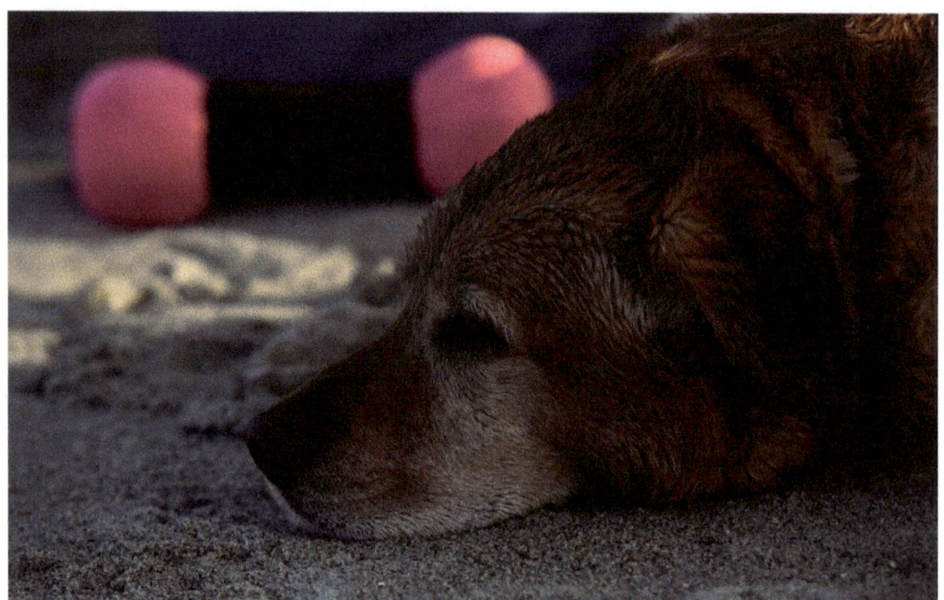

## Focus On: Documentary

For over a decade I worked as a newspaper photojournalist. Professional integrity demanded honest documentation. Set-up shots were a no-no for news coverage and Photoshop manipulation was frowned upon for everything. It is liberating to be free to create art and to play a bit more with my camera. Still, there are some basic tenants of journalism worth observing for even casual vacation photography.

For your own "news" of how you spent your vacation think about including visual clues that answer journalists' must list questions: *who, what, when, where, how, and why*? (You can cross off the last one. You don't need a reason; you are on vacation.) Documenting '*how*' is what you naturally do with your camera. You can eliminate that one, too. Remaining are who, what, when, and where. '*Who*' is usually easy to do; it is just a matter of consciously doing it. I am already finding it harder and harder to remember who was with me at which beach vacation. Taking a group shot is, of course, the obvious way of having a record of who was there. A sequence of shots in a compressed time-frame often better documents the day at the beach. Picture teens surfing, adults in beach chairs, 20-somethings playing volleyball, Aunt Eloise and Grandpa Mervin surf fishing. Whatever your compatriots are up to in a few sequential minutes answers the '*who*' and also records something about who they are at the particular point in their lives.

'*Where*' is also easy to do on Oak Island. The beach accesses have great big green signs with the street number on them and bright blue trash cans with Oak Island emblazoned across them. You can document '*where*' by using them.

'*When*' used to be the trickiest for photographers. Mercifully now, with most digital cameras, if you have remembered to set the date as needed, you should have the information somewhere on your computer. It is still probably a good idea to include in your OKI photo sequences a visual clue. You can often find one and make it part of a good shot. For instance, a great big banner will be stretched across Long Beach Road announcing the date of an upcoming event. Foliage provides an instant clue to the season; think daffodils versus mums.

'*What*' is the most important. The memories you preserve of your good times, doing what you and your friends and family enjoy most on the beach, will continuously appreciate in value over time.

Good beach photography requires appropriate light. Waiting until late on sunny day is one possibility. Using the shade of your beach umbrella is another one. Echo, our fox red lab, who has since died, was captured recovering in the soft light just within the umbrella's shade after repeatedly fetching his toy from the waves.

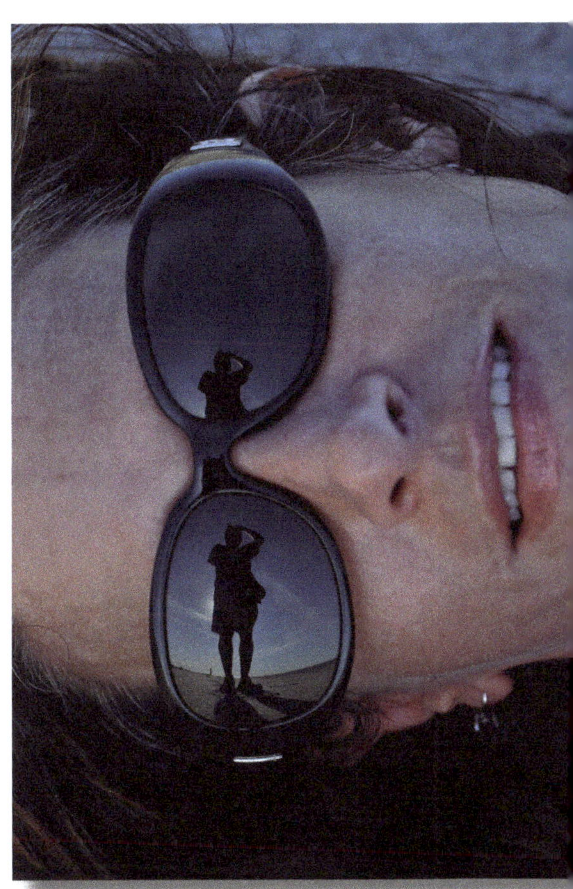

A third possibility is to intentionally use the harsh sunlight. Catching a full reflection in sunglasses works best when the sunglass wearer is in the shade and the reflected subject is in the sun. Or, create a shot like that below. It isn't intuitively obvious despite your having surely seen something similar through your camera's lens. Aim your camera in the direction of the sun, and you will see in the viewfinder virtually colorless silhouettes on the beach. The translucent tubes are, of course, the element in this frame that creates the visual "pop." Your translucent plastic beach toys will work equally well.

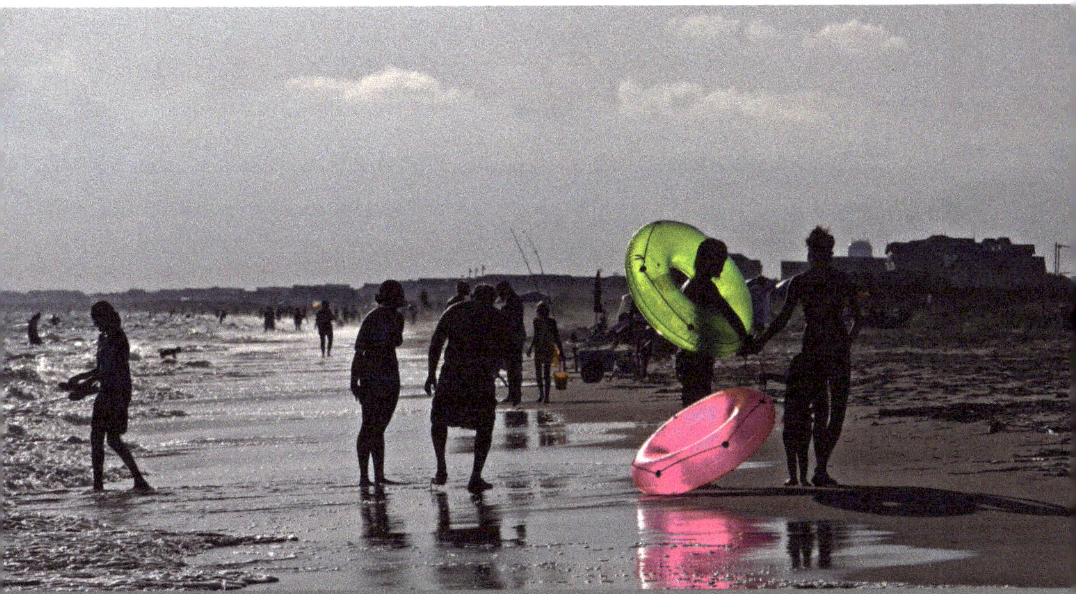

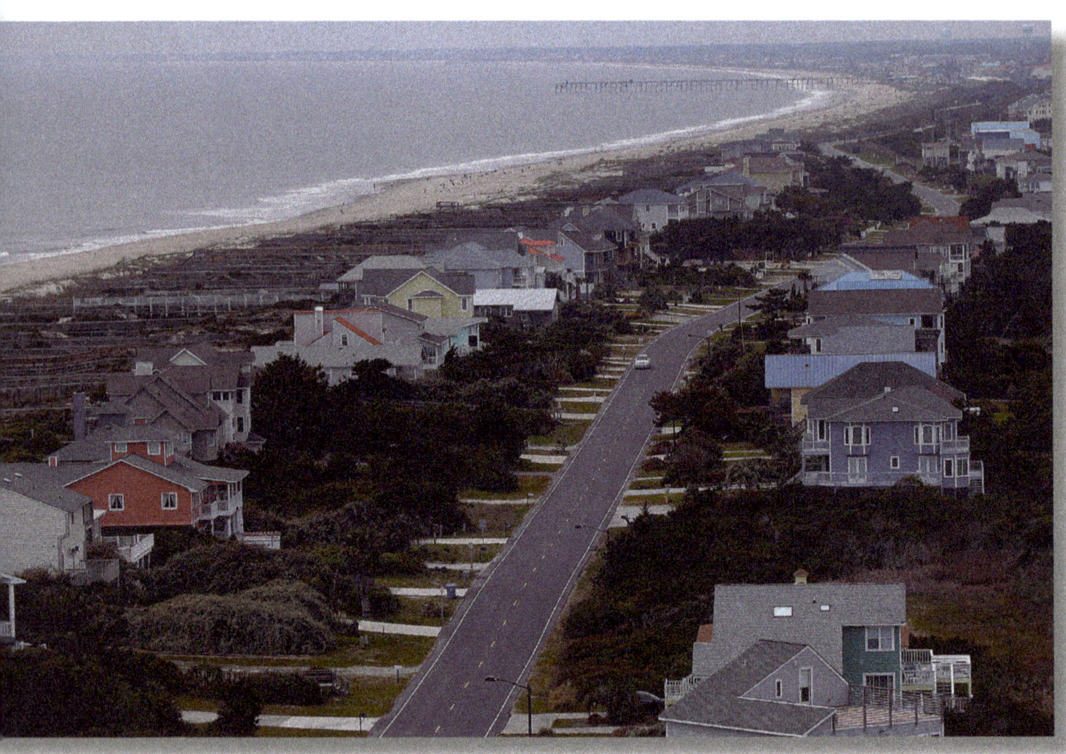

Oak Island boasts more than twelve miles of sandy beach. Little wonder that it was simply known as Long Beach when the island's beach was first developed for recreational visitors in the late 1930s. Where should you take that sweeping sandy beach shot to start your album or digital slide show? If you climb to the top of the OKI Lighthouse, you can take the shot that you see here, which includes all but the most eastern mile of the beach. Otherwise, as is so often the case, the two piers can assist you photographically. You'll have the advantage of both the piers' height and distance out into the sea to make photographing a huge swath of the beach possible. Try shooting from the Ocean Crest Pier to encompass both the Oak Island Pier and the sweep of sand from about the middle of the island to its curl into the Cape Fear River. Ideally, on a cloudless day, you take the picture in the morning so that the shadows are falling toward you. Shadows falling toward you will add a better sense of depth, adding three-dimensionality.

Sand on Oak Island morphs from the simplicity of that on the beach into dunes, bluffs, "caves," flats, crab hills, and castles. It is canvas to shells, seaweed, sea critters, plants, footprints, messages and people. The Oak Island dunes vary in size, vegetation, and shape along its coast, granting diverse options for inventive beach photography. They are protected from foot and vehicular traffic by an ordinance that both residents and visitors seem to conscientiously obey. Through the concerted efforts of Oak Islanders and respect of visitors, they remain remarkably unspoiled even though the Island hosts more than 20,000 visitors on a sunny summer weekend.

As you chose among the 60-plus beach accesses in the Town of Oak Island, most cross softly mounded dunes planted with sea oats and sprouting native plants. On the front side of the dune, some parts have been battered by the sea into a bluff. The stretch of beach just below the water tower at the end of the 29th Street scenic walkway pictured, is an example of the ever changing faces of the dunes.

Typical dunes unadorned are attractive as photographs. The inclusion

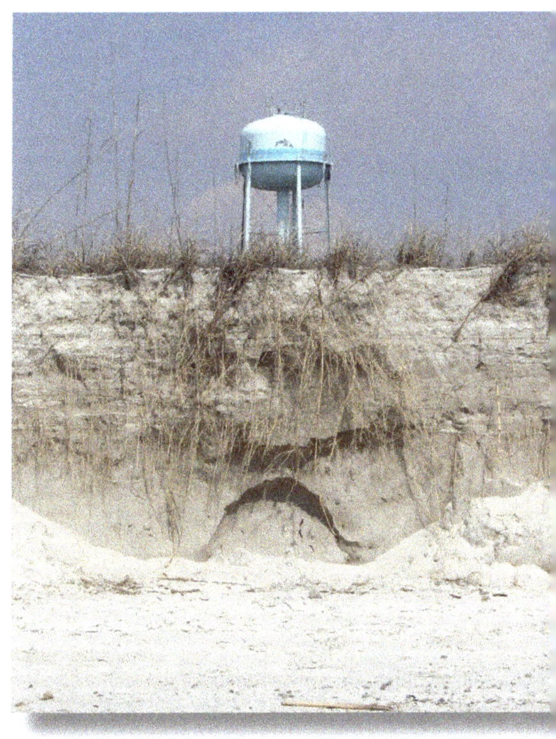

of some additional elements notches up the quality. Here the posts used to guard most of the Oak Island dune line,

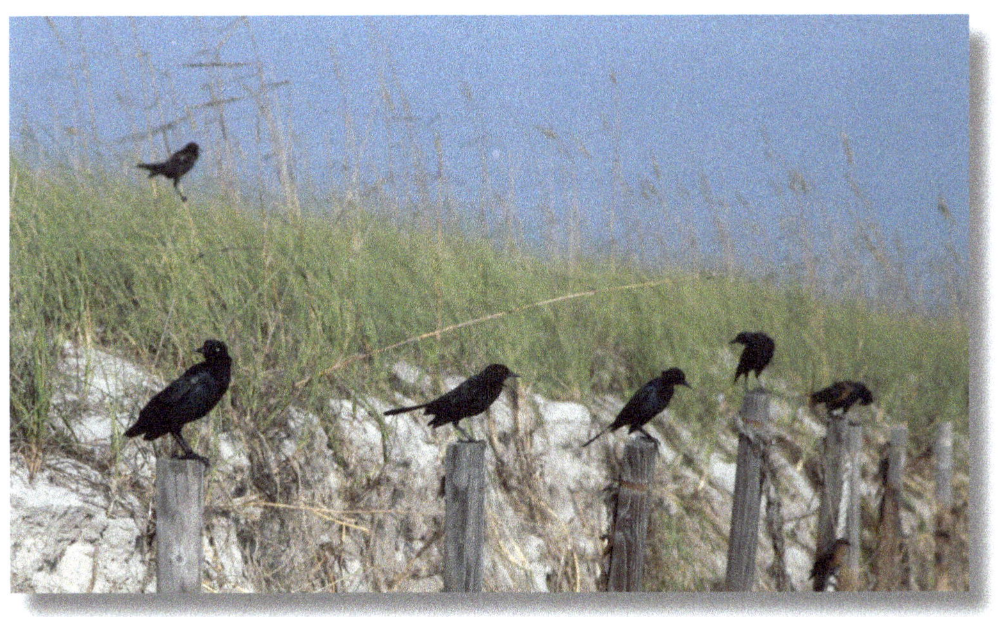

topped by a line of birds, distinguishes the photo from the plain vanilla dune shot. If you have some patience, birds will oblige. Some of my favorite sand shots are of simple sand patterns. The shot below is evocative in much the same way as a photo of undulating desert dunes meeting a sea are—but miniaturized.

Footprints in the sand are always intriguing. Where did he or she go and why? Go out to the Point where river silt mixes with the sand to find (or make) footprints as deep and undisturbed as those you see to your right.

For another mystery, visit the stairs to nowhere out at Dutchman's Creek. While some local undoubtedly knows why they are there, it seemed more fun to speculate than to track down the answer.

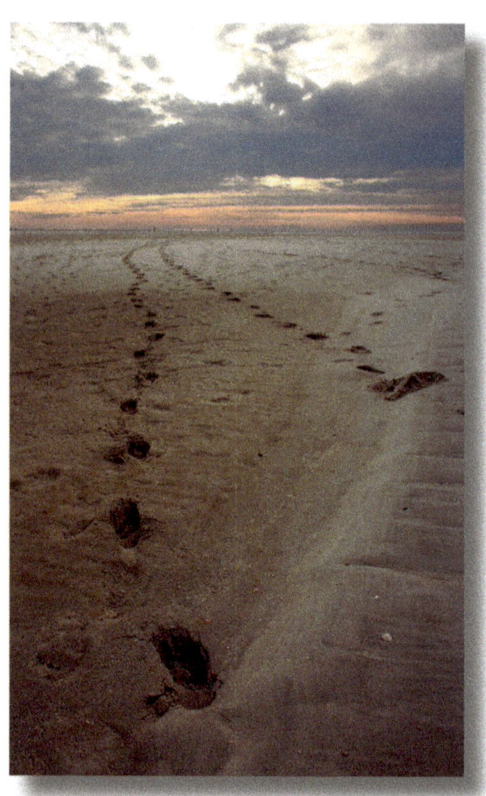

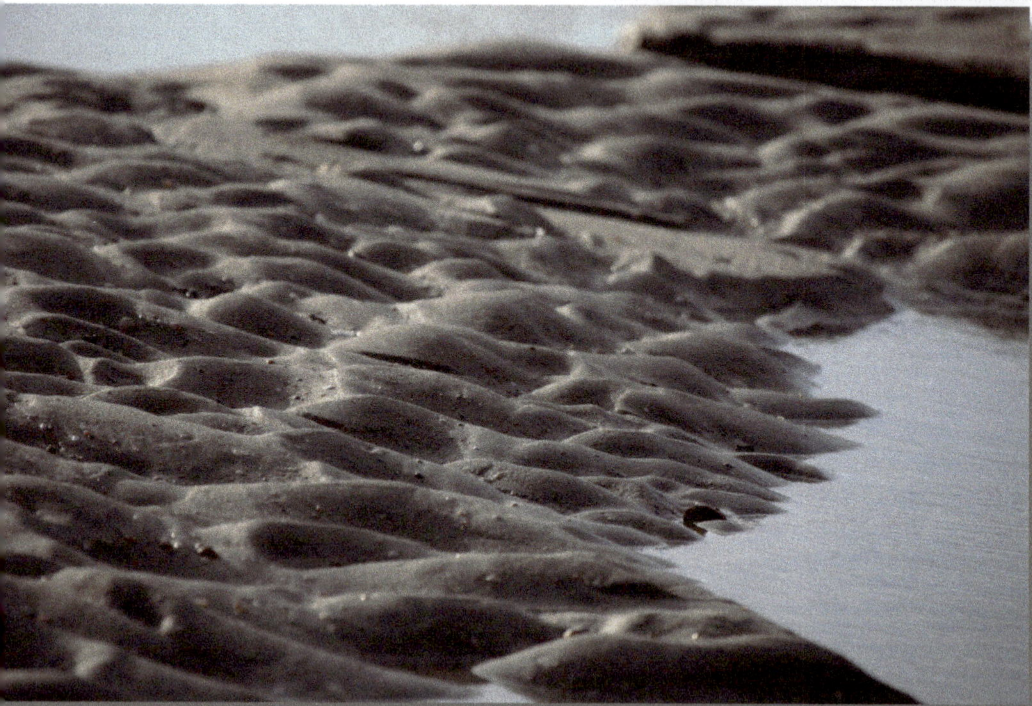

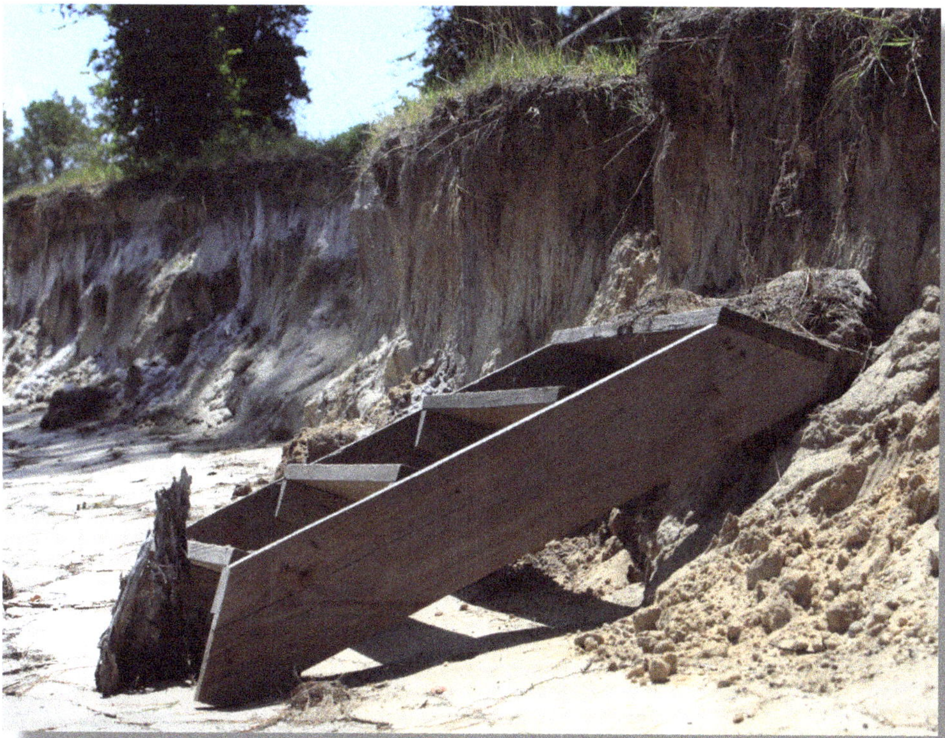

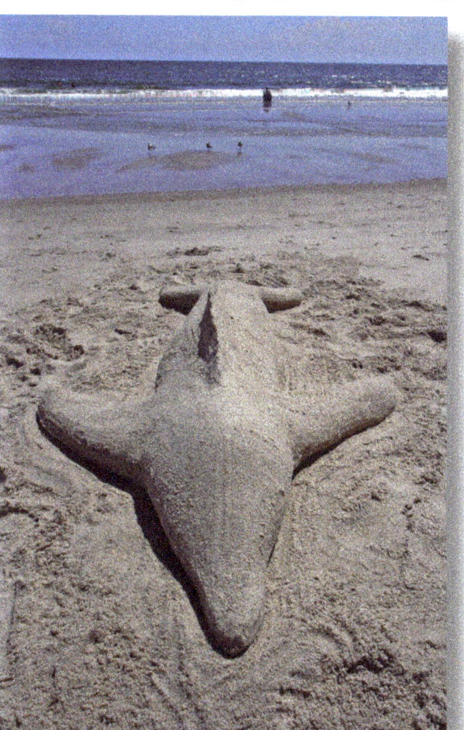

The relationship of humans to sand poses as the biggest of sand mysteries. Why do humans need to coat, cover, or bury themselves in it? Why do they spend hours building sand edifices only to have them be washed away? Whatever the reason, it's fortuitous for photographers.

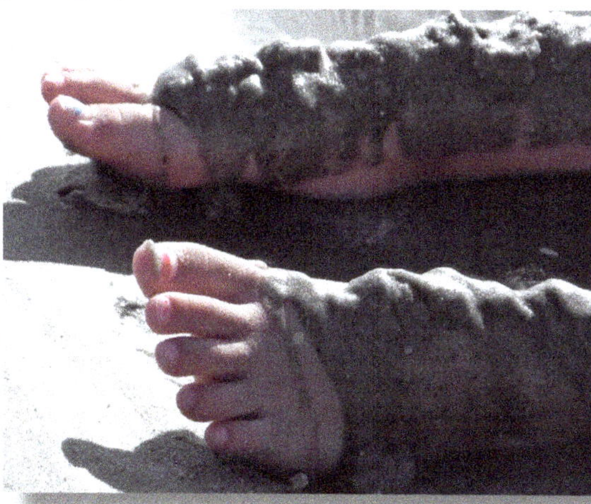

# *off the beach*

There is more to Oak Island than her beach. While the beach surely attracts tourists and home owners alike, there are approximately 4,500 miles of ocean shoreline in the United States to choose from. More and more people are choosing Oak Island. Why?

For most folk it is probably because of the Oak Island locals. Local plants and animals species are diverse and surprisingly plentiful. Opportunities to reconnect with nature is one of OKI draws. The local *homo sapiens* are also an asset, particularly for photographers. They tend toward whimsy in everything from landscaping to transport, signage to houses, interior decor to personal style. Whimsy is coupled with the dedication to keeping life simple.

"Come as you are" is an invitation that you will find offered with few exceptions. Visitors are often invited to "come as you are" to church services. The Barbee Library door featured a notice in the window this summer indicating "No Wet Swimsuits Allowed." (Oak Islanders don't actually consider bathing suits, wet or dry, appropriate library dress.) Restaurants more often than not divide between those where "Shirts and Shoes are Required" and where "No Shirt, No Shoes, No Problem." Through a photograph imaginatively composed using local signage in the "come as you are" spirit, you can create an attractive memento of your OKI experience.

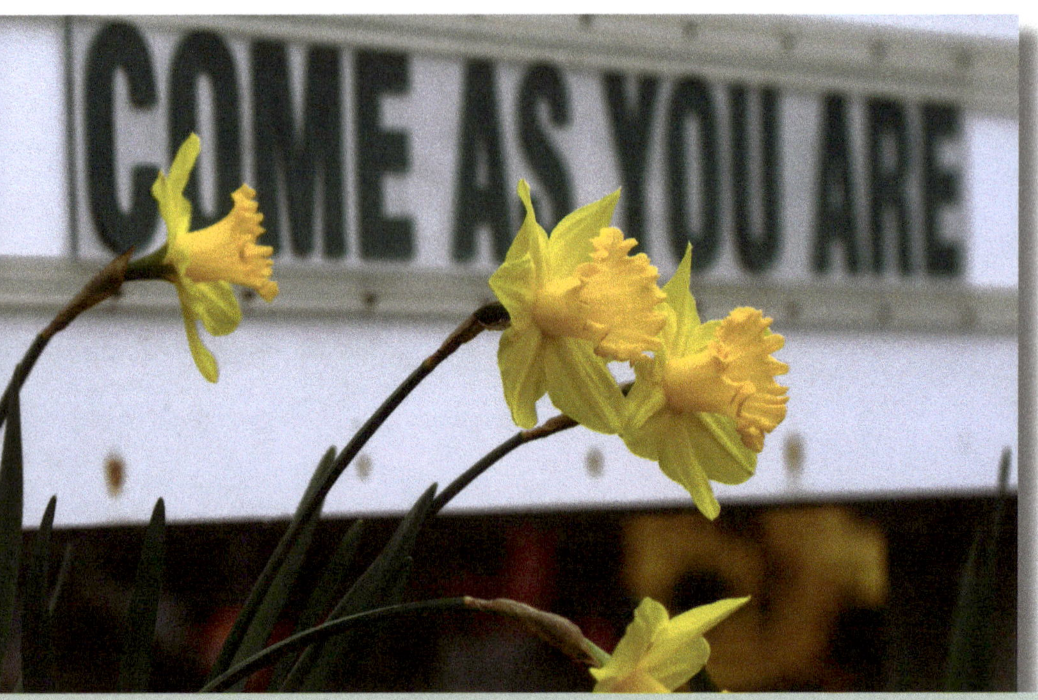

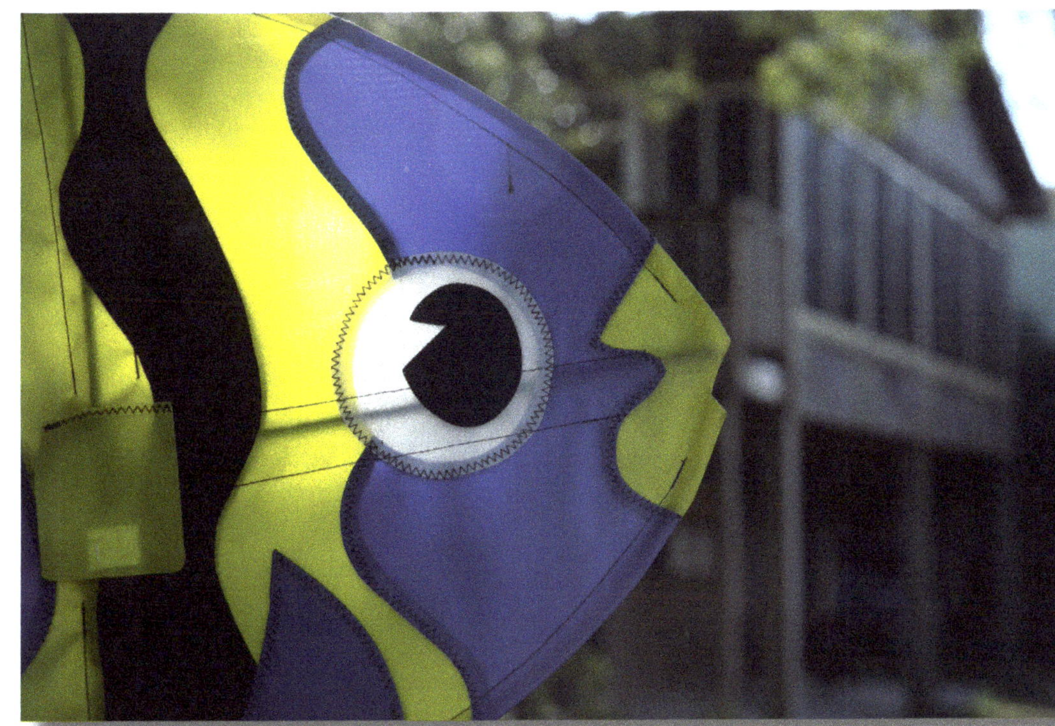

On the flip side to whimsy, Oak Islanders' devotion to simplicity makes photographing an essential vacation activity, even more pointless than it generally is. If you and your friends and family are similar to most, you will spend a good chunk of time off the beach, eating. Few things are less inspiring photographically than shots of folks sitting around a messy table, strewn with half-eaten food. Chances are, your old family vacation albums include those typical shots taken around a table; my family certainly has oodles of them.

Continue the tradition if you must, or, try more interesting alternatives photographically. To document your OKI restaurant experience, create a photograph of a decorative element inside or outside of it, with or without friends, or family as part of the frame. While Oak Island restaurants are seldom in scenic settings and/or the space is too tight and visually cluttered to make a desirable wide-angle backdrop, Oak Island restaurant owners, like Oak Islanders generally, decorate creatively with small elements that are eye-catching.

The few restaurants on the water are exceptions. Island Way and the Flying Fish Cafe, by the Ocean Crest, and Oak Island piers respectively, and Duffers at the Oak Island Golf Club overlook the ocean with exterior spaces that offer good photo possibilities. The Fish House, by the Blue Point Marina, joins them as places to go with your camera-in-hand.

As you explore Oak Island beyond the beach, you will find fodder for your camera wherever you go. The decorative yard element above is a typical pic-

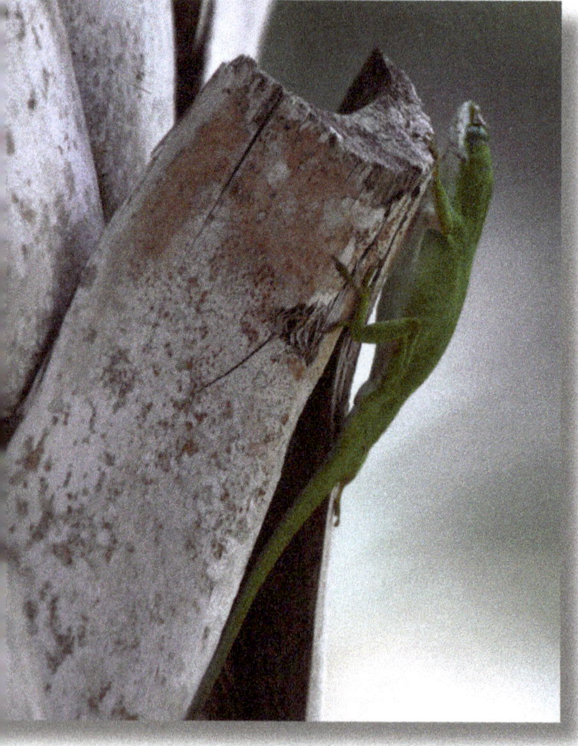

ture making find. This blue and yellow fish is eye-grabbing; the house in the background, shot in soft focus using a wide aperture, f/3.5, is perhaps the single most common house style built in the past couple of decades on Oak Island. You can spot plenty of eye-pleasing foreground elements to similarly frame structures and landscapes that typify OKI.

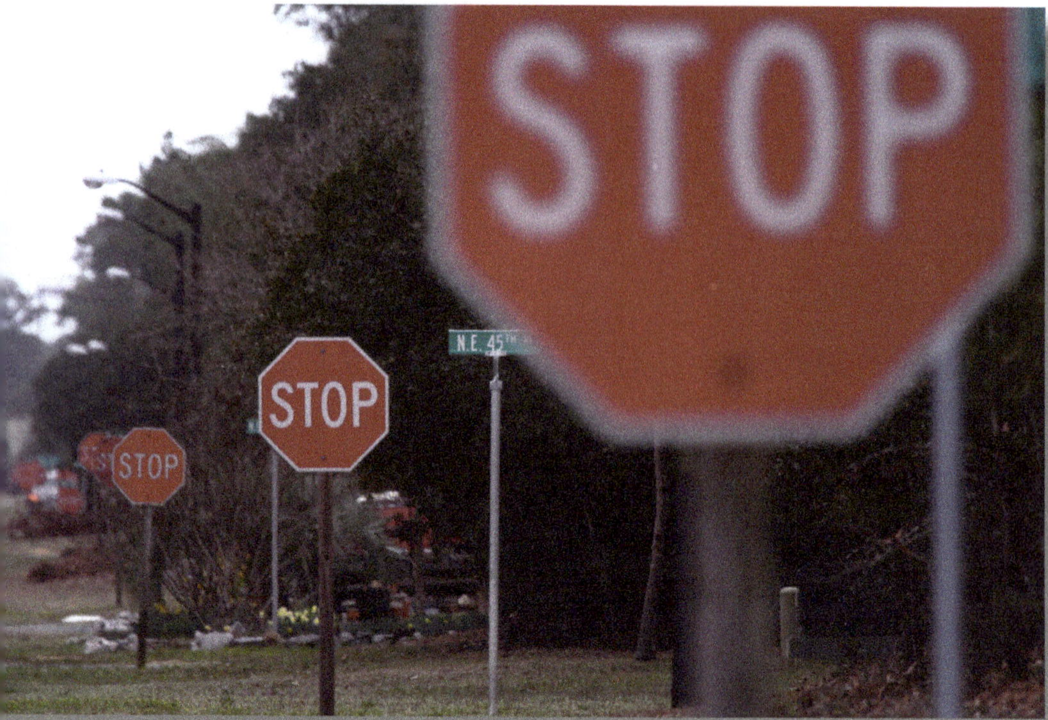

Occasionally, whimsy seems to even infect the bureaucracy. Oak Island has three working stop lights and a few scattered stop signs—except on East Oak Drive. As you will see above from the corner of NE 45th Street facing east there are ten stop signs in a half of a mile distance. In all likelihood there is a sound reason for the signs placement. As a photographer it doesn't matter, OKI's visual oddities are a gift to you.

In addition to humankind, an impressive representation of the rest of the animal kingdom inhabits the island, too. There are some sizable ones. You can see alligators on the Oak Island Golf Course and in some of the ponds and inland waters. Red fox abound as reminders of the pre-WWII era, when the island was largely marketed as a fox hunting destination.

There are smaller creatures, too. As you might surmise, a place named Oak Island would have squirrels and it does in abundance. Joining them are several members of the lizard family. Pictured on the left is a little green anole, most commonly spotted in the late afternoon and early evening.

It is tough to beat palm trunks as background. They make a fine backdrop with the interesting texture of the trunk colored in soft browns. The palm canopy creates a diffuse soft light that can be ideal for shooting with a long lens.

If you are on the island in the summer, you could see about 100 species of butterflies that are island regulars. You'll find them, as you might expect, on the subtropical plants growing at the northern edge of their range. You'll also spot them on the dune vegetation and sometimes even on the sand.

Every day on OKI is a good day to be on the island with your camera. Holidays will oblige you with especially easy pickings. The biggest one of them all is the Fourth of July. Southport, just across Cape Fear from Oak Island, has been celebrating the fourth for over two hundred years. Oak Island is an integral part of the hoopla. The Town, businesses, and homeowners participate in the celebration. The urge to press the shutter if you spend the fourth of July on the island is likely to be frequent and the results fruitful. Celebrations from Mardi Gras to the annual Christmas parade will also give you plenty of reasons to keep your camera busy.

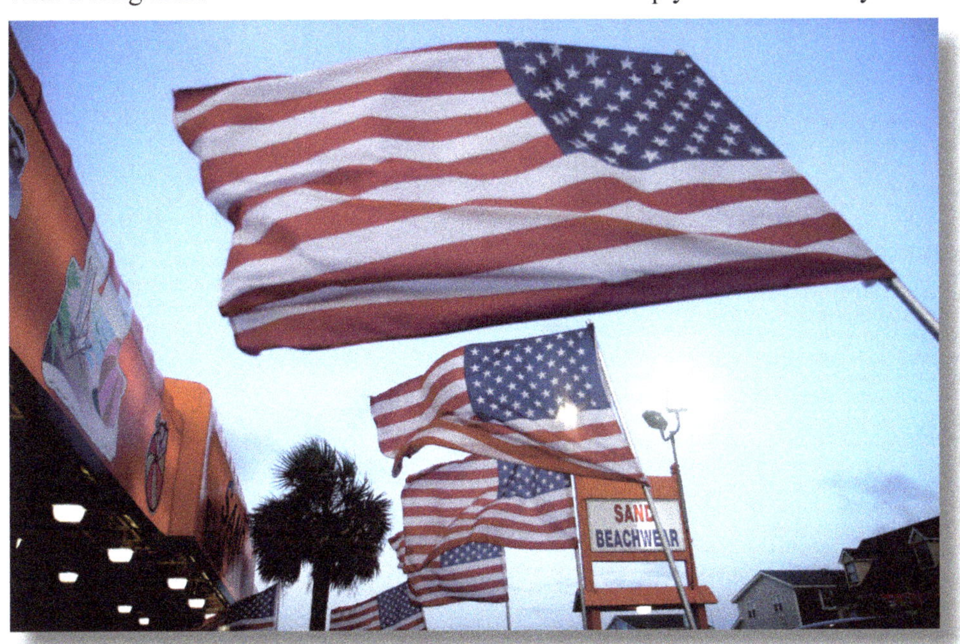

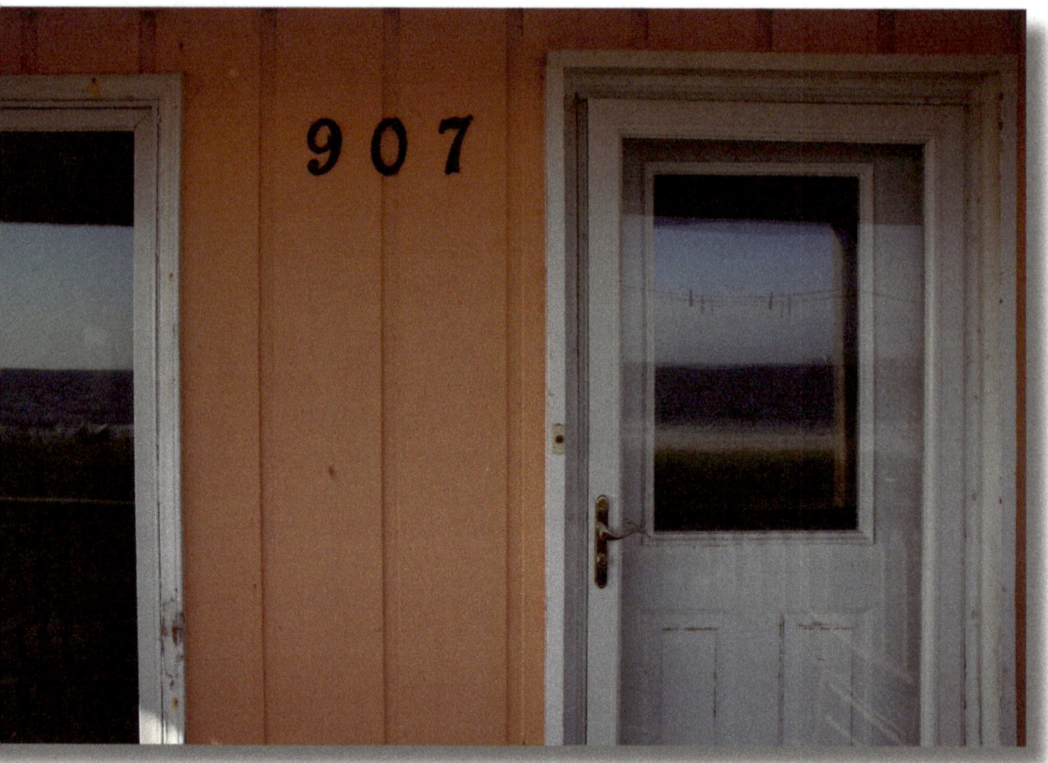


If you want to take home a picture of your beach house rental, chances are you can take one home that "shouts" Oak Island. If you want to take home shots that convey a sense of Oak Island as a place, a multitude of streetscapes, and shots of individual homes will let you do that. There are also shots that just ask to be taken because they make scintillating photos. Homes reflected on the interior waters, hexagonal and other many-sided variants, houses with brightly-colored swings, and samples of the ubiquitous house name signage are all potential frameables. As you explore the island you will stumble across many more.

If you have a first row beach house, check out your windows at the end of the day. If you are fortunate, the beach will reflect on your beach house windows just as it did on ours one Labor Day. The house number is a photo bonus as documentation of the *where* of your vacation.

Squadrons of birds flying over your beach house is a quintessential Oak Island scene that you can often observe with beach houses, even a couple of rows back. The seagulls flying over the beach house at right are typical. While there is no guarantee that you will see seagulls or pelicans, your chances are excellent. Or, sneak away briefly around dinner time to get a shot of your house just as the sun is setting; the simplest shot of a typical OKI beach house, in the glow of sunset, will forever warm the pages of your vacation album.

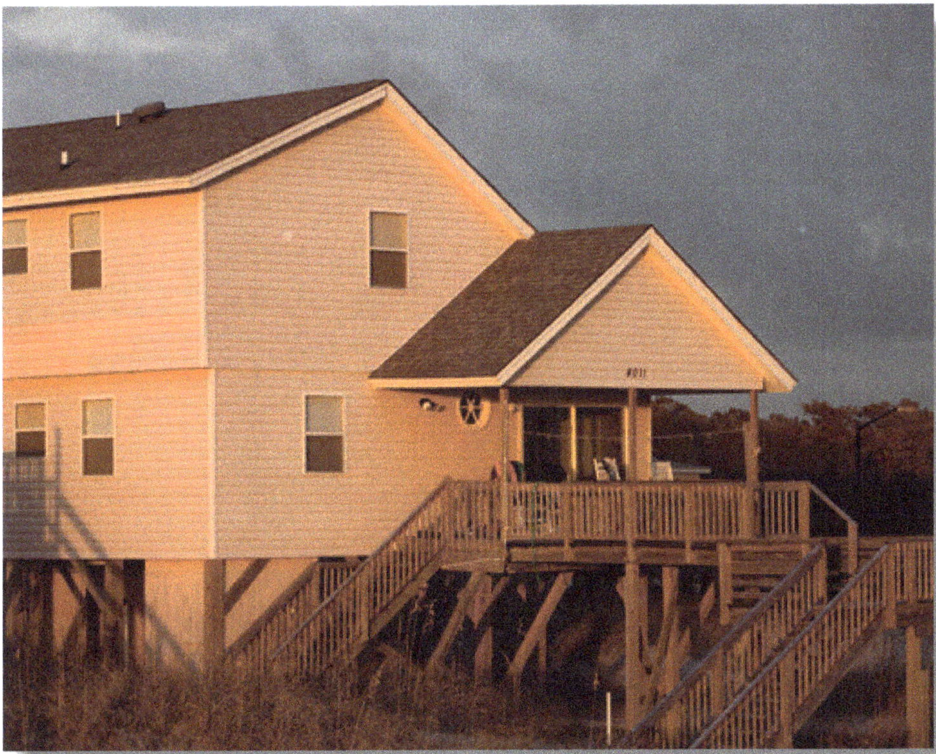

After checking off your own beach house on photo to-do list, the rest of the island awaits. You might spend a few minutes taking pictures of beach houses reflected in the water. Reflections framed in many variants make good visuals. Slightly rippled waters and dead still waters, reflection only (the upside down shot), and the subject and its reflection, are the best shots depending on personal preference and the conditions on a given day.

You might try photographing the rippled water of the ocean and the beach houses, as with the grouping on the next page. They are among a handful of house groupings that make a spread akin to the iconic "Rainbow Row" in Charleston. Here, instead of the brightly-colored doors, the houses are themselves multi-colored.

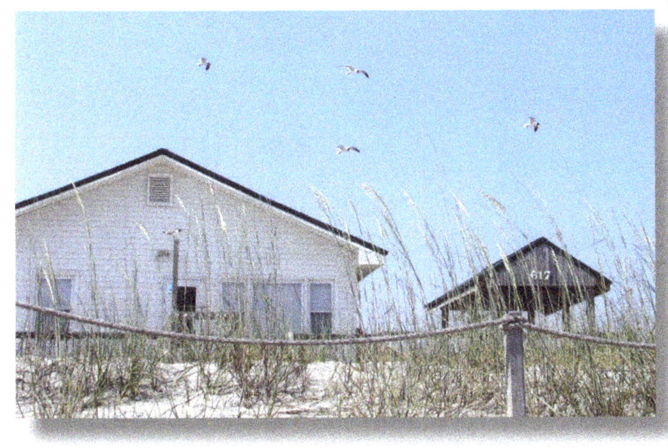

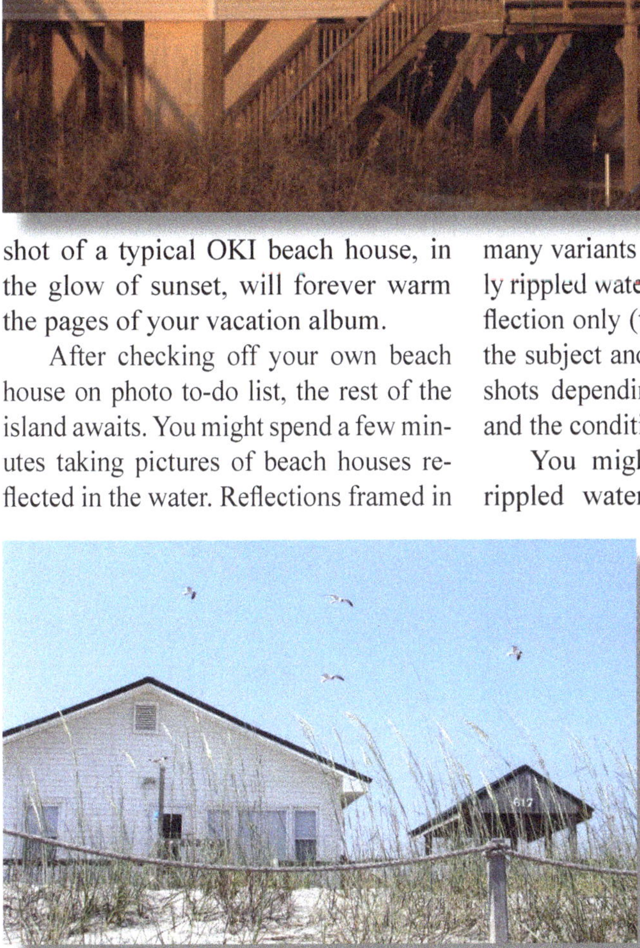

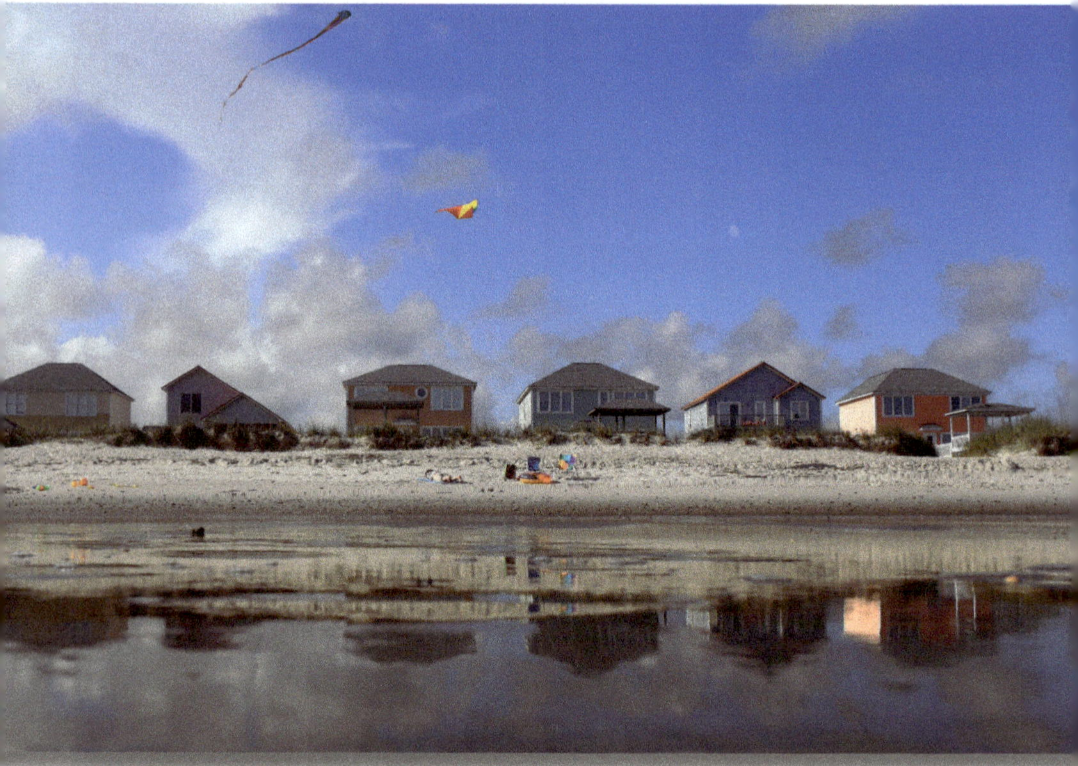

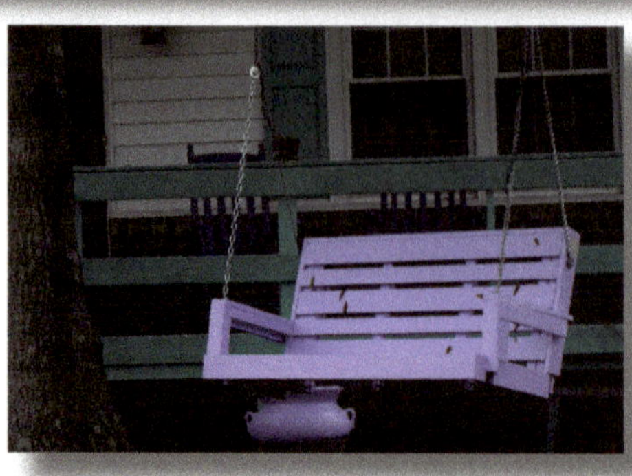

To take still water pictures, wander along the inland waters. You will find many places where the water serves as a mirror. The inland waters are just what you need to create mirror images or frame the upside down reflected house.

A whole lot of great photography comes from the small stuff. Just a quick flip through any travel magazine gives you plenty of examples. Because

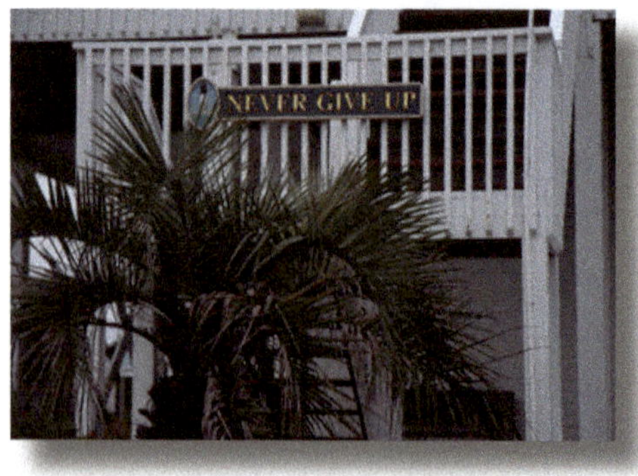


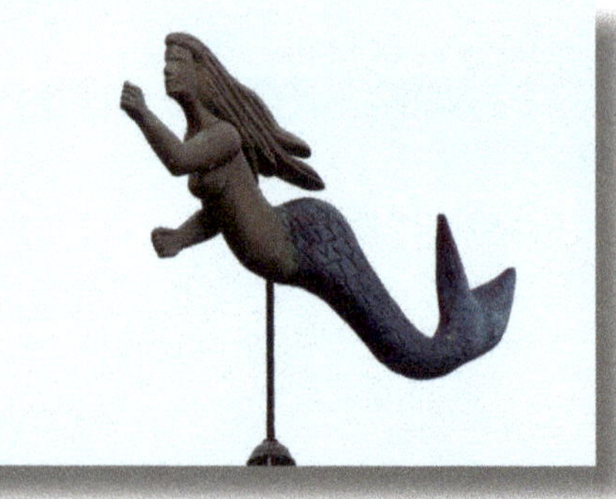

## Focus On: Reflections

Reflective surfaces abound on Oak Island with water being the most obvious. Reflections instantly add symmetry, depth, and line. Imagine a sailboat in the distance with its reflection softened by the imperfect surface of the water. That's an easy example.

Look around to find the less obvious reflections in windows, puddles, the chrome rims on a golf cart, or a rearview mirror on the handlebars of a beachcomber bike. These can all be fun. You can also use a reflection to add a foreground or background element.

Photographers use some techniques to enhance the effect of a reflection. First, if you are intending to use a reflective surface to create an image that closely duplicates it, have your lens as close to the plane of the surface as possible. On the water this usually means getting yourself and your camera to ground level.

Second, use a slightly longer focal length when shooting into a true mirror. Doing so will help keep you out of the image when trying to shoot directly into the mirror. The longer focal length will also bring the subject in the reflection closer, making it fill more of the frame.

Finally, look for reflected patterns on the wall or a nearby surface. Sometimes the light will shimmer as it is reflected from the surface. Using reflected light looks natural. Picture a wading bird plucking fish from the marsh. The glistening reflection will add light and intrigue to the photograph.

Oak Islanders enjoy architectural and landscaping details that celebrate island life, and, they don't take themselves too seriously, you'll encounter a myriad of details. These images of small decorations and vignettes are suitable for your wall or made into mugs, mouse pads, or note cards if you are into that sort of thing.

After discovering the many colorful and quirky details the island offers you may also want to seek out some of OKI's many-sided houses, a particular Oak Island penchant.

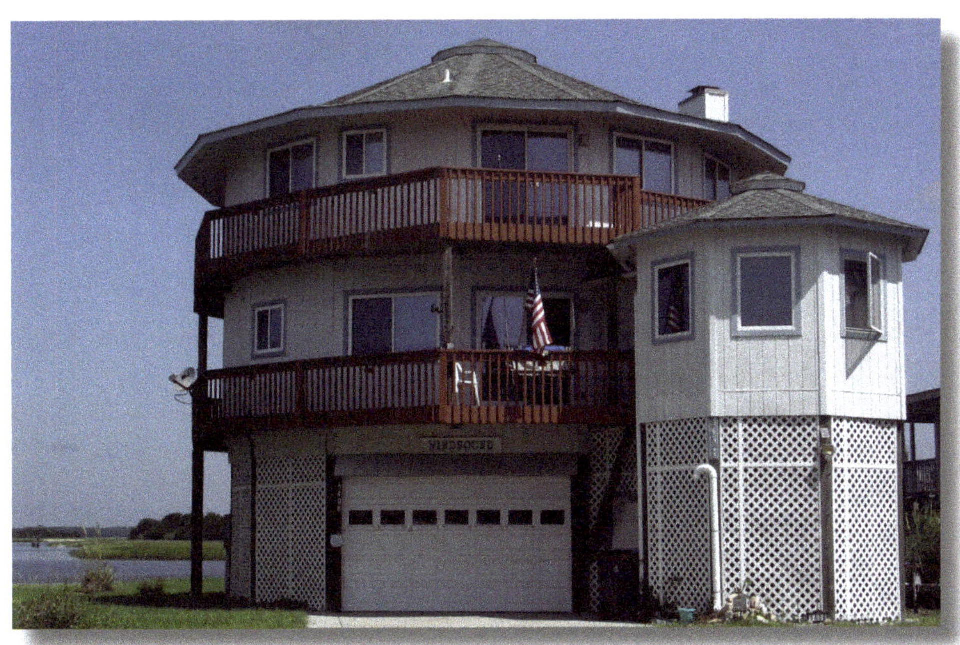

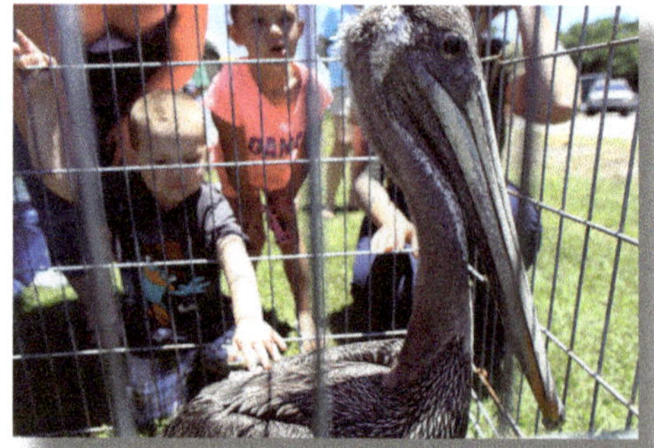

The Oak Island beach season unofficially kicks off around St. Patrick's Day with spring break vacationers and the annual Easter Egg Hunt; it peters out after the early December Christmas tree lighting and Christmas parade. Those two events, and the many sprinkled in between, are small scale by Macy Day Parade standards. Nose counts are in the hundreds, once in a while in the low thousands. As both a vacationer and photographer, I find them "right sized." You don't need to get to a 10:00 a.m. event at 6:00 a.m. to enjoy it or to get good images. Yet, there is still plenty going on.

For instance, Ride the Tide, the kayak float and race in late spring, draws a comfortably crowded field to the Davis Canal. It won't, though, be so mobbed by spectators to interfere with your shooting from the 29th Street Crossover vantage point for the race start or prevent you from following the kayakers with your car (or bike or on foot) to viewpoints along the canal and its finish.

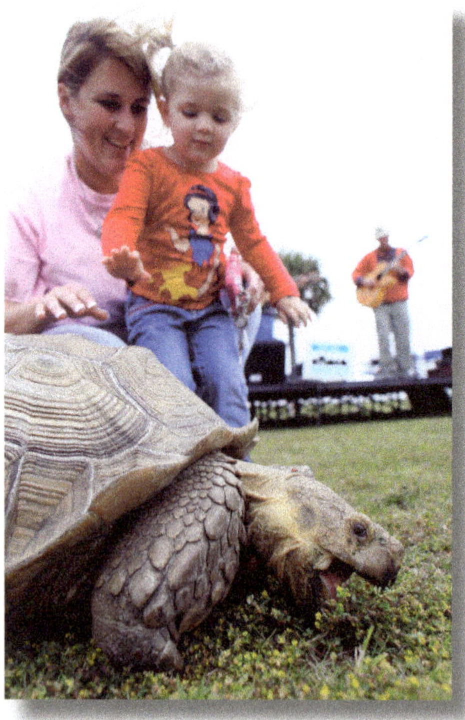

The Christmas parade brings just enough people to the island to create its one traffic jam each year. Events are intentionally family friendly. On Oak Island that includes people from the very young to the very old and their dogs. Oak Island dogs are generally as laid back as their beach loving Oak Island owners are. They not only share the beach on their leashes but seem to relish the hoopla of Oak Island events with their owners, too.

When photographing Oak Island events, I find myself wearing three different "hats." One is that of the family photographer. With my own family and friends, or when taking family photos professionally, I am apt to shoot clean images with a telephoto lens and subject(s) in sharp focus, with a blurred background created by a shallow

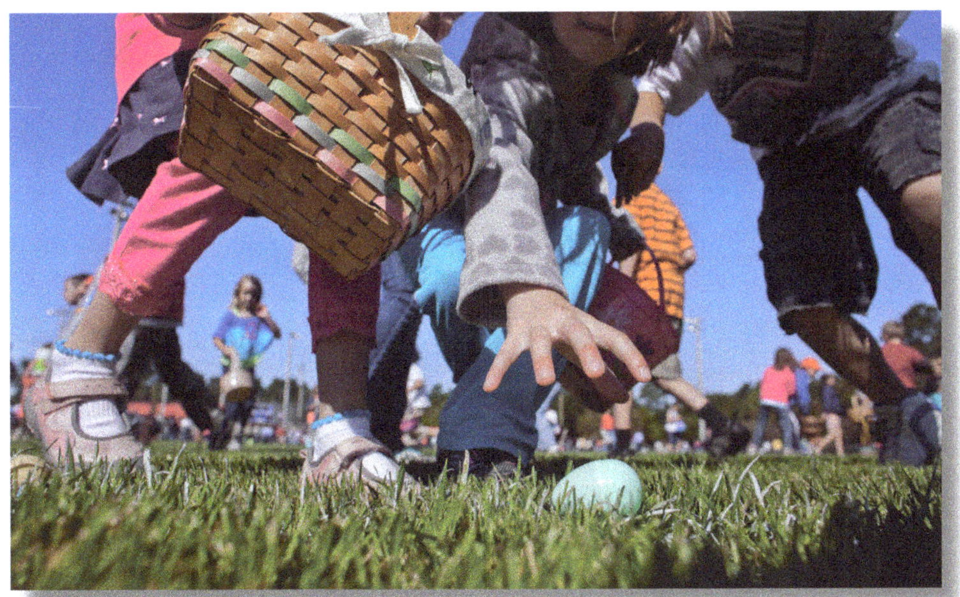

depth- of-field. My intent is to visually portray the subject's engagement with the activity. The blurred background seems to convey, subliminally, that the people experiencing the event is all that matters.

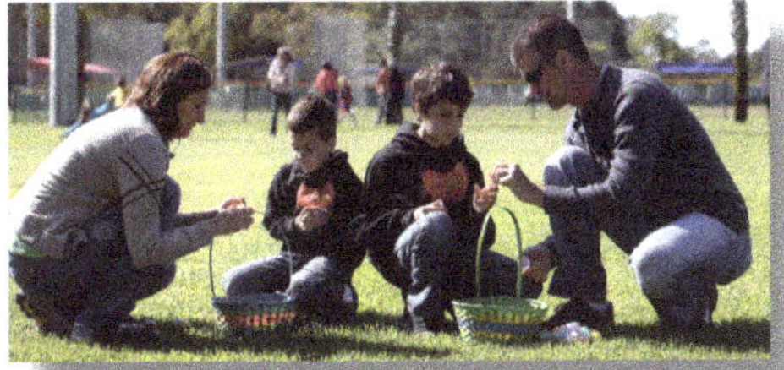

When wearing my photojournalist hat, my objective is to allow an absent viewer to be drawn into the event vicariously, and to do the same for participants, as the experience itself fades into distant memory. The techniques used are quite different from those used for good portrait photography. I look to find

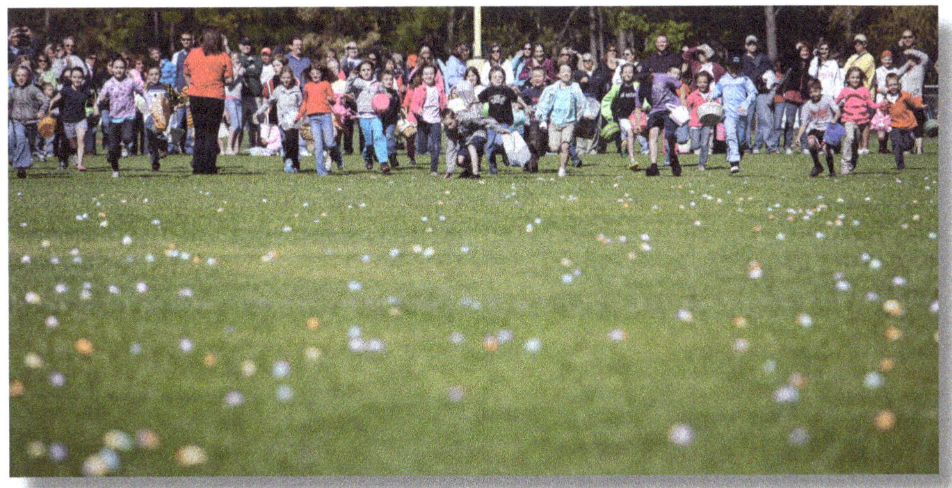

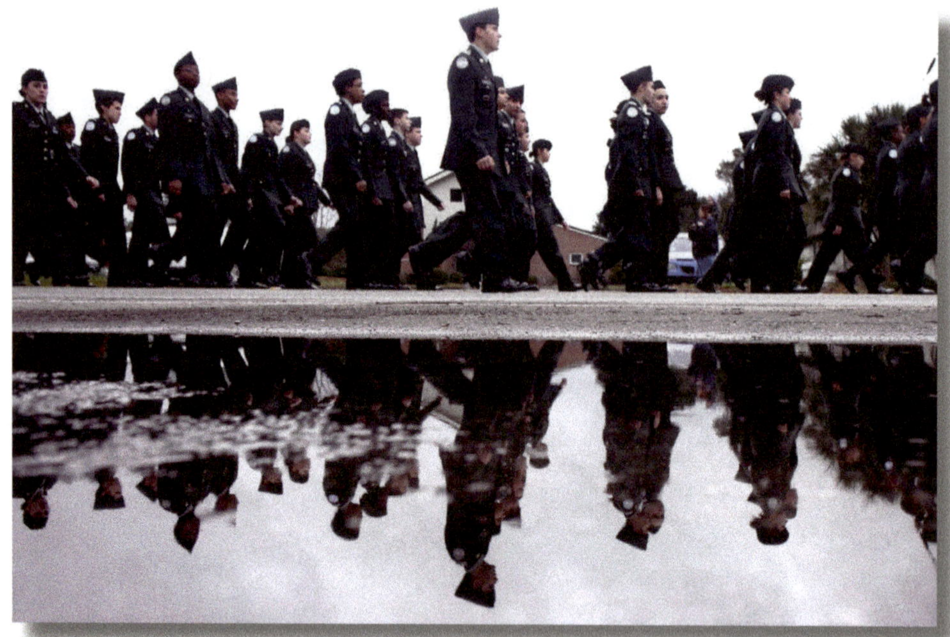

a way to create a "scene-setter" of people participating in the event. Setting the scene gives the activity scope and does not focus on one individual. One challenge, if you are doing a big picture shot, will be to set yourself up with a clean background. As in the Easter Egg Hunt shot on the previous page, it is usually possible to find a vantage point that gives you a natural background for Oak Island events and avoid some of the park's less desirable options: the chain-

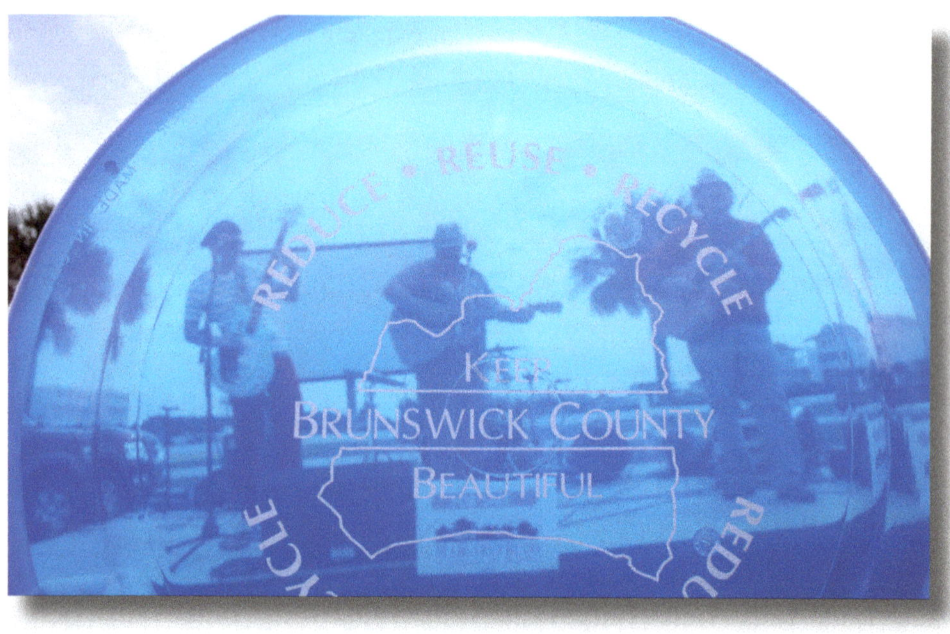

## Focus On: Depth-of-Field

As you are doing event photography think "hide and seek." As you are considering the background for your photograph, your best work will generally come from actively seeking out the best available option. The Oak Island Christmas parade, as an example, passes between two sides of Oak Island Drive from East 46th Street to McGlamery. You can backdrop your photos with uninspiring architecture, parking lots, plastic signage OR you can choose to shoot with a background of live oaks or iconic southern beach architecture. If you can find an attractive and unobtrusive background—use it. You'll gain context.

If you can't pick your background, think depth-of-field, specifically shallow depth-of-field. You'll want to open your aperture causing only the subject to be in sharp focus while the distracting background goes soft. The shot of the "reindeer" and his human companions to your right is an example.

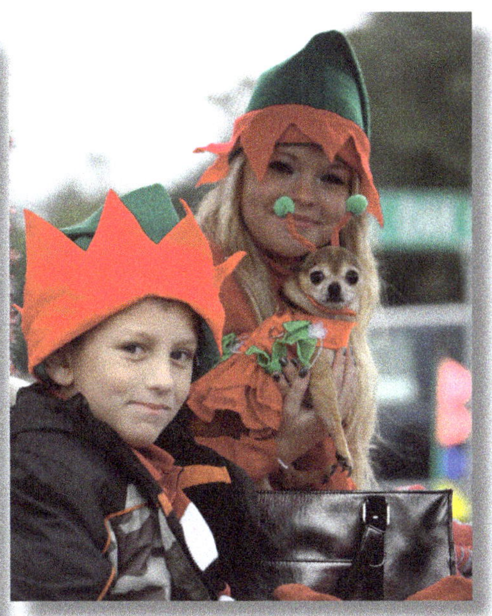

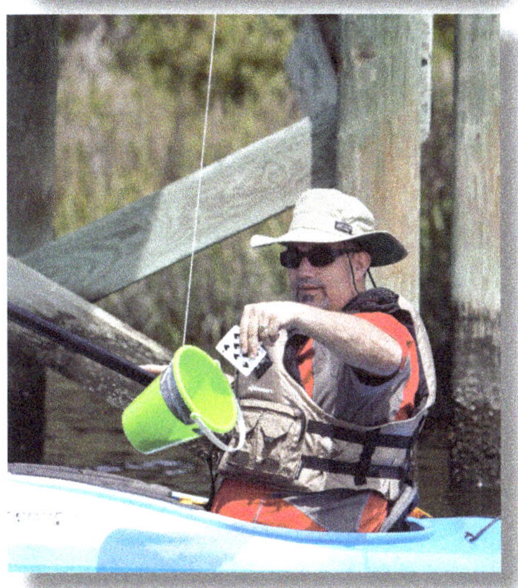

link fence, parking lot, and utilitarian buildings.

The standing water as foreground for the South Brunswick High School band's appearance in the Christmas parade was fortuitous. The standing water reminds us of the weather threat of that year's parade, yet adds an intriguing element.

Parades are, of course, always a bit of whimsy. This very small "reindeer" riding along with some parade elves makes for an informative portrait. The hats add all the context you need to realize it is during the Christmas parade.

The photographer "hat" that is most fun to don at these events is photographer as pop artist. (Think Andy Warhol, not Ansel Adams.) OKI affairs riddle themselves with unexpected possibilities. Who would have guessed Brunswick County Solid Waste\Recycling would pass out translucent discs used here to create a sense of the Town of Oak Island's 1st Crawl Environmental Festival; or the Town's Ride the Tide kayak races would include non-racing participants drawing poker hands from bright green buckets hanging against the weathered lines of the walkway.

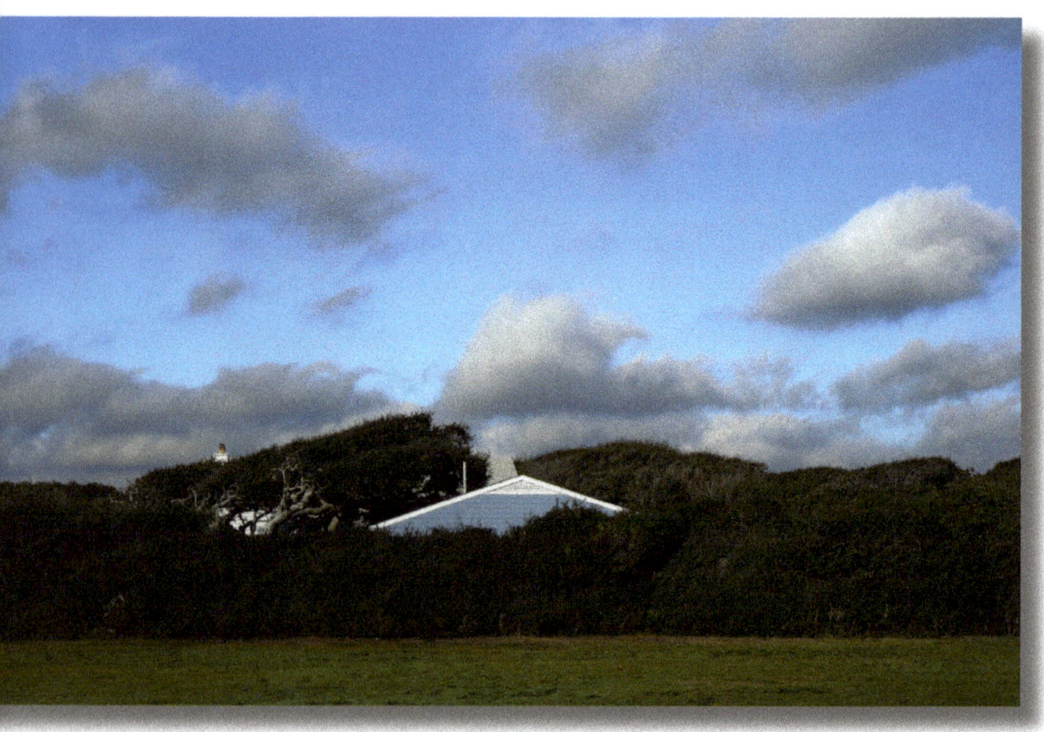

Where would you like to be: a coastal plain, the Old South, a Caribbean Island, the high desert, the Mid-Atlantic? You can virtually experience them all on Oak Island.

Before humans came to Oak Island, it was a native coastal plain; there were dunes, beach, maritime forest, and marshlands. Most of the island was maritime forest covered with live oaks, red cedar, yaupon holly, and pines. You can photograph the windswept live oaks much as they would have appeared hundreds and thousands of years ago. In the picture above taken at the corner of Barbee Boulevard and Beach Drive the live oaks appear to be take back the land from the encroaching blue house. Over at the Oak Island Golf Course the sweeps of live oaks form a canopy behind the club's restaurant and along the paths of much of the course.

Just a few hundred yards inland, the live oaks are upright and dripping in Spanish Moss shown in the photo on page 62. They are as Old South as can be. There are plenty of opportunities to find Spanish Moss draped over live oaks, the namesake of the island. It is even more fun to photograph the moss when you find it clinging unexpectedly. When bright sunlight streams through, it appears to glow. Position yourself with the moss between you and the sun.

Try working with the exposure compensation here, especially if the

## Focus On: Direction of Light

Having the sun at your back, as you were probably taught when you first used a camera, is a good general rule for group portraits (if the light is soft enough to avoid squinting and harsh shadows); however, when you are shooting to create memorable art, you should frequently break the rule.

Direction of light can include side lighting, backlight, uplighting, omnidirectional light, direct light and more. To add to the equation (and your confusion), there are often multiple sources of light, especially when using your flash at night.

A soft window light from the side can be very flattering to people, food and pets. By placing the twilight sky behind someone you create a silhouette—a form of backlighting. It creates a wonderful effect as the sun sets behind the dunes in the late summer and autumn. Try looking down on people strolling below the pier. On one side you'll have the shadow falling away from the camera leaving a flat image. When you backlight the image and the shadow falls toward you, the photograph suddenly shows depth, contrast and imagination. The direction of light adds a sense of three-dimensionality to an otherwise two-dimensional image.

Translucent objects, like a colorful innertube, can appear to glow when backlit. The vast ocean can be sparkling with the sun hitting at the right angle.

Try rethinking blind adherence to the rules even with your group photographs. Put the sun behind the group on a lightly overcast day. You can create a unique look by rethinking the direction of light. You can always take the safe shot by playing by the rules, or you can go with that creative spirit by thinking in a new direction.

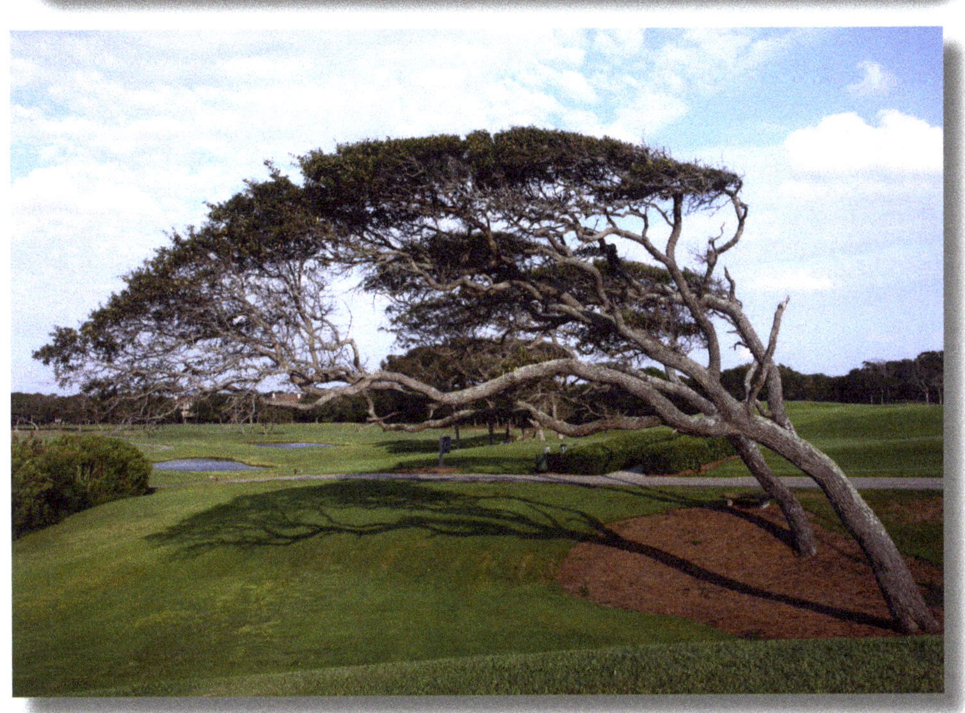

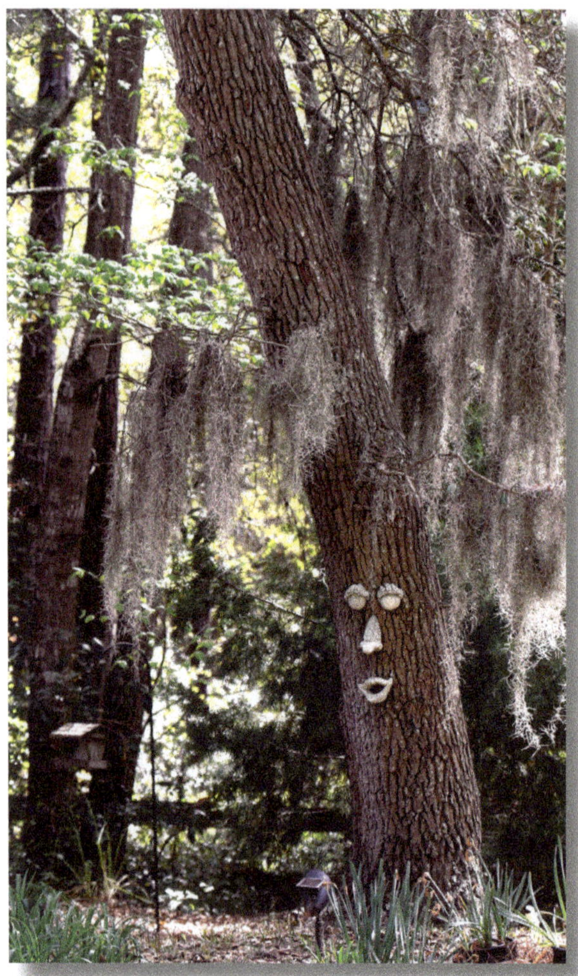

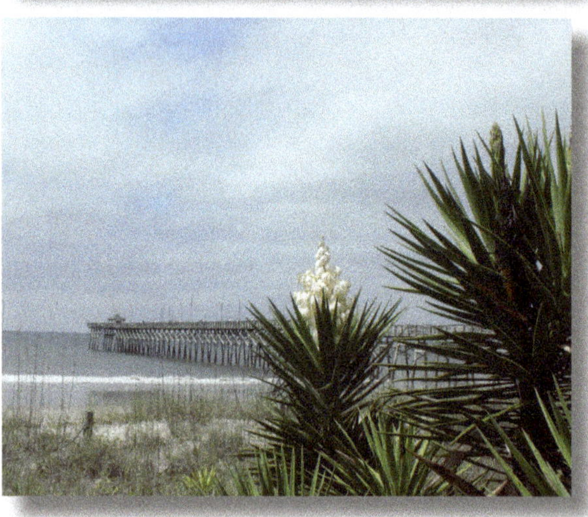

sun appears in your image. Bracket by taking the same photo at -2, -1, 0, +1 and +2. Give it a whirl.

In many places on the island. Some native plants look to be from southwest high deserts. The Spanish bayonet, a yucca plant, is the most common. It is often found in really hostile environments. In the "Blue Skies" subsection you see it growing in nothing but sand. That is brutal, and seemingly incongruous for a plant so stunning in bloom. Treat this rugged beauty with respect. Its "bayonets" are really sharp; they will puncture your skin if you back into one.

The Spanish bayonet is only one of OKI's hardy native specimens. Out at the Point, the Dollar Weed to the right was growing like a single survivor escaping from a formidable block structure. The little plant compelled shooting it with a shallow depth-of-field. Visually, the pattern of the blocks is a good compositional element, but nothing about the detail of their surfaces make them deserving of sharp focus.

Few plants are as eye-popping as the Indian Blanket Flower. It self-propagates along the dunes in as brutal of environments as the Spanish bayonet and Dollar Weed, but with the colors of florists' favorite flowers. While the kite in the same color palette as the flowers was an unexpected element for this frame, the color of the flowers are typical beach colors. Clothing worn by the people you are with, an umbrella, or beach toys will match or complement the Indian Blanket Flower when used as foreground or background.

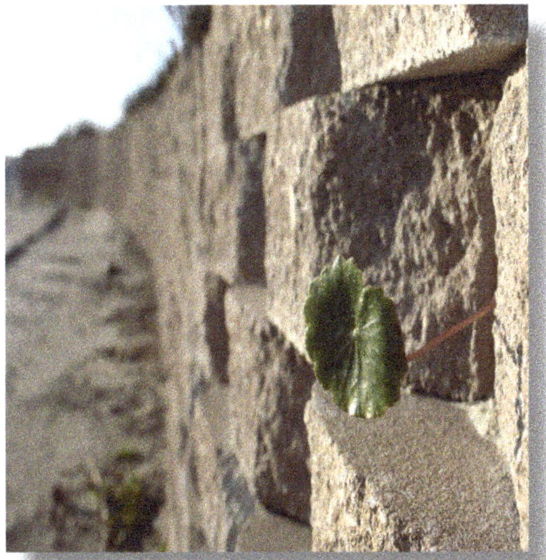

If you like the Caribbean, Oak Island can provide. Oak Island is in a transitional location at the northern edge of the subtropical range. It is your good fortune; you will see unexpected interaction between northern birds and subtropical plants. For instance, in palms you can find cardinals perching, woodpeckers pecking, and mourning doves nesting. The startling incongruity makes a unique frame.

In the challenging coastal environment plants struggle to survive. Dead trees, overwhelmed by water, are the classic stuff of wetland photography. This plant didn't survive, but is still useful to this ibis ruffling its feathers and to passing photographers.

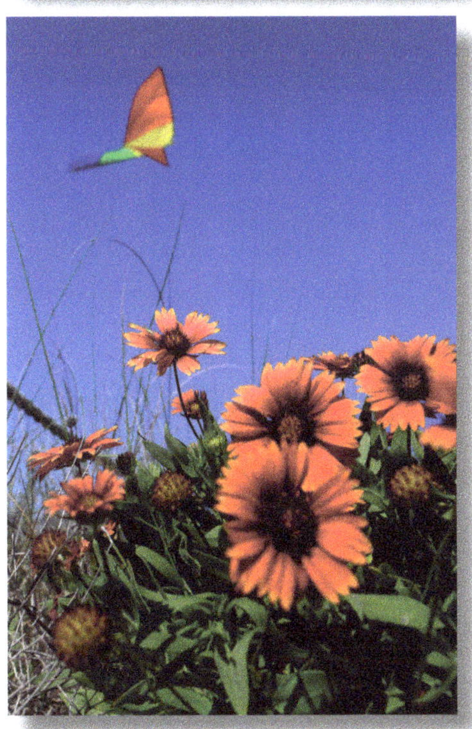

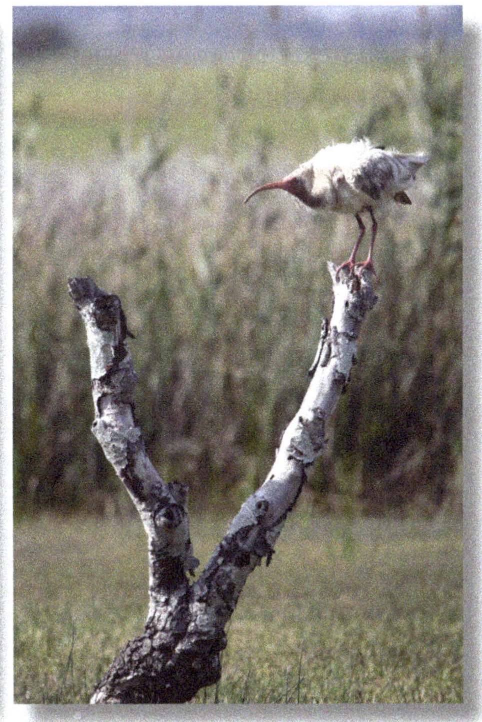

# *history*

History buffs will be disappointed in the quantity of historic sites on Oak Island. For those, though, on the island on the weekdays between Labor Day and Memorial Day, a visit to Fort Caswell on the Baptist Assembly property will compensate with quality. Similarly, the Oak Island Lighthouse, accessible all year round, is a historical treat. Here you will learn a bit about the engineering used to construct the next to last traditional lighthouse built in America. Imagine the sights seen from its top, as it and its predecessor lighthouse guided cargo ships, fishing boats, recreational vessels, pirates, and German U-Boats safely past the dreaded Frying Pan shoals.

The paucity of historic properties is in itself interesting; there are two reasons for it. Oak Island was largely unnoticed until the 1930s. Seemingly, it was only occasionally visited by Native Americans before being "discovered" by Italian and Spanish explorers in the 1520s. Neither the Italians nor Spanish exerted much effort to claim to the land. So, instead it became part of the British claim to what is now most of our eastern seaboard. On August 1, 1727, the Governor's Council granted Oak Island to Maurice Moore, founder of Brunswick Town to the north, for a sixpence. OKI continued to lay undeveloped for more than 200 years, until Ernest Felder Middleton recognized its potential, bought and developed it, and opened it to the public in 1939. By 1954, when Hurricane Hazel made landfall, there were, according to the State Port Pilot, 357 structures on the island, of which five remained on their foundations. While some of the structures that washed into the marshlands were rescued, Oak Island's historic built environment mostly spans a mere 60 years.

So what can you do with your camera? Go out to Fort Caswell during the off season; pay the modest fee to explore the property on a self-guided tour. It is a photographer's treat. The fortifications themselves couldn't be better designed to shoot patterns, textures, lines, colors, shapes, and shadows. The vistas are among the best along all of Oak Island. From the eastern tip of the Island, you look directly across the mouth of the Cape Fear River to Bald Head Island and Old Baldy, North Carolina's oldest standing lighthouse, visible from OKI since it was built in 1817. The eastern end of Caswell Beach is the best place on OKI to watch big sailboats scoot across the same water passage used by the Spanish to attack the British up north in Brunswick Town in 1748, and by pirates of all ilk from the 1600s through the 1700s.

Face north, and you are looking at the Garrison House in Southport, the last remaining vestige of Fort Johnston, which was completed in 1754. If you spend anytime along the northern coast, you'll see the Bald Head Island Ferry cross one direction or the other between Southport and Bald Head Island, a modern legacy of a time when visitors to Oak Island, as well as Bald Head, were most likely to arrive by water.

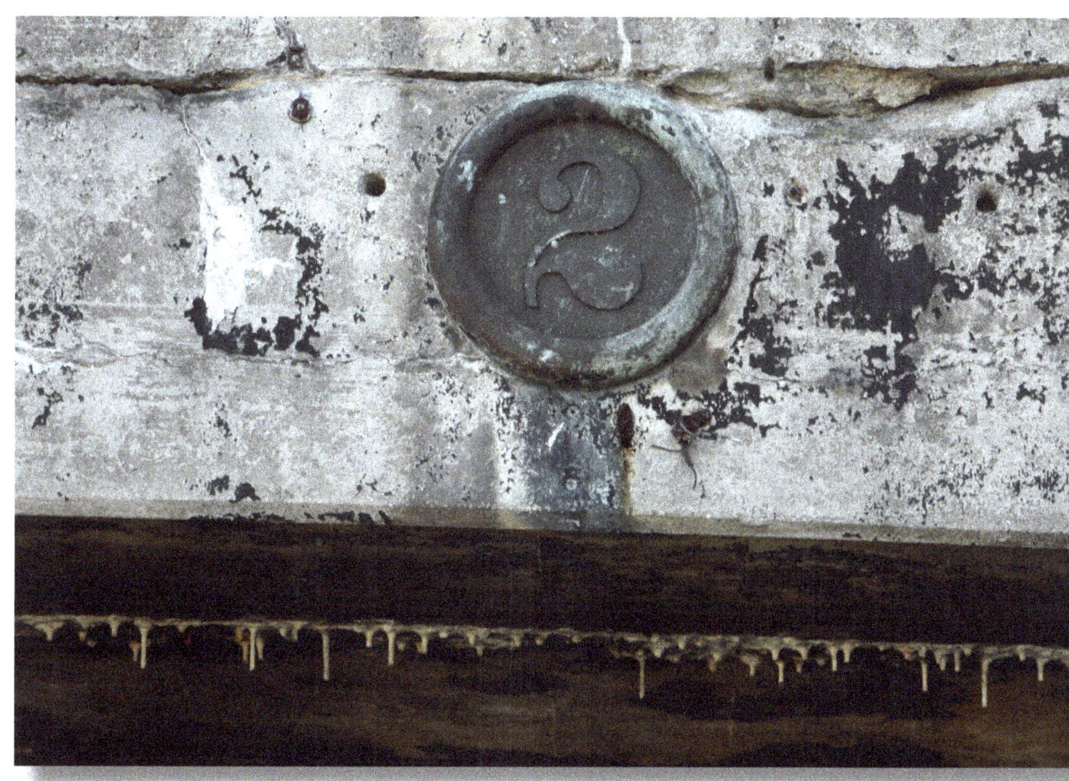

When you start exploring Fort Caswell, you'll do some of your best camera work when concentrating on the fort's details. Think small and fill-the-frame as with this corroded "2."

The lighthouse presents photo possibilities that will likely remain etched in your memory if you partake. Those of us, though, who have joined a group to trek to the top can attest that it is not for the fainthearted. Unlike the typical North Carolina lighthouse that was built with spiral stairs, the Oak Island lighthouse was built with ship's ladders. If you are game and want to photograph what the climb is like, set your ISO to 800 or thereabouts and your camera to aperture priority. You'll want to have a wide aperture to enable your camera to match it with a fast shutter speed. The folks climbing up the stairs will be moving. While they won't be going all that quickly, climbing stairs requires much muscle movement with attendant motion blur. I did this from the top platform, intentionally using the lighthouse windows as the source of natural light.

If you want to settle for a shot of the interior itself, without the climbers, you can do that from the bottom of the staircase.

Besides planning to bring home photos of what would typical "historic" photos, I like to take pictures of things that I am quite sure will someday be thought of as historic. Oak Island has added a second bridge, and the construction was often photographic. The work involved barges and cranes, men and machines. While I took some doc-

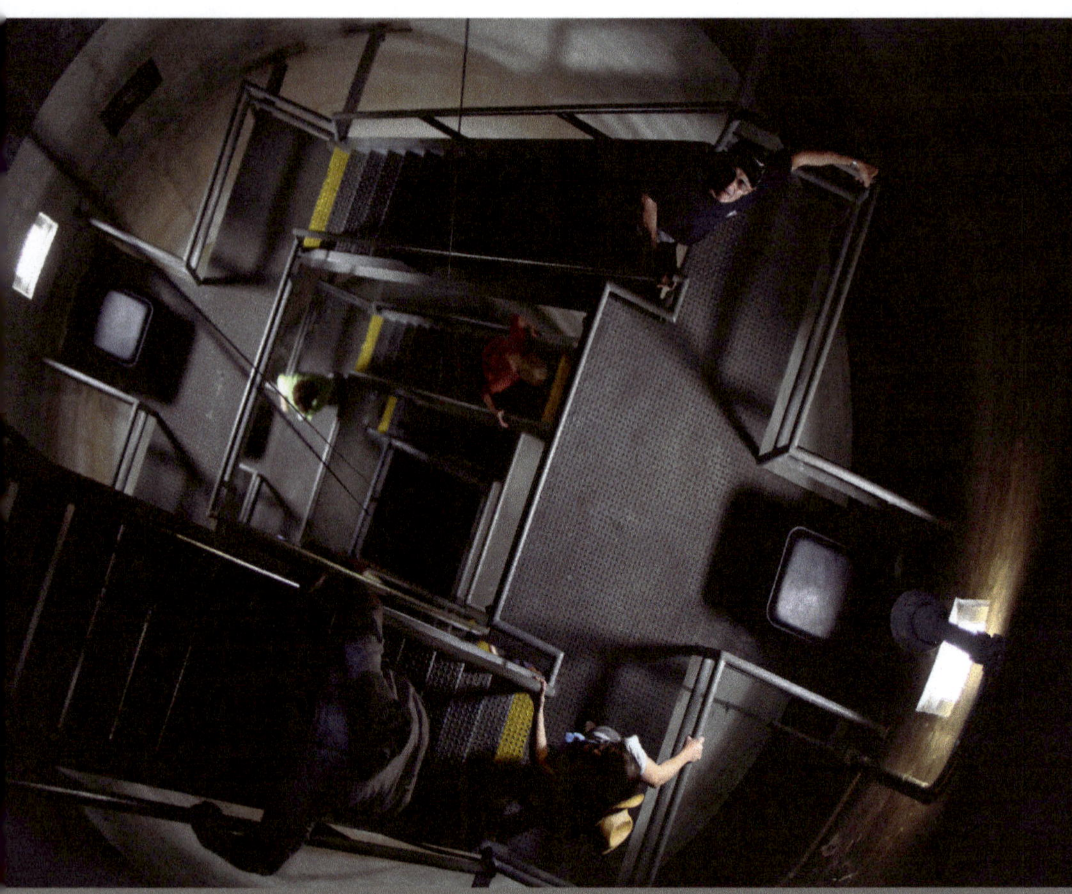

## Focus On: Pattern

A row of identical birds creates a pattern as does a structure built by humans. Architects have been using the mathematical principles of nature for eons. So have artists.

The goal with pattern is to find subtle variations that lead the eye to surprising elements. Repeating positive and negative space catches the eye by creating a sense of movement. When that pattern is interrupted, it creates a focal point.

There are two examples on these pages. Above we have a staircase which creates a swirling effect despite not being a spiral. There is much variation in the pattern from the yellow stripes to where the people are positioned.

The construction of the new bridge at right might remind a viewer of a referee's jersey. The pattern is so stark and strong, it becomes the focus of the image as opposed to the bridge itself. The construction of the new bridge was a bit controversial and not a black-and-white process.

On Oak Island, you will see lots of patterns to capture with your camera. Try looking at the pattern you see with a long lens to compress the spaces, aka stacking. Likewise, with a horizontally-stretched pattern, like a picket fence, try using a wide-angle lens to increase the scope of the pattern.

Don't forget to change your vantage point; often a pattern will emerge by getting up high or even shooting from ground level looking up.

umentary style photos, this shot, taken before the road was laid, is emblematic of the extraordinary visual elements one frequently finds at construction sites. Although I don't do a lot of black and white work, this frame was so much about line and contrast that it cried out to be freed of distracting color. It also seemed particularly appropriate for something shot as a "historic" photo.

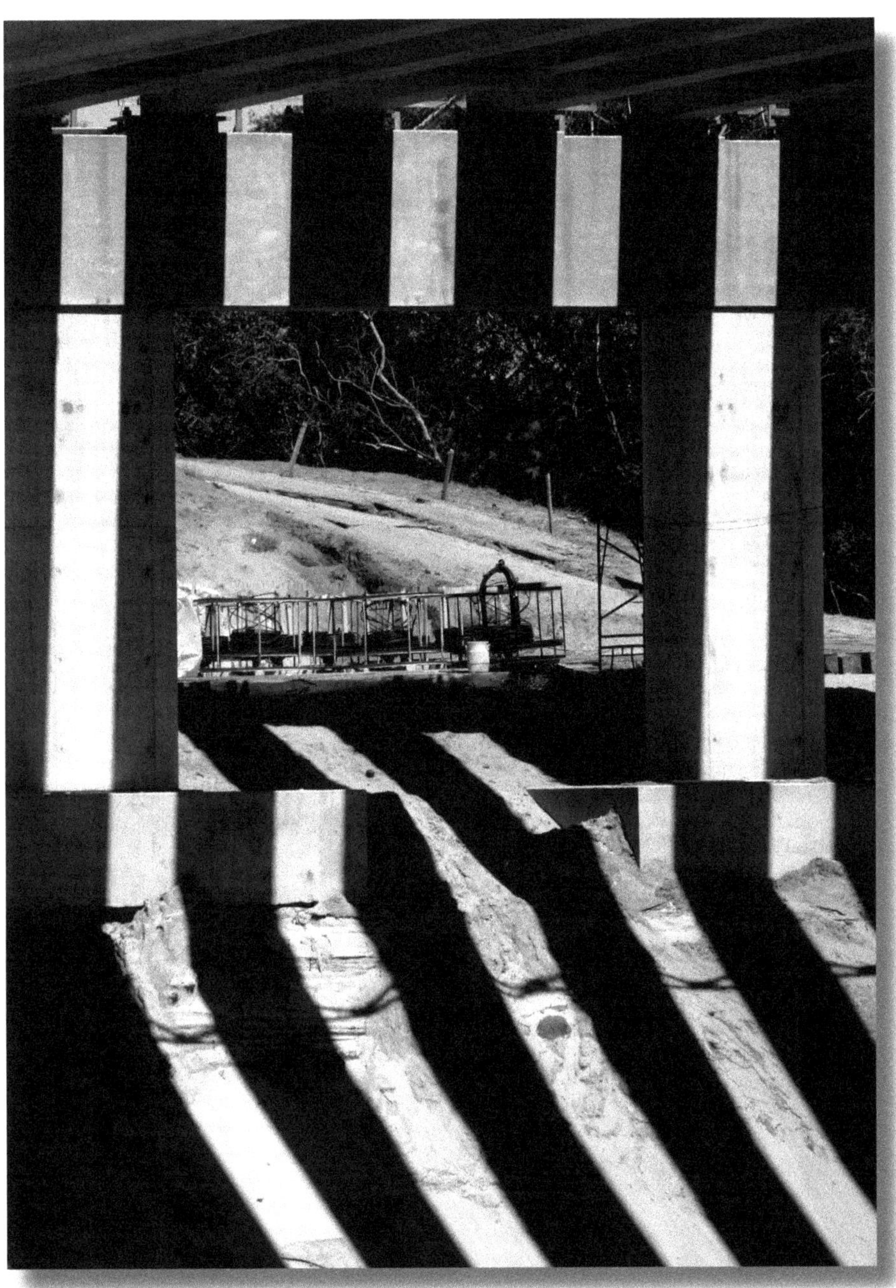

# *sports*

Sports enthusiasts may be surprised by the variety of athletic activities offered on Oak Island proper and the Oak Island mainland just across the bridge. Photographers will enthuse at their venues. The Oak Island Golf Club is nestled among windswept live oaks and berry-dripping yaupons. The Oak Island Par 3 Golf Course at South Harbor features turtles, herons, and cormorants on a course nestled into a undulating terrain. In the springtime, the disc golf course, with its azaleas in bloom, is reminiscent of the Masters venue in Augusta.

Sky diving at the Cape Fear Jetport is better done without a camera, but you can photograph your friends and family or total strangers engaging in the sport, framed with numerous creative foregrounds against some wonderful backgrounds. The volleyball courts at the beach await your camera, with the Oak Island Pier in the background as you face southwest or the Oak Island Lighthouse in the background as you face northwest.

Sports participants in all of the photographic venues will oblige with plenty of fodder for practicing stop-action photography. If you are young enough or have youngsters along, the skateboard park is a fine venue for honing your sports photography skills. The venue itself, comprised of cement and chainlink is wildly different from the beauty of the aforementioned sports spots. The drabness of the skateboard park works surprisingly well photographically. Think contrast. Brightly-colored skateboards and typical tropical-colored beach attire, pop out from the grayness of the cement.

Outside of the organized sports venues, locals and visitors engage in cornhole toss, volleyball, cycling, and pick-up games of popular American sports.

For more than a decade, I spent much of most weeks taking sports photos professionally. What I did then, when creating photos for newspapers, and what I would encourage you to do is the same. While the whole gamut of photographic techniques used by professional are applicable to sports shots, we'll only explicitly consider three here: vantage point, depth-of-field, and panning.

Whether you are using a fast enough shutter speed to create the stop-action sand blast from Sergio Garcia's club on the PGA tour, or a sand shot by an amateur at the Waves4K.I.D.S. charity tournament, the technicals are the same.

Likewise, if you are following Tiger Woods with your lens or a golfer at the Oak Island Golf Course, the shot of an impressive finish is enhanced by a bit of variation from the obvious. The alligator tee box markers cried out to be included. Get down low, or at least hold your camera near ground level. Vantage point here distinguishes this from the basic shot that any of you that follow golf have seen over and over. It is unique to Oak Island.

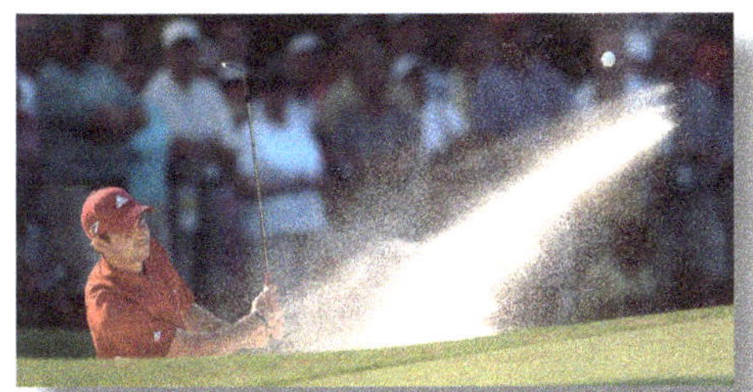

It is sometimes useful in sports photography to take depth-of-field on a path less taken. You'll want to have sharp focus in the middle of the frame, with both the background and the foreground blurred. A typical use of the technique is for basketball when you would like to have the net in soft focus, the shooter and the ball leaving his fingers in sharp focus, and the crowd in the background blurred. At the disc golf venue at "Bill" Smith Park, a similar construct works.

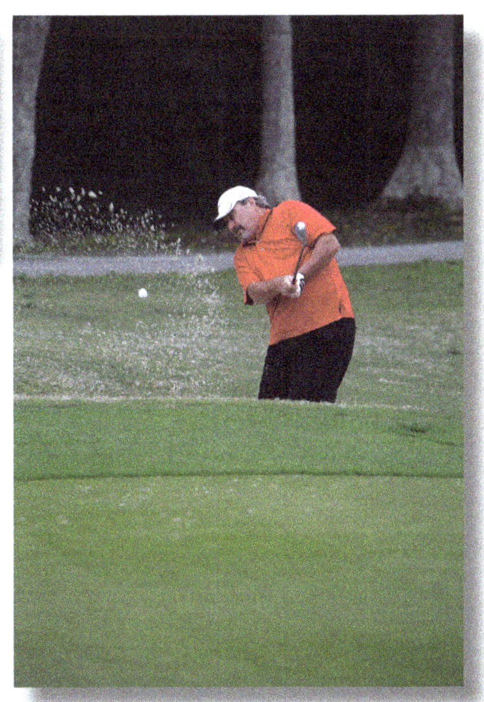

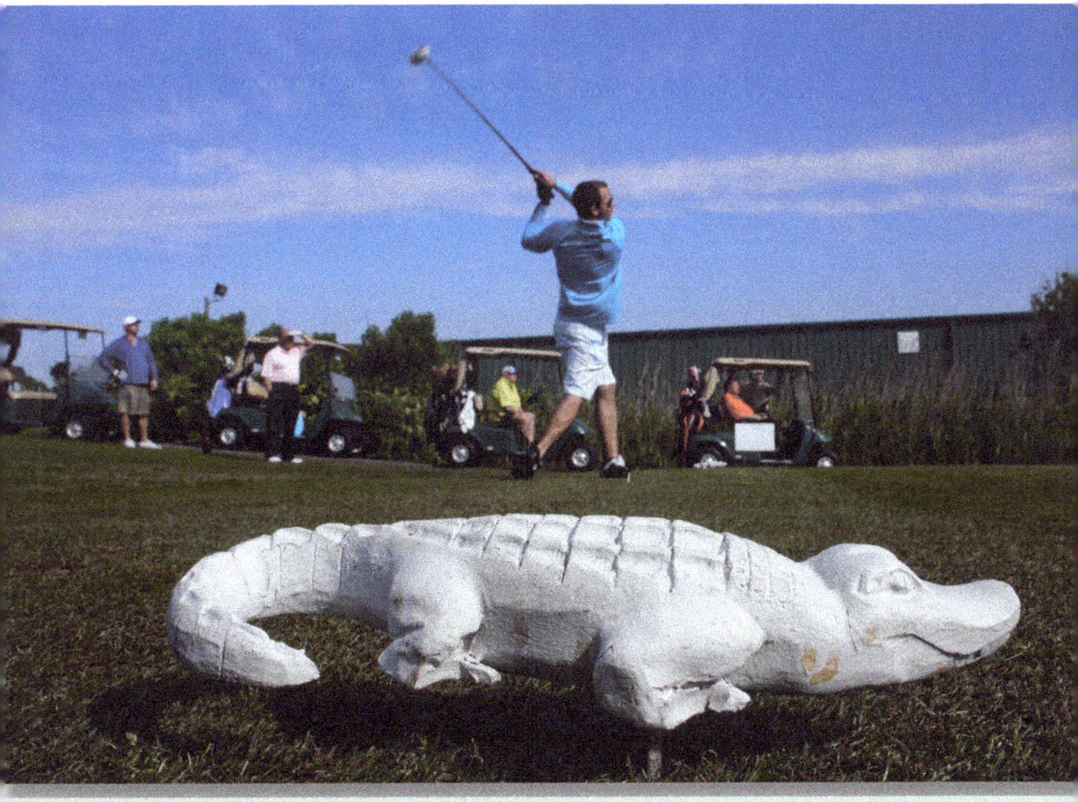

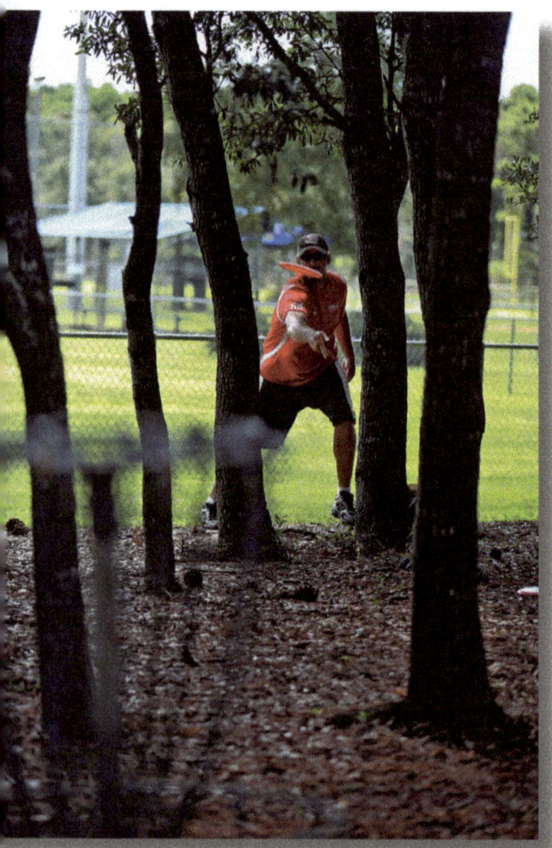

Nothing is more OKI than the annual Surf Off. Typically there is little wave action, making it a bit less thrilling, but still challenging for the participants. It is perfect for practicing your sports photography skills. Use panning of one surfer racing to the waves. It creates an effect that mimics the soft focus created by a large aperture. Only the featured runner is in sharp focus.

In the final photo, a fairly open aperture is used to create the desired depth-of-field to feature a single surfer while providing sufficient context to capture a sense of the event.

## Focus On: Panning

Panning is when the subject is held in the same position in the viewfinder regardless of the background or foreground position, resulting in a sharp image of the subject but a blurred background/foreground.

This technique is especially useful in low-light situations where stop action is just not feasible. It can add a sense of motion to an otherwise static image.

Pan-action shots are done in lateral moving objects, such as a beachcomber bicyclist cruising the beach. Set your shutter speed to a 1/30 of a second slower. As the biker passes, keep their head in the exact part of the frame as you "pan" the camera laterally with the motion of the subject. The subject and the bike will be sharp, the spokes will seemingly disappear, and the surroundings will be blurred but recognizable.

Try this just after sunset or on a dreary day by following sandpipers as they dart in and out of the water.

With image stabilization, you can often shoot at a slower shutterspeed when panning. Nothing will help, though, unless the subject is moving linearly. As an example, panning works on a bicyclist but not on a jogger who is also bobbing up and down. The biker's head and wheels will be at a constant level.

You can pan vertically, too, as with a child jumping up and down in one spot on a pogo stick. You can't pan both ways simultaneously.

The panning technique is used by sports photographers on the cusp of being able to stop the action outright. A surfer on a dreary day laterally moving across the frame is an example. The photographer might have a shutter speed of a 1/125 or a 1/250 of a second which doesn't quite stop the motion; therefore, panning can give the illusion of stop action while not entirely looking like a pan-action blur.

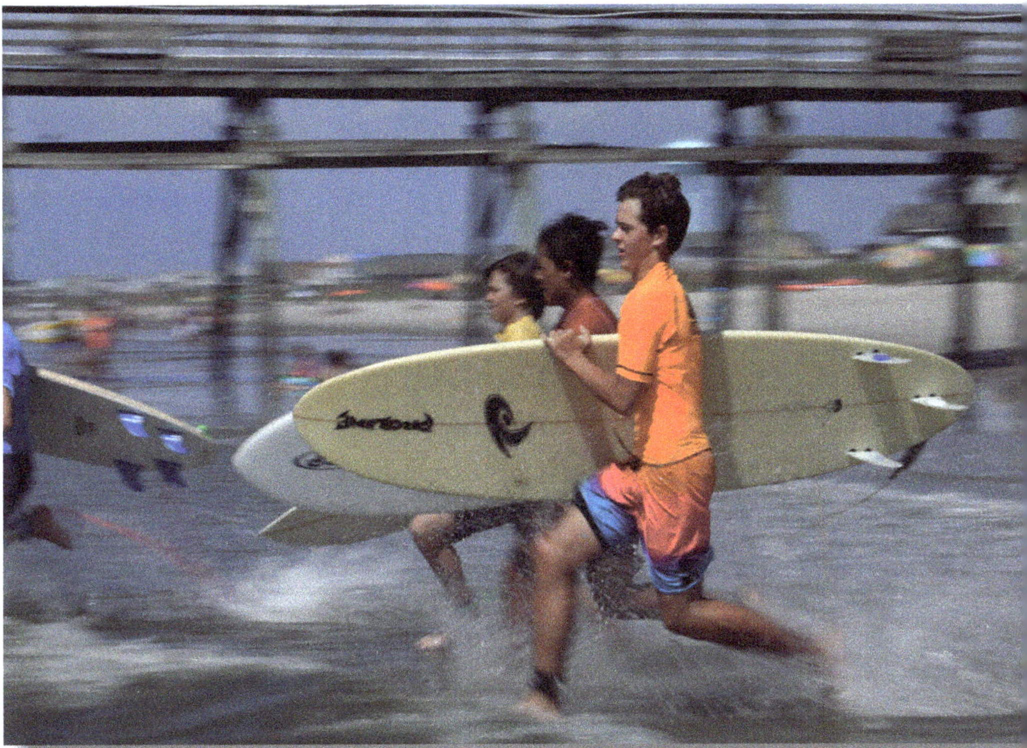

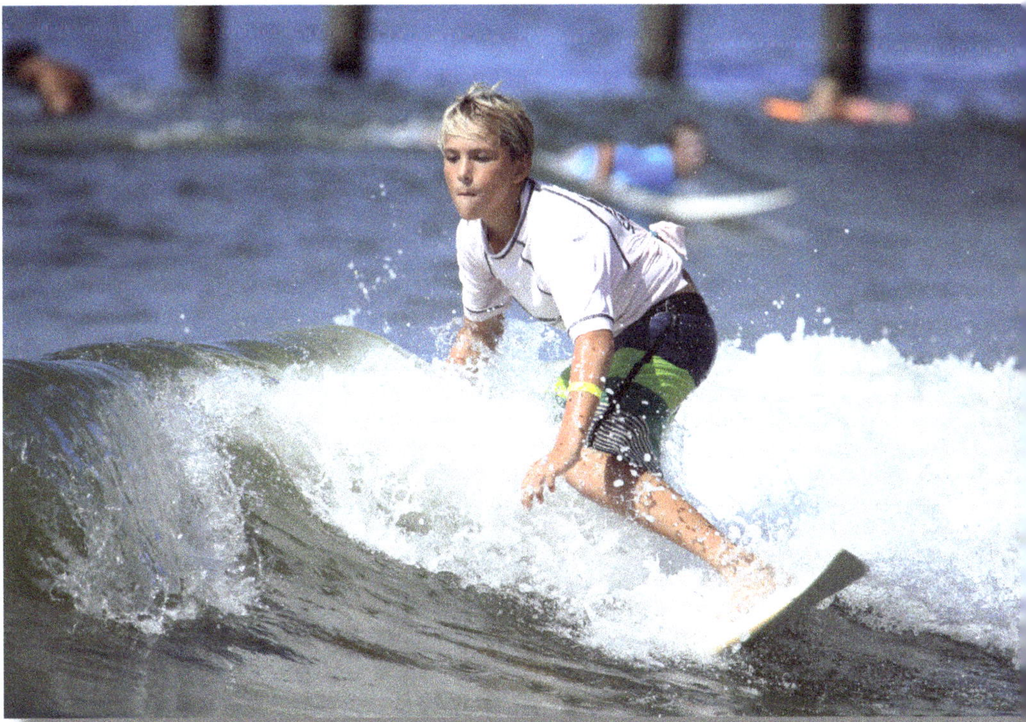

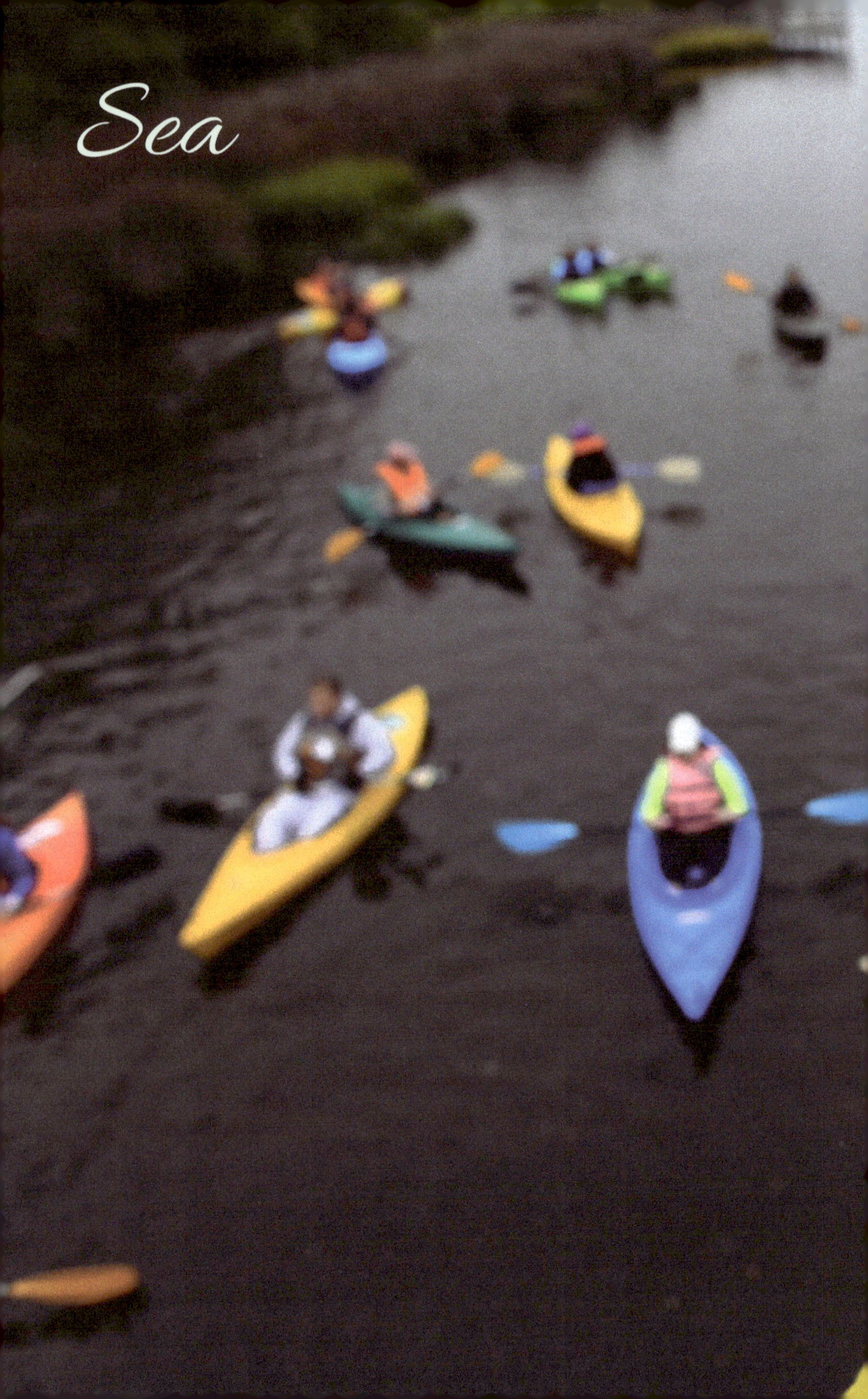

# Sea

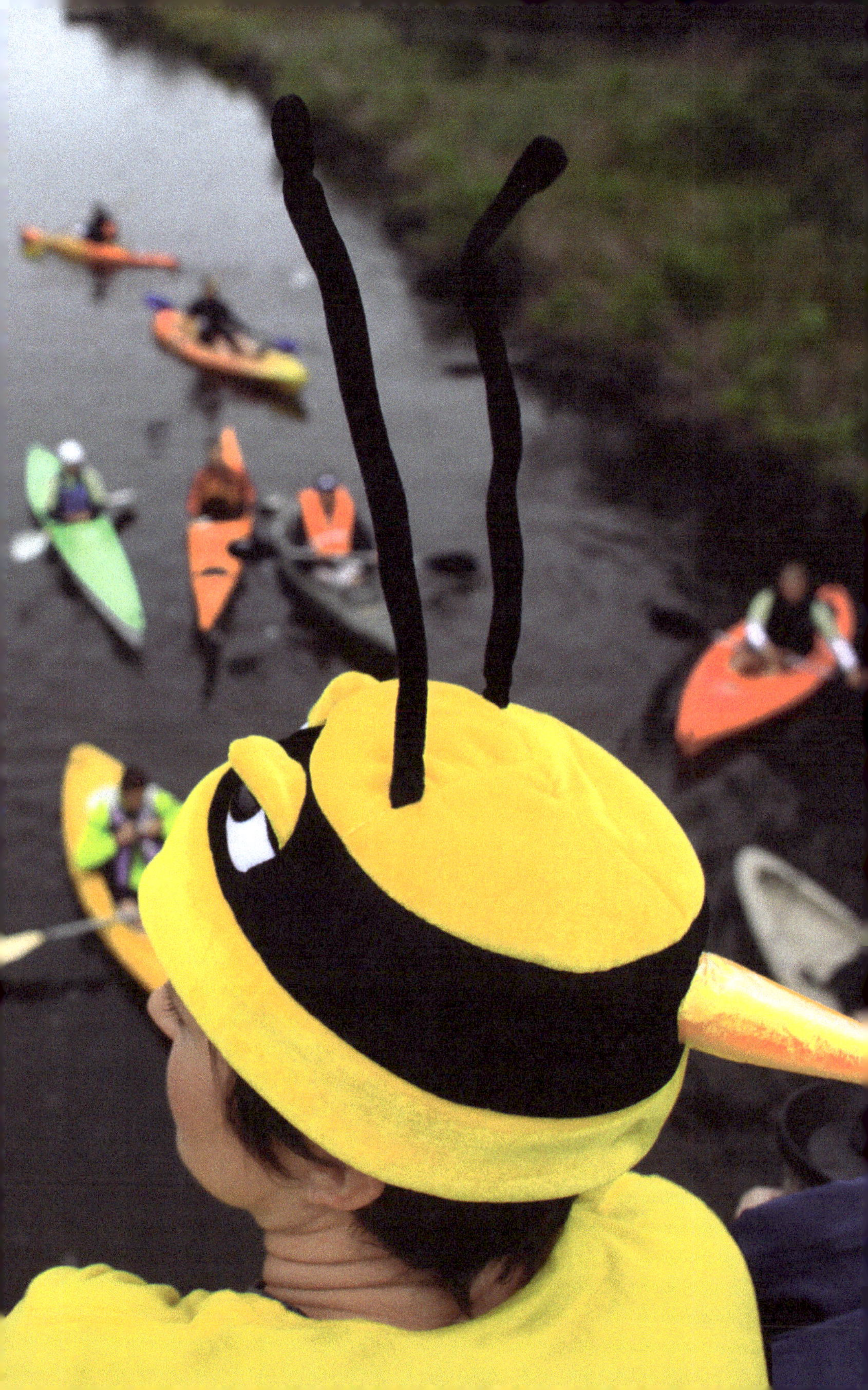

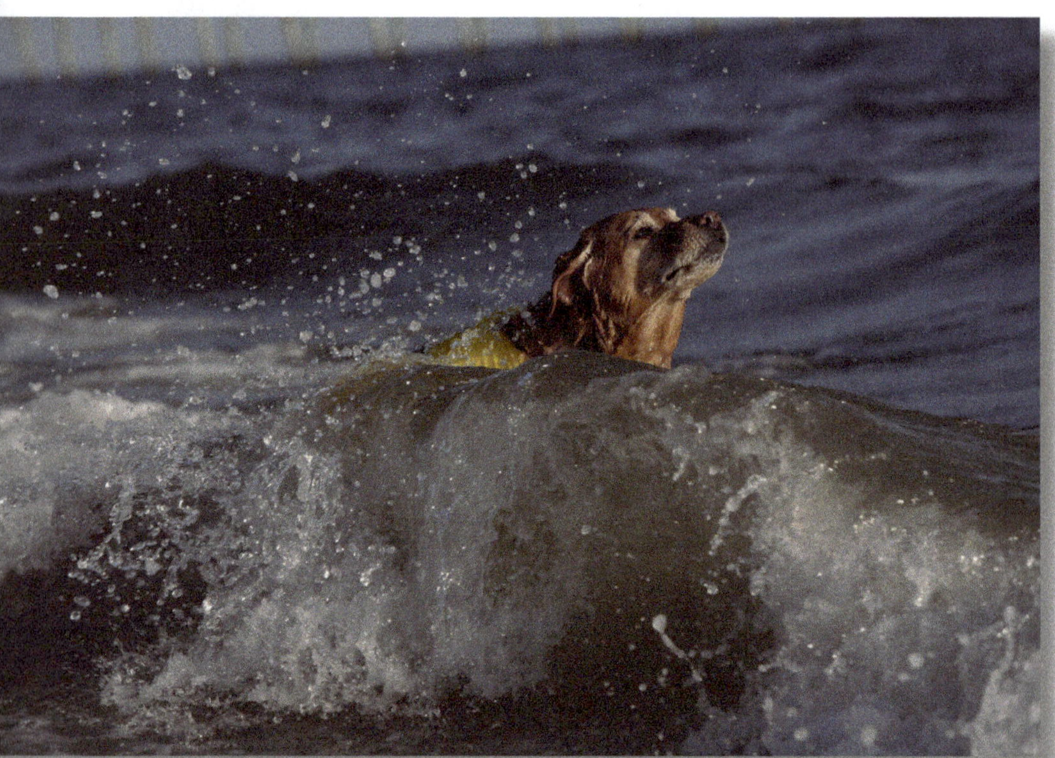

Water as subject, water as background, water as foreground, water stop actioned, water motion blurred, if water doesn't get your creative juices going nothing will. Most of what draws residents and visitors alike to Oak Island takes place on, in, or by the water. It should surely be a part of your OKI scrapbooked memories.

Casual photographers, though, seldom take pictures of their dogs, siblings, friends, or strangers simply doing what people and their pets do most at the beach—splash in the waves. A camera "sees" what your eyes see, too, but your brain will likely ignore. The splash of a wave halos the splasher with translucent glowing droplets. To approximate the shot above you'll need a shutter speed of approximately 1/1000 of a second.

Even many inexpensive point-and-shoot cameras will be able to do that. The focal length of your lens may be a bit more problematic. This shot was made with a 180mm lens from the shore. If you don't have that much focal length, you can risk going out into the wave with your camera (not recommended), crop the frame using computer software, or visit the nearby CVS at the end of Long Beach Road to crop and make your print.

Finally, you'll want to take advantage of the glow of the light on your subject and the translucency of the droplets. The darker ocean water will contrast

## Focus On: Motion Blur

The term "still photography" was coined to distinguish it from the newer "motion pictures" or "movies." In still photography we capture a single frame as opposed to the multiple images that are looped together to give the appearance of movement in motion pictures.

In order to give a feeling of movement in a singular image, photographers use the motion-blur technique. Motion blur is created when a single object is exposed on the film or camera sensor in multiple places along a path. It is opposite of stop action, which freezes the object in one part of the film.

Some uses of motion blur we illustrate in this book are shooting fireworks, water flowing around the pier pilings, and children spelling "OKI" with sparklers. Earlier we highlighted the panning technique, which is one form of motion blur.

Motion blur gives us a sense of action in a still image creating a visual energy. In the fireworks example, the glowing burst travels from the launch pad to its apex before erupting into multiple fragments. The burst and those multiple fragments are exposing different pieces of film grain, or pixels in the digital age, to create the motion blur captured in the image.

When trying to set your shutter speed to achieve the correct amount of blur, think about the percentage of the frame, or sensor, that the object is traveling across. If the moving object takes up most of the pixels, the slightest movement will cause motion blur.

If the object only takes up a small portion of the frame, you will need a longer time value to get the same sense of motion even though it is traveling at the same speed. In the photo below, the foam in the foreground appears to move faster than the foam at the right center even though it is all taken at one shutter speed.

In other words, the blur is not entirely dependent on the shutter speed or the speed of the object's movement; the blur is more prominent the greater the distance the subject moves relative to the area of the sensor or film.

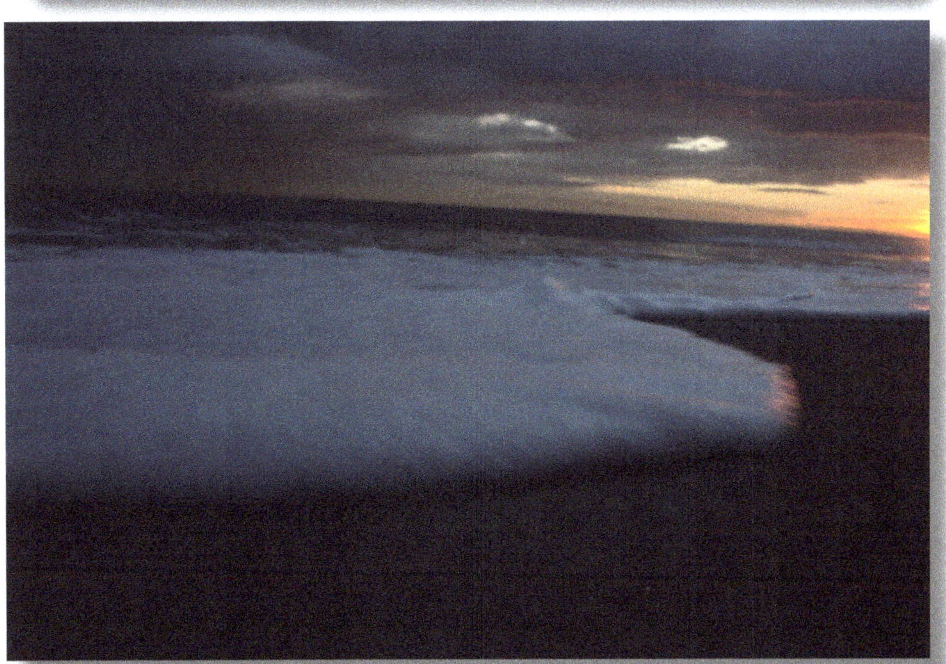

with the droplets, while the short exposure duration will have the splash suspended in mid-air.

Big sweeps of water beg to be photographed. Little bits of water are no less intriguing. For either photos of droplets dangling after a rain or bubbles sitting in stationary objects you will want to have the sun, glowing through the water, behind you.

OKI is not Hawaii, with its huge forceful sweeps of water. Usually though, during any given week, there will be periods with some notable wave action. That always entices some surfers and a whole lot of boogie boarders. These two intrepid souls demonstrated how to do it, as the OKI surf swelled prior to Long Beach being buffeted by Hurricane Hanna. Your surest bet at getting a surfer shot is to set your camera to shutter priority, so you can ensure sufficient speed and carry a long lens. You can often use one of the two piers as a long lens work around. The wave action near each of OKI's two piers is good. Walk down the pier until you are at the wave break. You will then be close enough to work with a normal length lens.

The Atlantic Ocean is not Oak Island's only photo-worthy body of

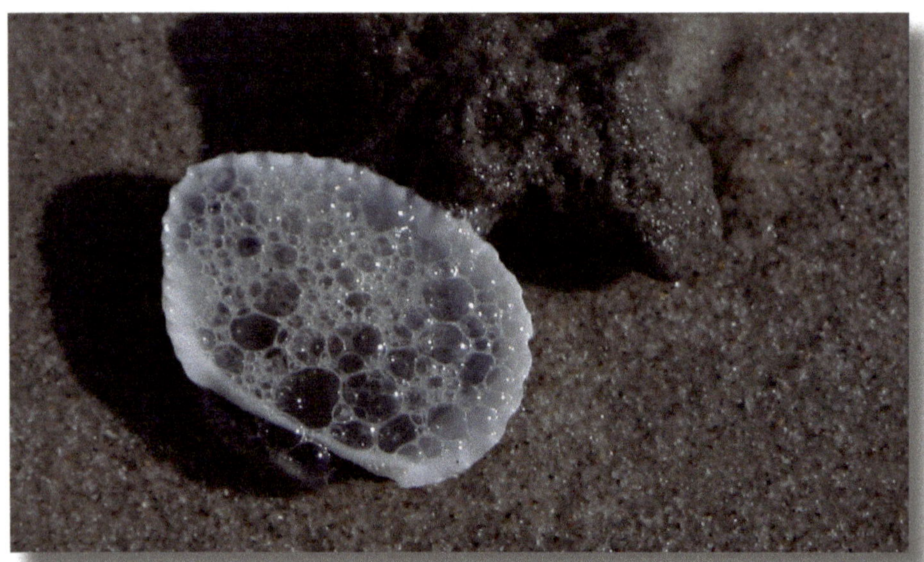

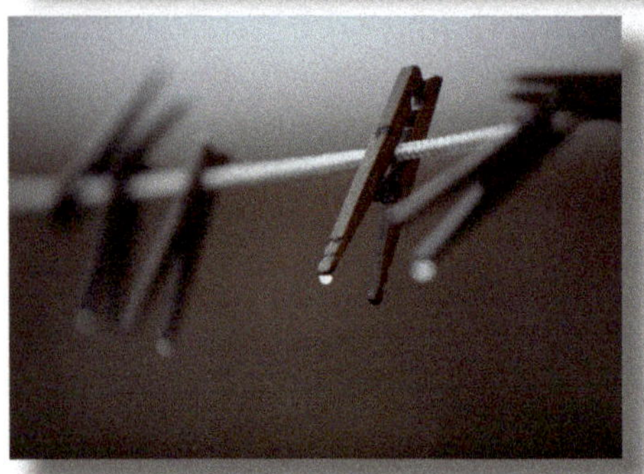

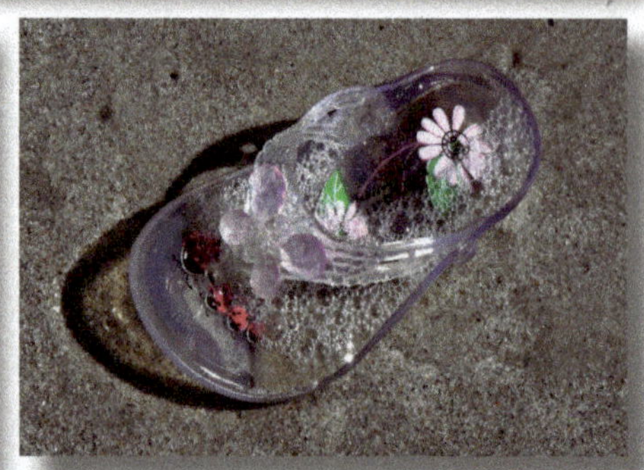

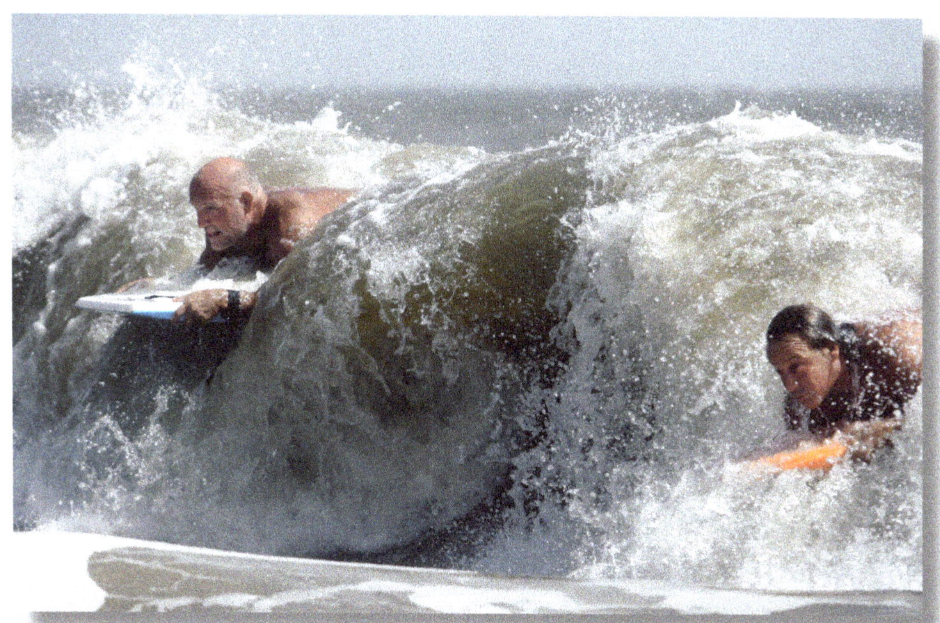

water. All beach towns have beaches, but Oak Island has scenic inland waters, too.

If you ignore these other liquid attractions, you will miss out on the total OKI experience. The waterways are ever-changing due to the tides and seasons. Use the waterways and their banks to create leading lines, which seemingly transport you to the distant horizon, even in a two-dimensional image.

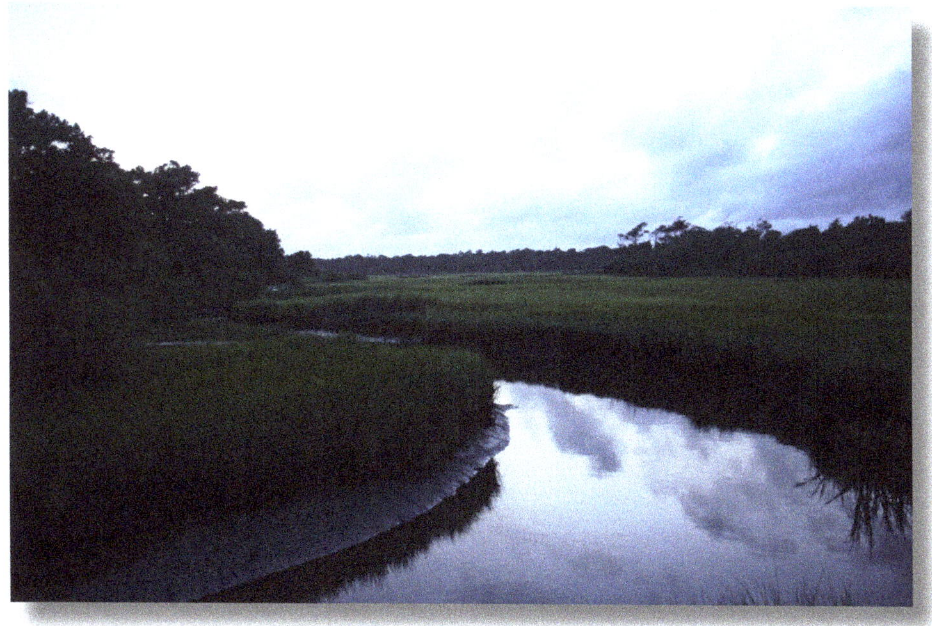

# fishing

Fishing is taken seriously on Oak Island. Emmy Award winning, television pioneer, Clay Cole, in his book *Sh-Boom,* written while retired to Oak Island, noted that he lives in "a quaint little drinking village with a fishing problem." Fishing is found everywhere. Anglers can be seen on boats, piers, beach, and docks; fishermen are offshore, near-shore, along the Intracoastal, on the inner creeks, and trolling in Cape Fear and Lockwood Folly Rivers.

Experiencing the fishing crowd on one of Oak Island's two piers is an essential component of a visit. Aside from the piers being the easiest way to actually cast your bait, these weathered wooden structures are unsurpassed as a place to create photographic artwork.

From the vantage point of the beach, look toward the pier facing the sun. You will notice silhouettes. Look for patterns of poles, posts, and people to capture an iconic memory of your visit to the pier.

Making pictures on the pier is a blast. You can use the campy fish scale doorway to pose the kids, stand on one of the raised benches to capture a different angle of an angler baiting his rig, or play with different focal lengths as family members reel in the big catch. The piers present an ideal place to exercise creativity in using different focal points and exploring foreground, middle ground, and background. There are lots of lines, shadows, colors, and patterns on almost any given day on the deck of the pier.

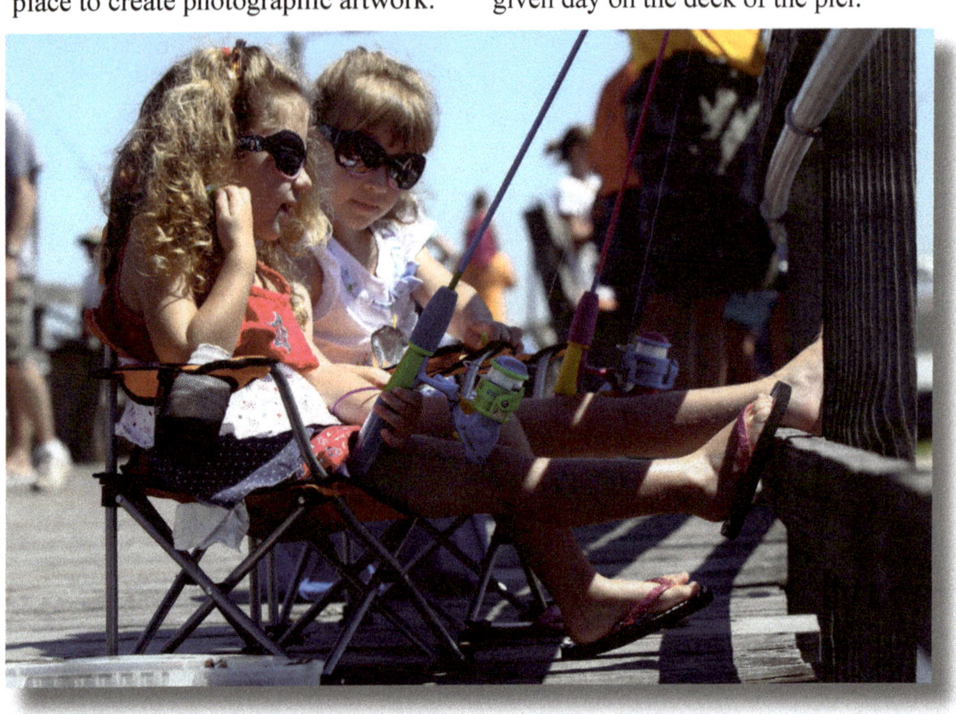

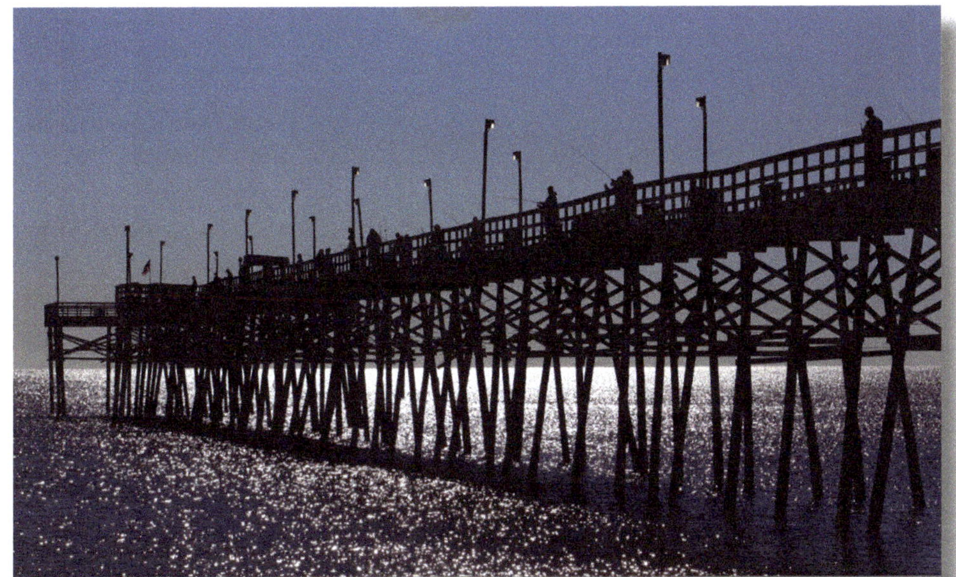

Discover the 21st Century. Women have joined the ranks as top ocean and river anglers on Oak Island. Nearly a decade ago the Town of Oak Island began a two-day program called W.A.I.T (Women Anglers in Training); it is partly why more women are anglers now. The women's fishing movement encourages younger generations to the rod 'n reel sport. Women have added vibrant colors to fishing photography, too.

These two young ladies at left were part of the the Town of Oak Island's Kids Fishing Derby in June 2013. Taking a "clean" picture on the pier is difficult with so much potential clutter in the background. Using a shallow depth-of-field (a wide aperture) will help background elements, such as the light posts, be additive information elements as opposed to a distraction growing out of your subject's head. A second recommendation to aid in your pier pictures is to get closer to your subjects. Close proximity will help your background become a soft focus scene.

Fishing is an around-the-clock activity. As the evening encroaches, diehard Oak Island fishermen use the tidal creeks as their source for crab dinners or to catch bait for the next day.

While poles big and small are staples of fishing gear, castnets are the tool of choice at the end of Davis Canal. If you haven't tried to throw a castnet, know that it is really tricky. The effort is worth it though; local fish are a lot like Oak Island natives, they like the local southern fare. Castnetters bring in mostly shrimp and menhaden, which if the big fish are biting, seem to suit their tastes. If you try your hand at learn-

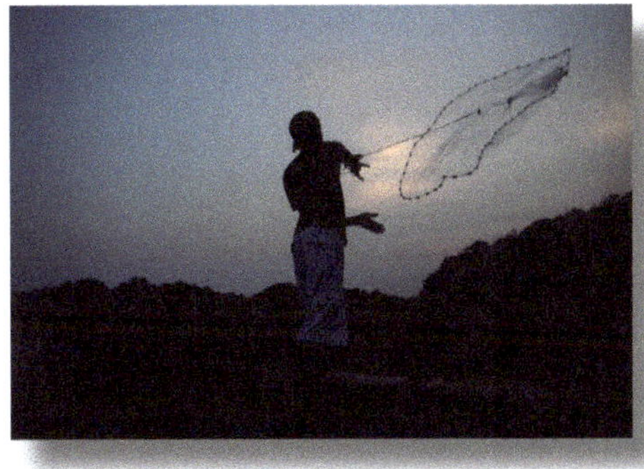

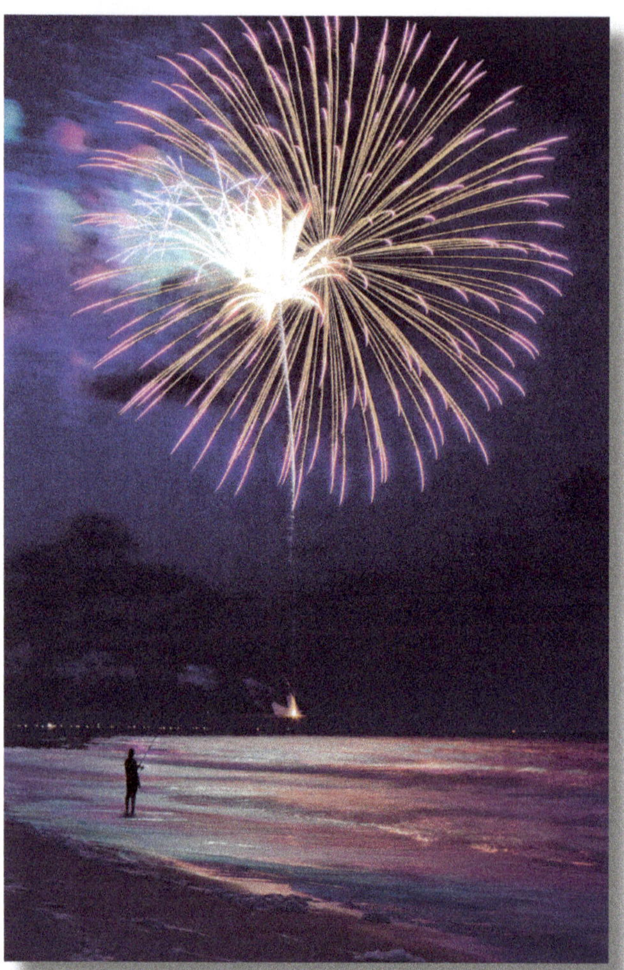

ing to castnet, have a friend photograph the experience as it will certainly lead to some early laughs and a good memory.

Even though I have seen the occasional fishing aficionado casting into the surf after dark, finding one in my viewfinder during the Town of Oak Island's fireworks display, scheduled for July first on Beach Day each year, was a bit of a surprise. While I wouldn't bet on replicating the shot, fishing is such an OKI passion that if you scout the beach, your chances are good.

On a bright sunny day try taking a detailed picture of your bait fish as you let it out. The sunlight off the waters

## Focus On: Lens Perspective

In all photo images, elements in the distance appear smaller than they actually are relative to foreground elements. The effect intensifies as you decrease the focal length. As you take a picture of your two young nephews with your pleasantly plump Aunt Betty, shooting your nephews carrying their fishing gear ahead of your aunt will make them appear a bit bigger than they are and your aunt look a bit smaller. (If this seems like cheating, shoot guilt free; reversing their placement would be equally distorting.)

You should generally take pictures of people with them looking up at you so their eyes are fully open. For those with double chins and jowls you get a "two-fer," standing above your subjects will cause them to automatically stretch out the sagging skin a bit.

As you translate this into your fishing pictures, combine the two techniques. Take the picture of the day's catch with the fisherman holding the fish out from his body and looking at it above eye level. The fish will look a bit bigger than it is and you will help ameliorate the squinty eye syndrome so ubiquitous near sand and water.

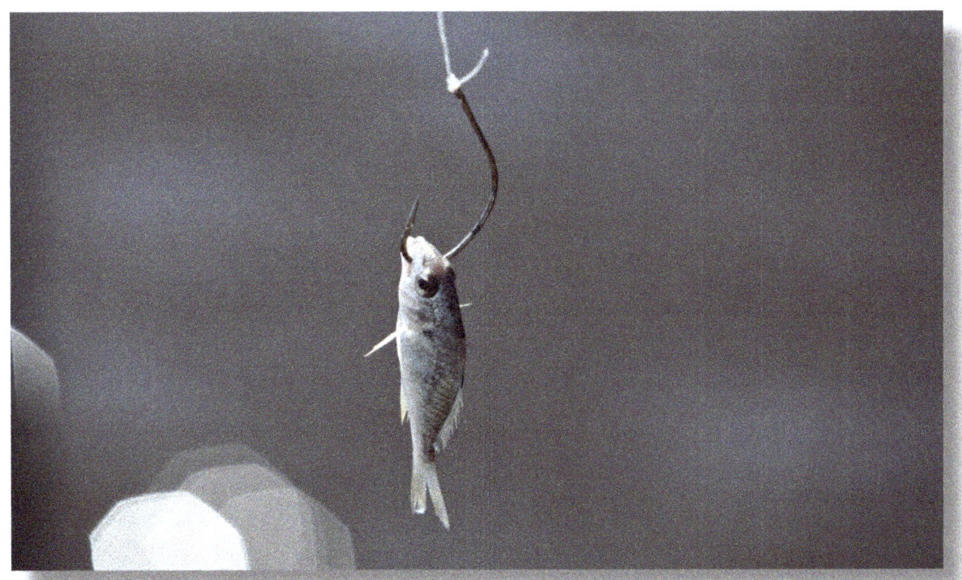

below the fish makes a backdrop that appears a bit surreal. The ocean water will be a soft, even backdrop. Combine that with the sparkles in the water that are distant from your lens which appear as aperture-shaped white spots. The final effect is a very clean photo of your baitfish with a little pop of flare.

For the catch consider using a wide-angle lens. Below, using a 24mm lens and getting as close as possible, made the catch appear a bit larger than it actually was. For evidence supporting your fish story, this ploy is beneficial.

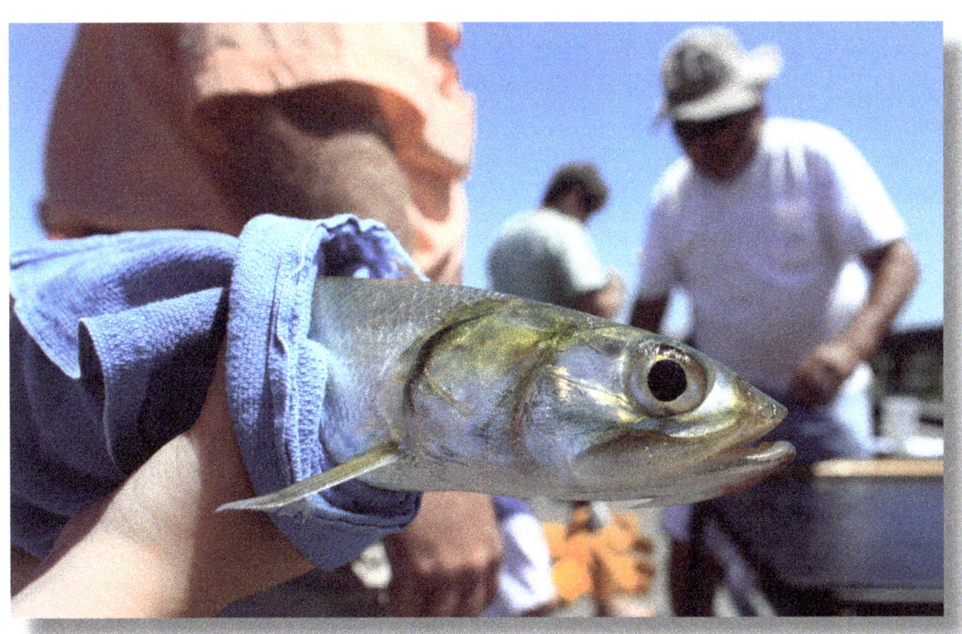

# boats

Boats appear to be everywhere when you visit the island. Watercraft are seen from the beach, on the Intracoastal, and mid-island along Davis Canal. You'll spot vessels at the Blue Point Marina at SW 57th Street, at the South Harbor Marina on the Oak Island mainland, and at both Dutchman's Creek as an industry providing good fortune to locals and visitors who can buy locally caught shrimp. During the shrimp season, which starts as early as April and is most reliable from July into November, shrimp boats can be seen in the evenings. Sometimes they are visible trawling throughout the night.

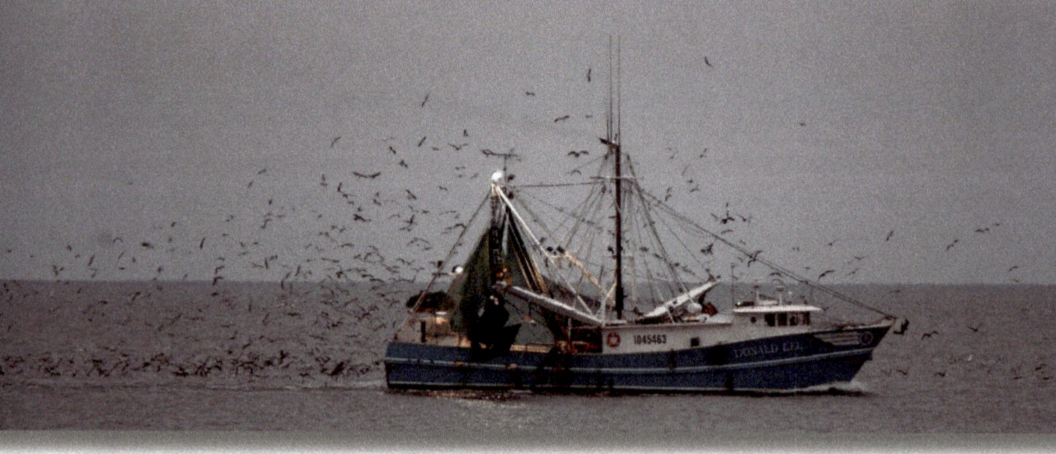

Villas' private marina at NE 54th Street and its adjacent public boat ramp.

Boats sit in many front yards, too, which sometimes gives the impression that Oak Islanders are boat rich and house poor. The common sight of a humongous boat sitting next to a modest cottage is more of an indicator of priorities than wealth. Big boats and little ones from kayaks to yachts are all popular with residents.

Of all of the boats you'll see, the shrimp boats just offshore in the Atlantic are especially riveting. Shrimping has been important to North Carolina since the early 1930s. It still survives

To catch a shrimp boat after dark with your camera demands particular attention to light control. It will be tough, unless you are able set the ISO on your camera. I set my camera's ISO to 800 in the above photo and still needed a fairly wide aperture of f/4 to allow for a fast enough shutter speed to freeze the swirling masses of birds. The movement of the shrimp boat and birds means a long exposure is not a viable option. If you have suitable equipment, the night shot is particularly emblematic of Oak Island and worth the bother. If not, there will also be some shrimp boats out before dusk that make good photo subjects, although not quite as iconic.

While lone working boats parallel the shore, crowds of boats dock at the marinas. Blue Point Marina, the only public marina on the island itself, brims with charter fishing boats and those of local hard core fishing enthusiasts. They bob alongside the recreational watercraft of the locals and visitors. It is a wonderful place to have fun with your camera taking pictures of the unexpected, and practicing less used techniques.

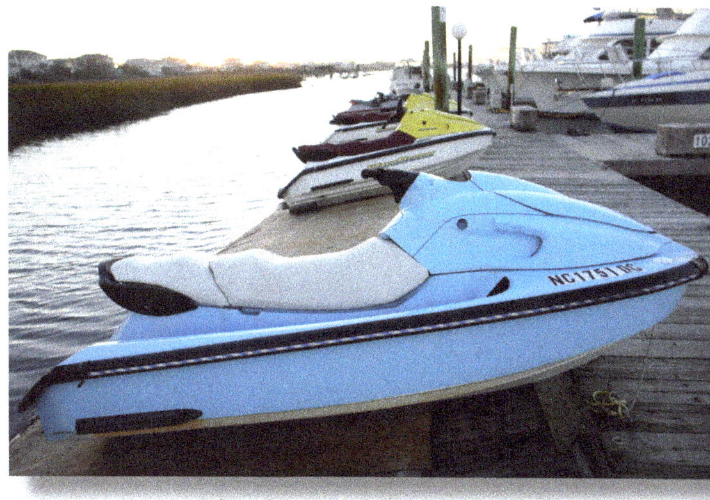

Is the top right picture a study in using color, line, or pattern? Or, is it a photographic story of recreational jet skis going head-to-head with fishing boats? Photographically, the shot uses line to make it three-dimensional, a technique discussed in the next subsection inset. Additionally it plays the color pop of the deep aqua jet ski as foreground against the soft colors of the evening sky, water, and other boats. The soft feel of the background is created by using a wide aperture setting of f/4.

For a bit of fun, the shot below is unexpected, symmetrical, and has distinctive use of color. Photographically, the effect is created with a wide-angle lens, much like the big fish illusion.

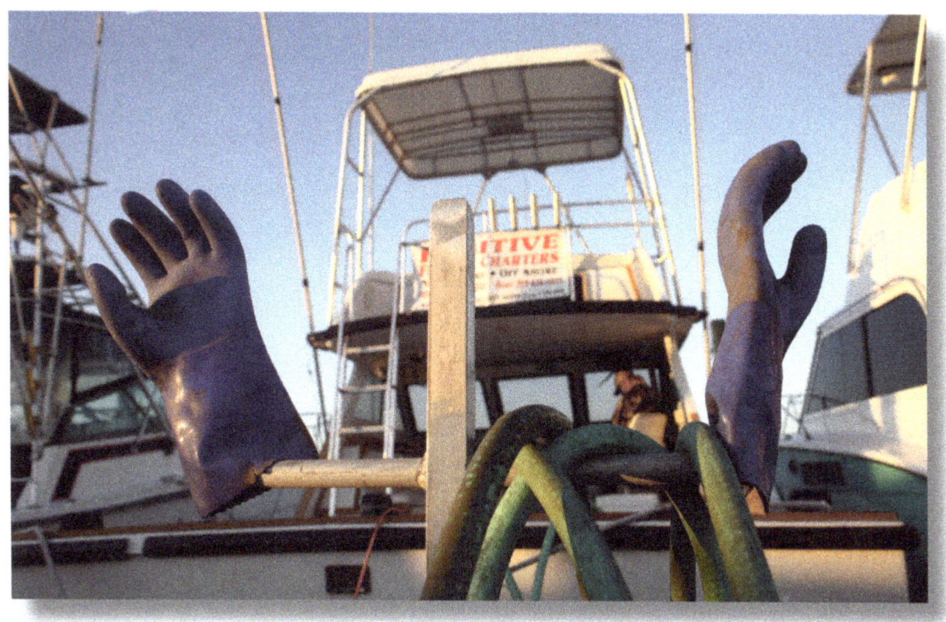

## Focus On: Vantage Point

Taking the photo from a child's vantage point is a classic example of seeing things in a new way. A small child is limited to looking up. It is no wonder why kids love to climb a tree. It gives them a different scope.

In photography, changing your angle-of-view can be quite dramatic. Try shooting a crab from its eye level. This will create drama and put the viewer in the world of the crab.

Raising or lowering the camera a few inches can make a big difference when in close proximity to your subject with a wide-angle lens. Is there a light post or telephone pole directly behind someone? Lower the camera to make it disappear beyond the subject.

A crowded beach at standing-eye level can suddenly become expansive from a raised position, such as the elevated pier. Getting horizontal, as longtime State Port Pilot photojournalist, Jim Harper, did as he worked the angles at the 2013 Ride the Tide is part of what separated him from the nearby amateurs.

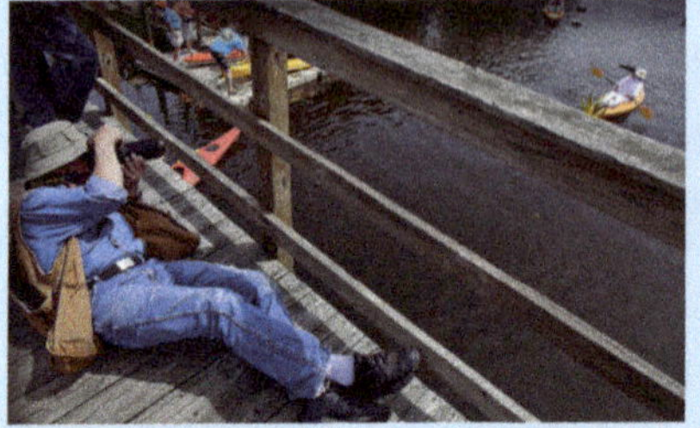

The working gloves in the photo are, of course, not almost as tall as the fishing consoles on the boats to the right and left.

If you travel east of the island, you will find sailboats bobbing at anchor in a cove just south of the Wildlife Boat Ramp on Fish Factory Road along Dutchman's Creek. Some of the boats are visiting; others are floating homes. A second marina called the South Harbor Marina is found a bit farther south of the cove. A variety of sailboats and powerboats are docked long-term with many of them functioning as house boats, too.

For boats on the move, powerboats outnumber sailboats in Oak Island environs. Recently though, the Cape Fear Yacht Club has added many small sailboats to the waters as part of their summer sailing camp program for young sailors in the making. Not only will this encourage the upcoming generation to fill the waters with more sailboats, it provides a chance for a nice photo. While the usual photo opportunities are of single vessels or a completely fortuitous mish mash that, by happenstance, work together in the viewfinder, this

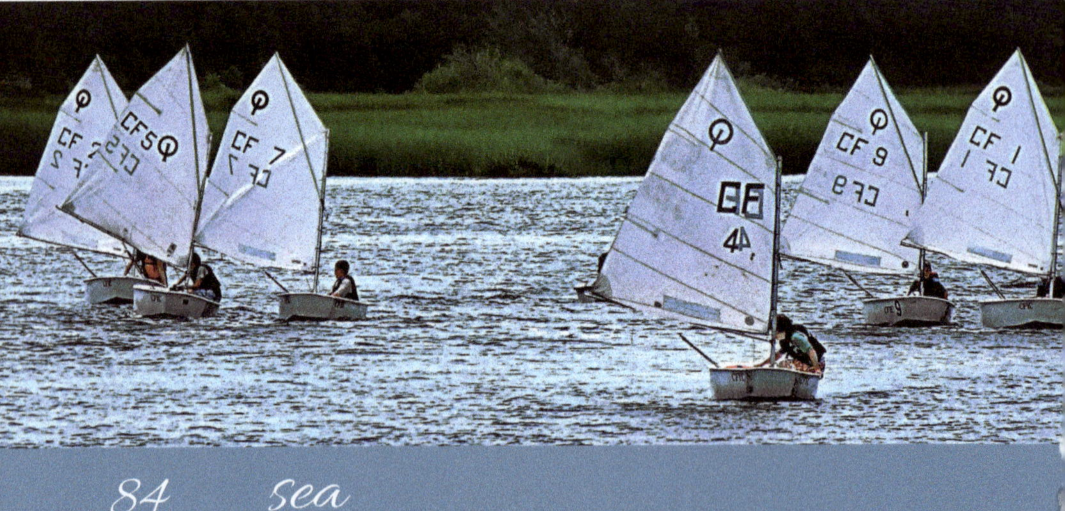

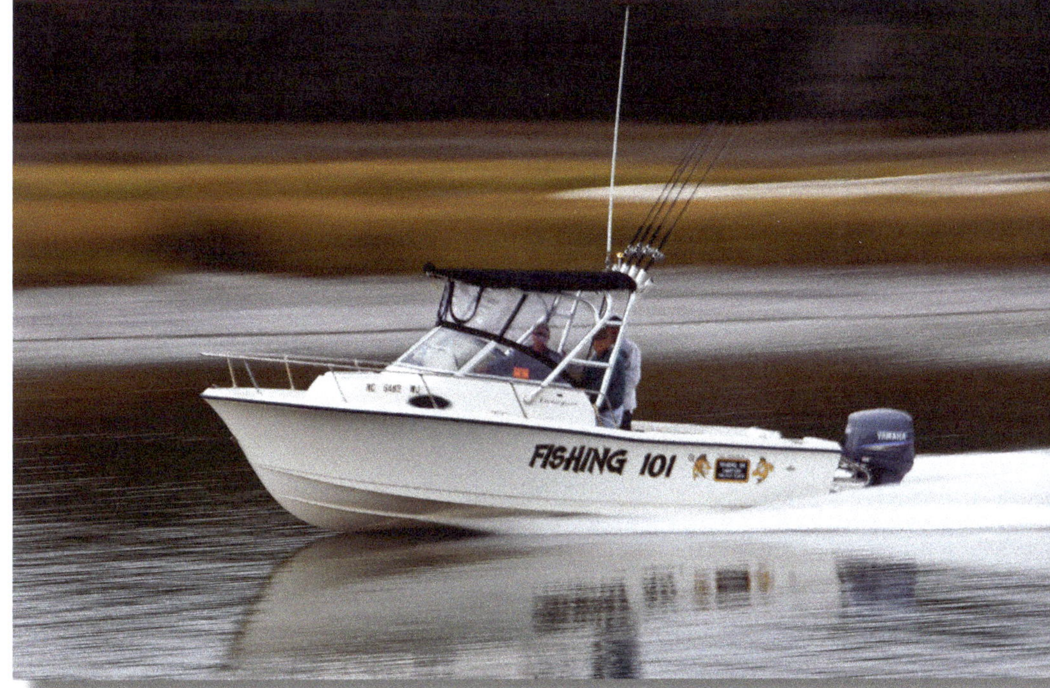


matched set of little sailboats floating along Dutchman's Creek to the left is a boon photographically.

To see really big boats, from enormous sailboats to yachts, to even the occasional barge, the Intracoastal Waterway is the place to be. You'll see the most impressive vessels on the Waterway in the spring and fall as boats are moved between harbors in the Caribbean, our southeastern coast, and our northeastern coast.

The best places to photograph big boats on the move have both interesting foregrounds and attractive backgrounds. Good places include Waterway Park, May Moore Park, Old Bridge Road, and the South Harbor Marina.

Boating photos can also test your skills. The above photo is a pan-action photo, which creates clean lines and a nice reflection. Keep in mind though, that the boat is moving up and down as it skims across the water. A really slow shutter speed will be ineffective.

Oak Island is not just about the big boats. The island is populated with about as many kayaks and canoes as people. Probably the easiest place to launch is by the Rec Center between SE 30th and 31st place as shown in the "Land: Events" subsection; there are rollers to facilitate the process. The 30th Place West Canoe Dock is only slightly more challenging and arguably offers more photogenic shots of the inland waters and on the waters. It is located on the northwest end of the island which is the least developed with the widest swaths of inland water.

# piers and walkways

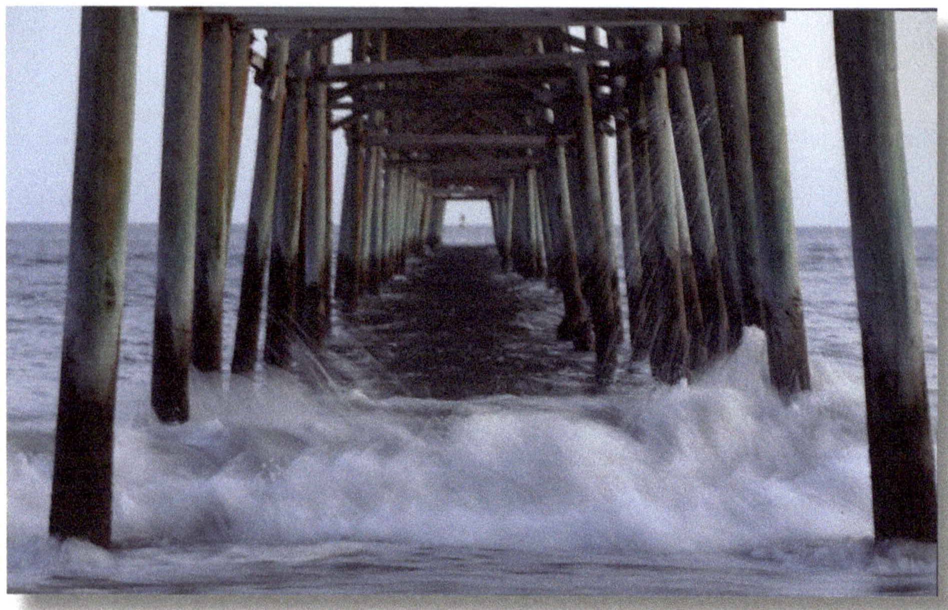

Oak Island's piers and walkways make it easy to create photographic eye candy. These wooden formations can be the subject themselves, a nice photo backdrop, a prop, or you can simply document your time enjoying activities on, under, or near them.

You have almost certainly, at least, seen the two piers if you have been on the island. On a clear day they are visible from almost any spot on the beach, even those miles away. As discussed in the "Fishing" subsection, they offer wonderful photographic possibilities.

Unlike the piers, the three Town of Oak Island walkways are possible to miss altogether. Missing the walkways would be a pity; they are each unexpected portals to the natural world. They were built for utility; Oak Island is bifurcated by the Davis Canal and/or Montgomery Slough for a little more than six of its 12.6 miles. In order for the folk on the north side of the water to walk to the beach and those on the beach side to get to Oak Island Drive, the town created three wooden crossovers that begin off Oak Island Drive at SE 9th, 20th, and 31st streets and end at 9th, 19th, and 29th Place East, close to their respective beach accesses.

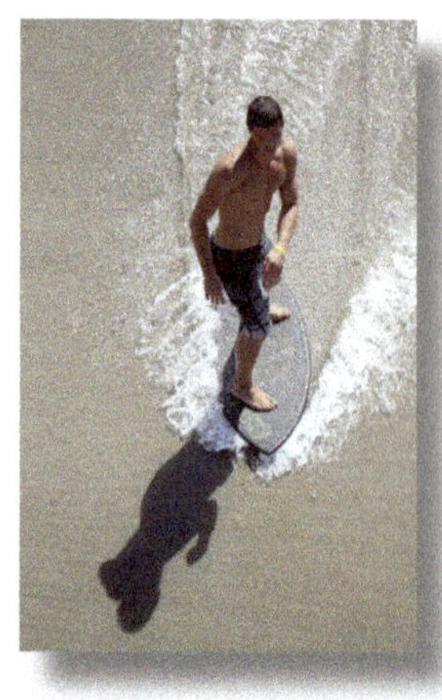

The crossover walkways span the marsh. For you as a photographer, they can be used successfully as photo

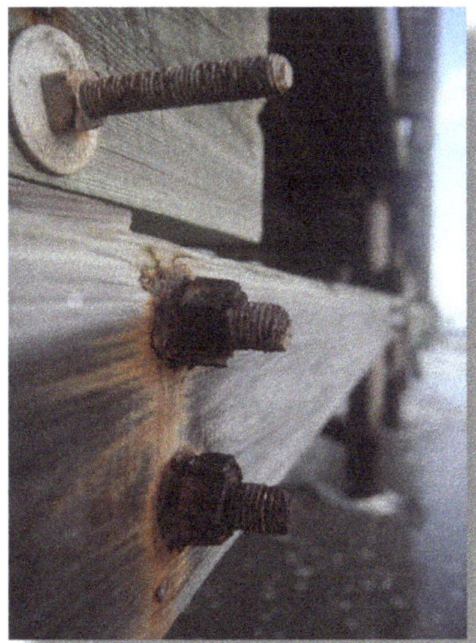

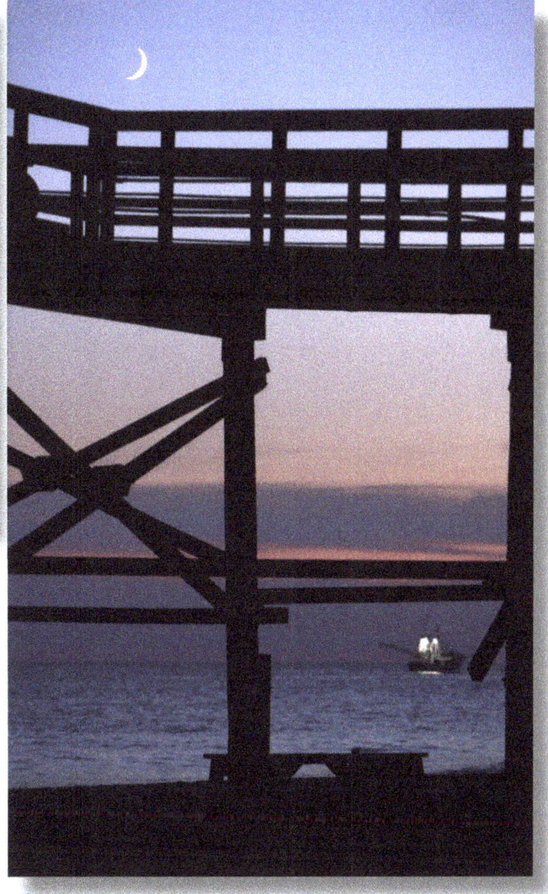

subjects, as they stretch the expanse, with their rails creating a pleasing radial symmetry. The crossovers are also great sites for making portraits of your friends and family. The background is essentially the horizon.

Additionally, for you the vacationer, the walkways are sanctuaries from motor vehicles. As

## Focus On: Line

A line is not always straight nor visible.

In terms of photography, artists try to use leading lines to keep the eye moving. Another use of line would be to visually organize or compartmentalize different areas of interest.

The above two photos use these techniques. The photo of the bolts has the viewer moving past the rusty fasteners to tell the story of why they are corroded. Meanwhile the moon and boat photo has used line to create a grid which is a graphic delight in itself.

The photo of the walkway you will see on page 89 has curved lines that meander from foreground to background.

The general rule is that horizontal lines and vertical lines create stability while diagonal lines add a bit of drama and motion.

Try using line to create shapes. Often these shapes are not literal. An example would be the strong triangle created in the shovels photo on page 41.

The key shape is the triangle. Look to create multiple triangles or at least one dominant one as you compose each photograph.

Using line, especially to create shapes, will take your images from snapshots to wall worthy artwork.

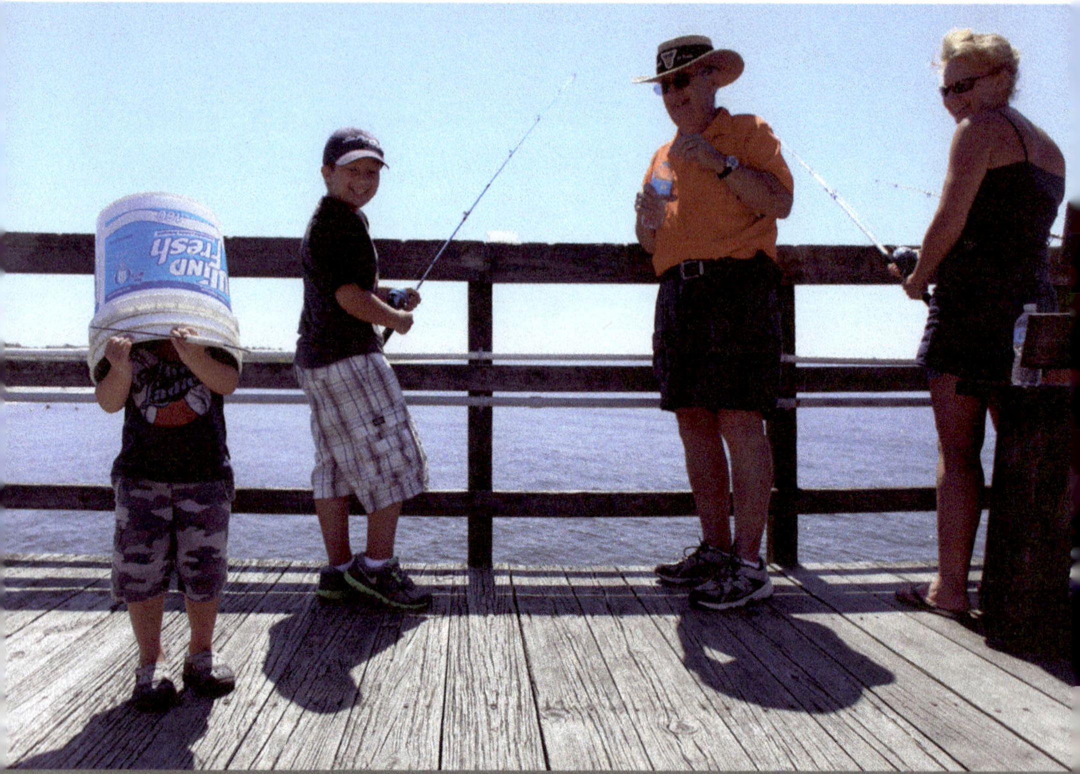

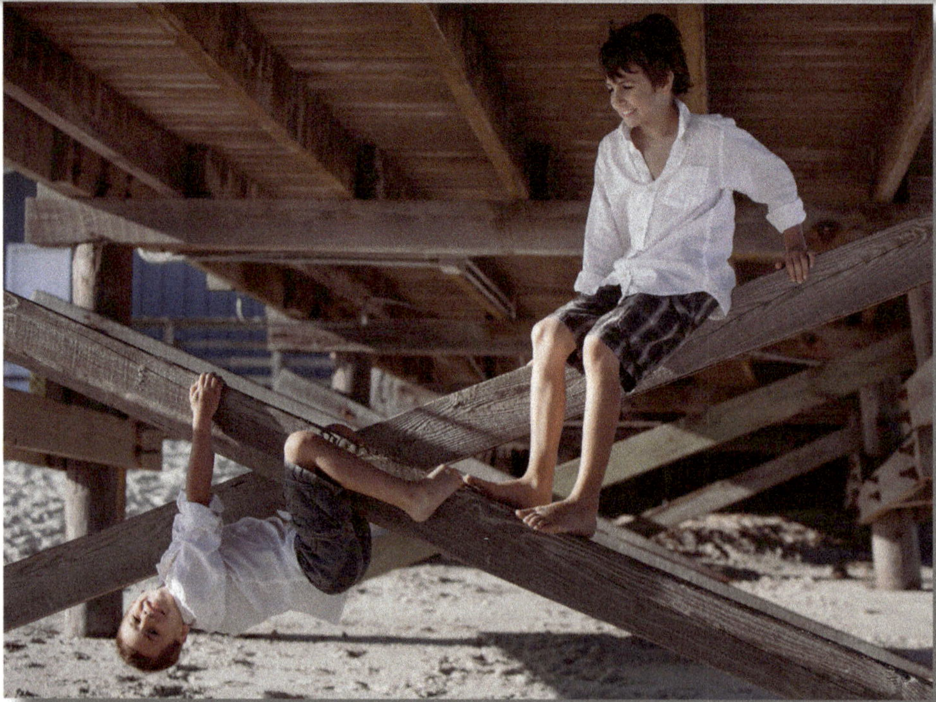

the sun rises or sets, not only are your photographs tranquil, but your present reality is serene. Once you take the photo, you can recreate that quiet, calming place in your house by making a large print for your wall, or using the image as a screensaver. It will be your photography—not some stock image of a place you haven't experienced.

The two large-scale wooden piers and three walkways are complemented by private piers and walkways, the large Caswell Beach walkway across the street from the OKI Lighthouse, and those owned by the Town of Oak Island as a part of its parks system.

A jaunt out to Waterway Park is always a good bet, if you are carrying your camera. The lines of the pier and the park's walkways are wonderful framing elements.

You can explore the waters *sans* camera, too. Biology experts are aplenty in Brunswick County and occasionally lead free learning activities for kids and adults in conjunction with the wonderful staff at Oak Island Parks & Recreation.

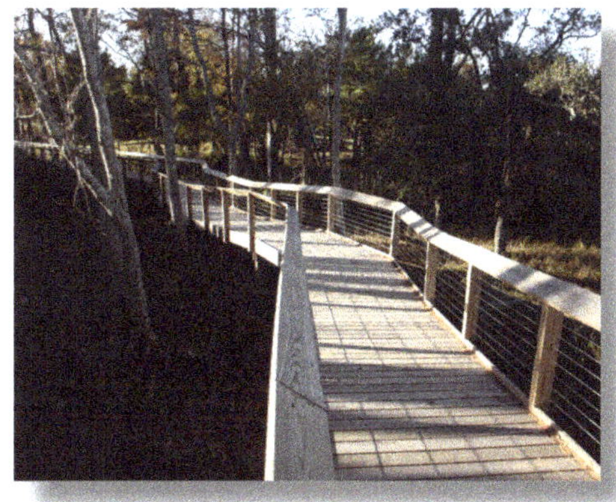

The picture below at Waterway Park is of a lesson on using a seine net to capture all sorts of creatures. As an example, the Intracoastal is a nursery for puffer fish. Children are fascinated; even most adults have never encountered a real one in the wild. Crabs, shrimp, and bait fish are also plentiful.

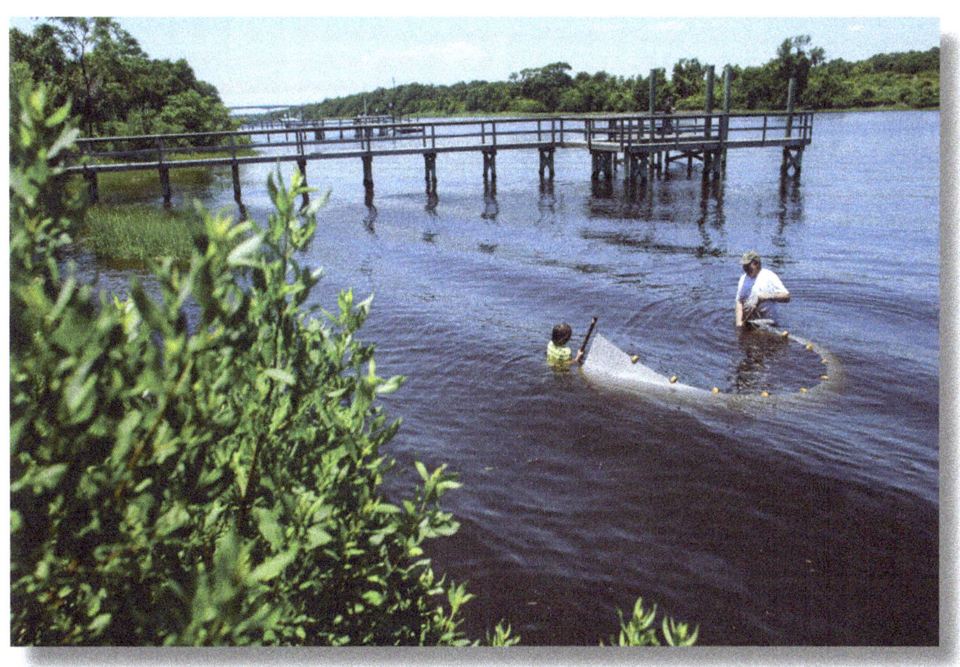

# wading birds and waterfowl

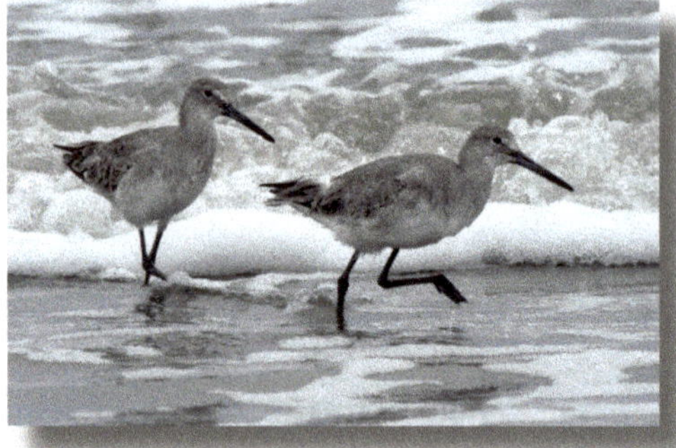

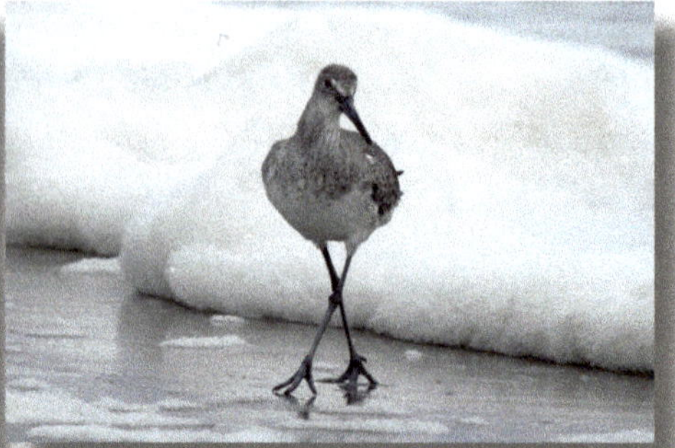

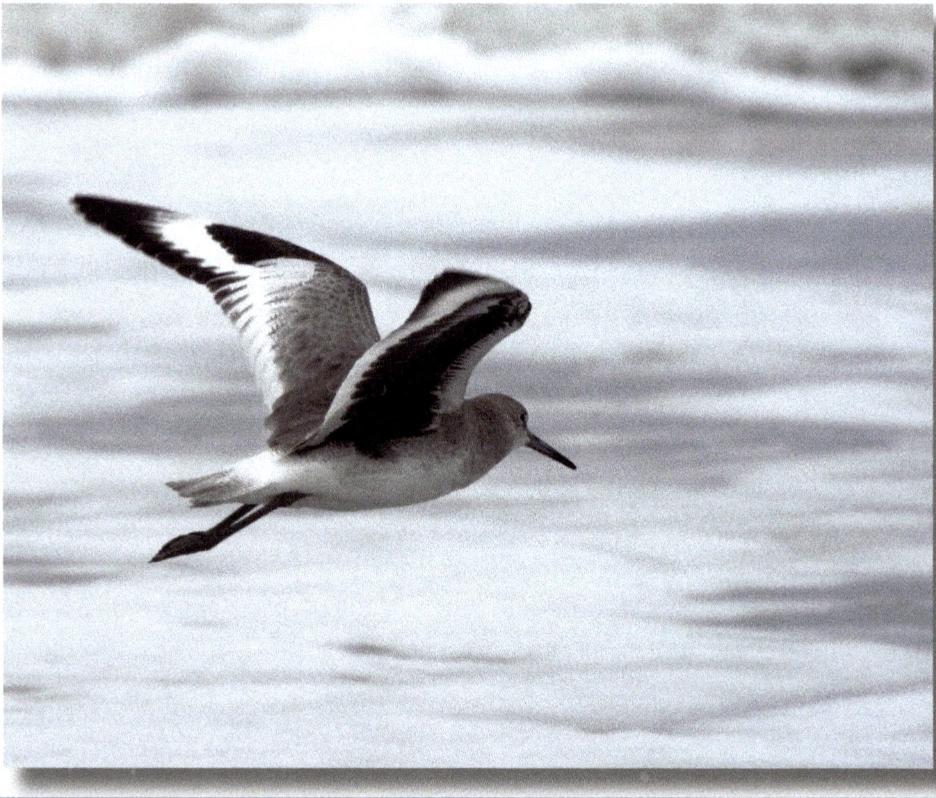

All along Oak Island's beaches sandpipers amuse Oak Island visitors. The willet is one of the most common. He isn't as skittish as some pipers, and if you do spook him (and are quick enough to photograph him transformed) your picture of him airborne will be as good as the one on the beach. The willets cavort with their smaller sandpiper friends the sanderlings, plovers, and dunlins. These are particularly fun to watch. I used a fast shutter speed of 1/1600 of a second to freeze the action of this diminutive bird, pictured on the top of adjoining page 91, during a sunny late afternoon. You can compare the

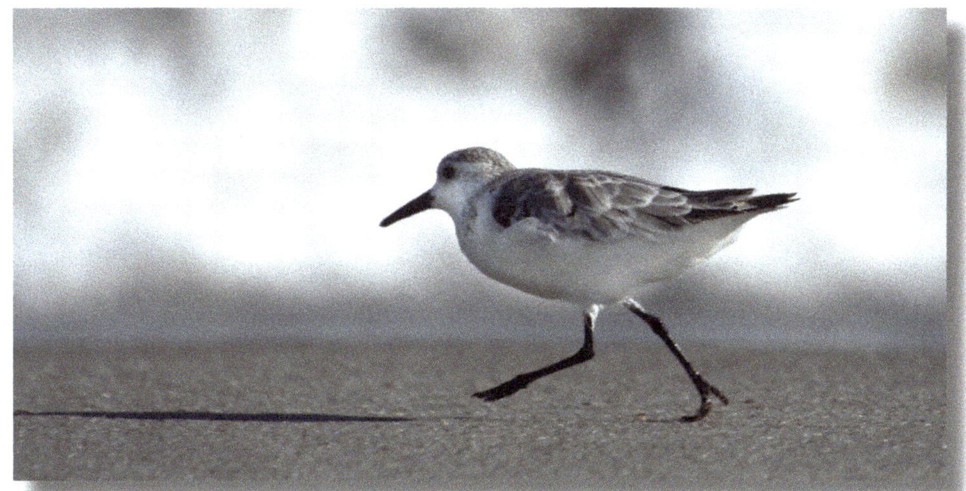

flat light of an overcast day, when the willet photos were taken, with this in full sun.

Often they scurry about with their little legs moving so quickly, they blur to the naked eye. You can use them as a good opportunity to practice taking the same basic shot at different shutterspeeds. Try setting your camera to shutter priority and taking a handful of shots from about 1/30 of a second to your camera's max.

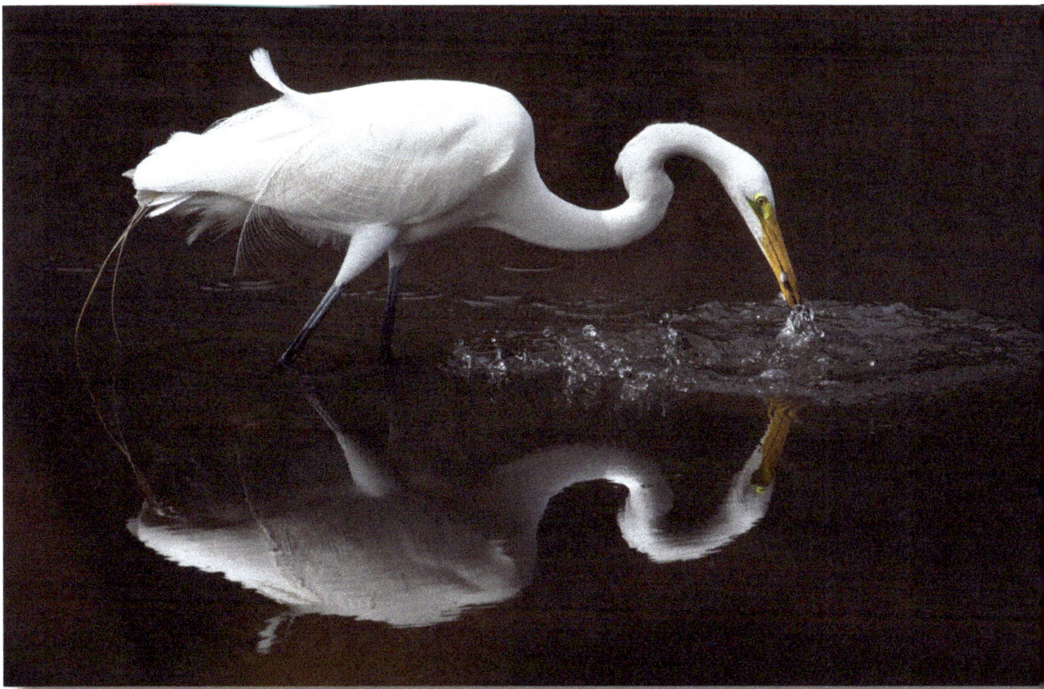

While the sandpipers dominate the beach, most of the Oak Island wading birds are along Davis Creek in the middle of the island, on the golf courses, or

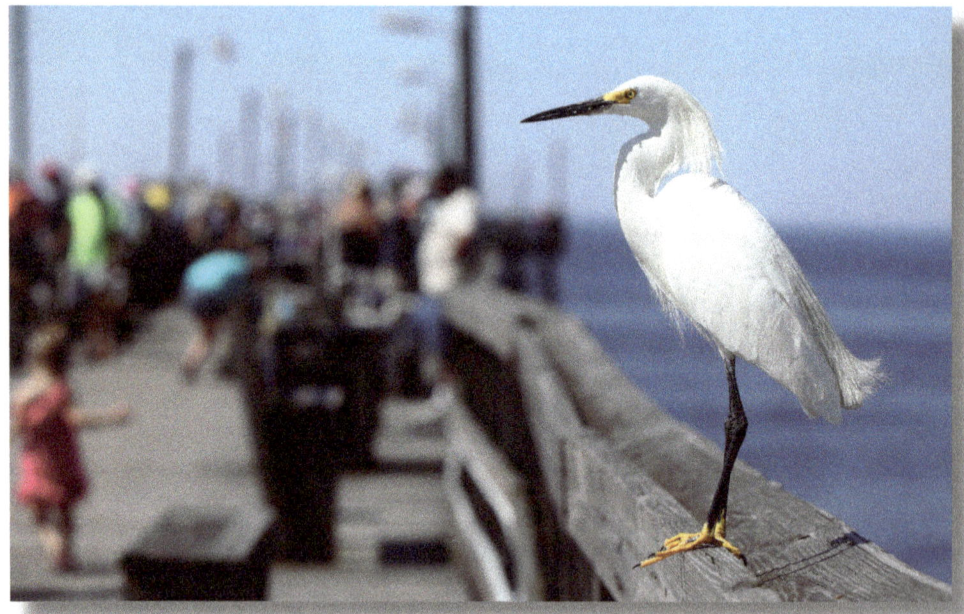

on the Town of Oak Island mainland by the creeks. A good spot to see both herons and egrets is the eastern end of the canal on SE 40th Street. If at all possible, sneak up on them, or if you are willing to devote a chunk of time to photographing the birds, consider using a blind.

The vegetation at the north end of SE 40th Street provides a natural blind. Often one can pick a spot, sit still, with camera-in-hand, and wait for a heron or egret to begin fishing nearby. The street ends of the SE and SW streets on the canals often work similarly. You can use your spot to surreptitiously photograph your bird wading, or you can do much as a hunter does, and scare him after you have him in your sights and catch him in flight.

Varieties of herons and egrets are so common that if you spend a bit of time at the wading birds' usual habitats along the inland waters, you should get a good shot. If you go out to the Oak Island Pier, you may be rewarded with a less common photo op.

For whatever reason, a snowy egret has been a commonly observed visitor next to and on the Oak Island Pier. While egrets are bountiful near marshlands and brackish canals, they are much less so in salt water and waves. Plus, egrets are normally flighty around people. This one seems fearless.

Like wading birds, waterfowl are plentiful on Oak Island, especially during the winter. There are the Mallards, Northern Pintails, Canada Geese, and Gladwalls found all along the East Coast. You will also find Buffleheads, Hooded Mergansers, Red-breasted Mergansers, Ring-necked Ducks, Redheads, and Ruddy Ducks with their eye-grabbing shapes and colors. A good place to start on a photo duck-hunt is on the north side of The Point at the far west end of Oak Island, or check out kayak launch sites at 57th Place on the west end and Smith Park Access at the back of William "Bill" Smith Park.

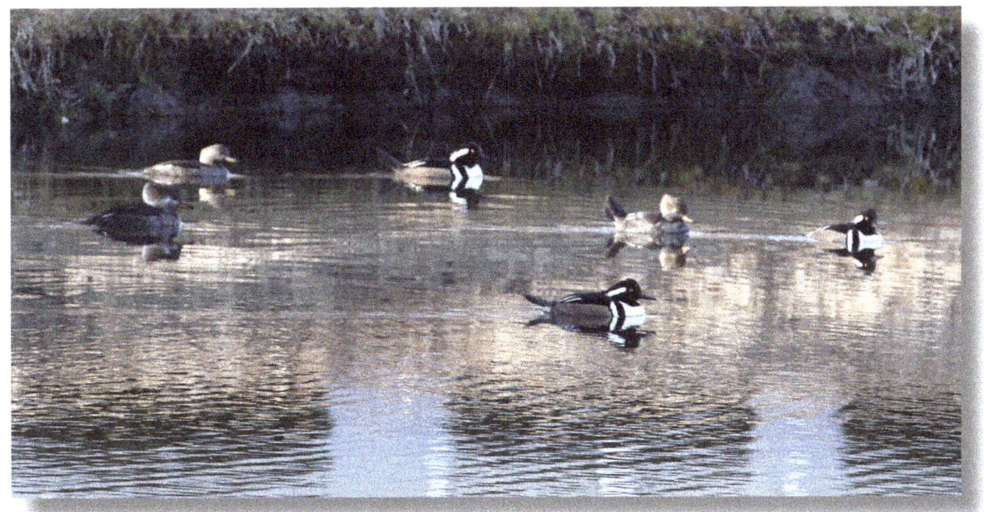

The ducks share the waters with loons, grebes, geese, and swans. This little fellow, shown at Waterway Park, seemed to express his gratitude to Mary Ellen Rogers, founder of the Sea Bisquit Wild Bird Sanctuary, after she nursed him to health and had just returned him to the wild. He soon returned to doing all the things loons like him are supposed to do, but seemed, for just a bit, conflicted about that prospect.

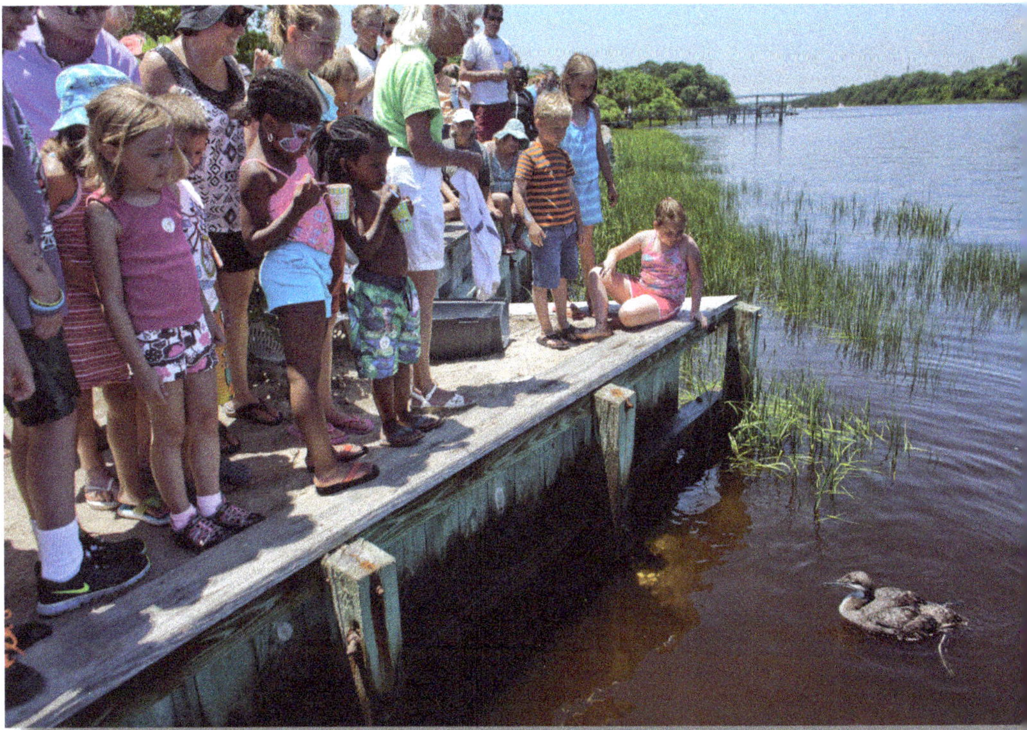

# sea creatures

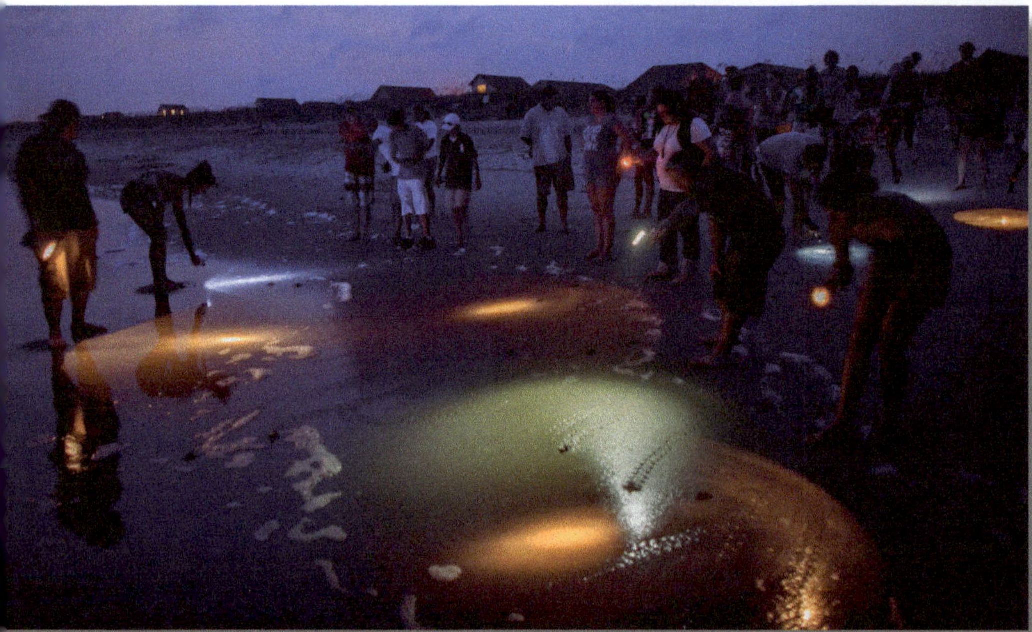

Oak Island hosts many water creatures. Crabs, oysters, alligators, jelly fish, and turtles dot the waters. Loggerhead turtles are local favorites. Sixty-two loggerhead mothers who birthed 6703 baby loggerheads were counted in 2012. While it is possible, through blind luck, to encounter a mother loggerhead on the beach one night, your chances, however, are slim. You do have some chance of seeing hatchlings make their way to the sea. The Ocean Education Center at 49th Street and East Beach Drive and the Oak Island Recreation Center at 3003 E Oak Island Dr. keep track of the turtle nests and can give an estimated time for when an existing nest will "boil." You won't be using the photographic equipment required for perfect lighting. Nature protects the turtles by making them sand colored and

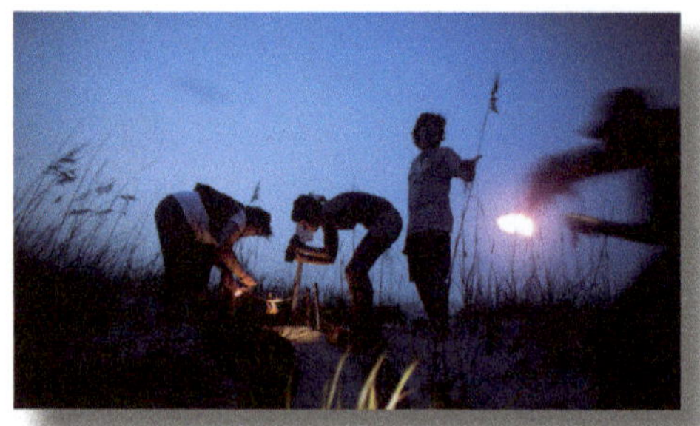

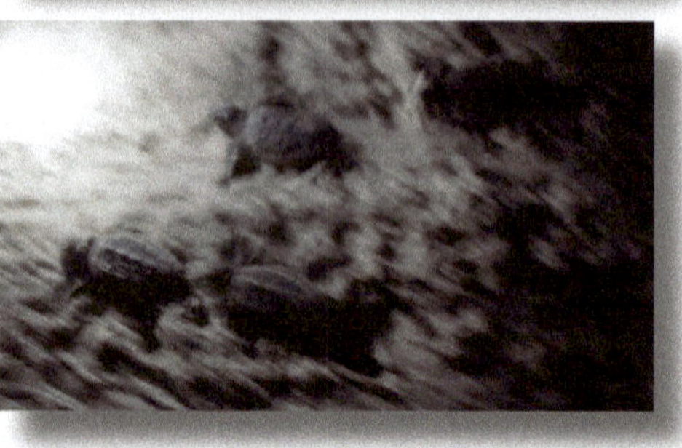

programs them to travel by night. Turtle nest "parents" and volunteers shining bright white lights in front of the turtles will be your only available light source. Other light sources including, of course, the lighting systems professional photographers would otherwise bring, disorient the hatchlings, endangering them. Even so, you can capture the spirit of the experience.

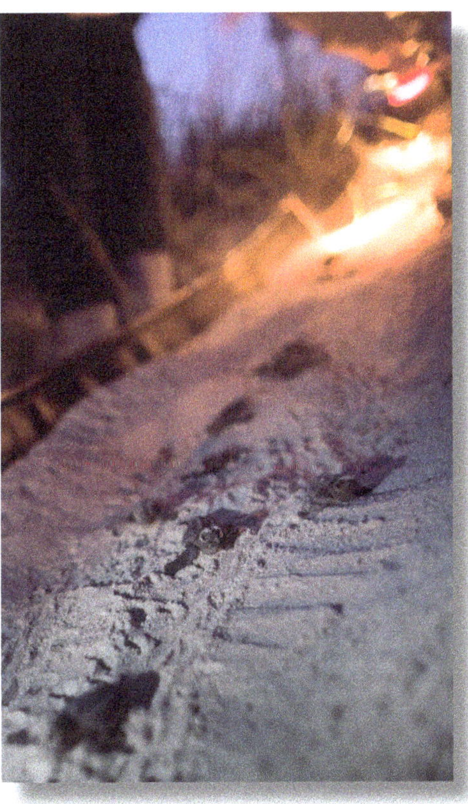

Forty-four human onlookers stood awed, watching 31 waddling turtles wend their way to the sea on this night. The experience itself seemed fanciful but the photos forever document the reality of the event.

Luckily for us photographers, most of Oak Island's sea creatures are easier subjects than little turtles. Adult oysters are easiest of all. Their shells form unmoving oyster beds, which are both prevalent and accessible along the Intracoastal Waterway. The beds are home to crabs and fin fish and are often topped by shore birds. May Moore Park, the Crab Dock, Waterway Park, and the Oak Island Nature Center, along Yacht Drive, are especially good places to watch the birds and water creatures inhabiting the beds interact, and to see fishing enthusiasts fish the beds (and have their canny catch outwit them, as they use sharp oyster shells to cut fish lines).

Oak Islanders appreciate the importance of oyster beds, but there doesn't seem to be much emotional attachment. Crabs, on the other hand, are an Oak Island passion. Fiddler crabs appear in droves at Waterway Park and at the west end of Yacht Drive. The mud flats beside the pilings next to the Davis Canal walkways are also good spots to watch hoards of them strut their stuff. When I am taking pictures of most crabs, I generally try to get low so my eyes are the same level as their eyes. I will set my camera to shutter priority if they are scurrying about and I want to do a stop-action shot.

While fiddler crabs are abundant and, thankfully, daytime creatures, making them fairly easy photographically, ghost crabs, flitting madly along the beach glowing in the night, are usually a bigger challenge. The one on the next page was busy with a construction project one August afternoon seeming-

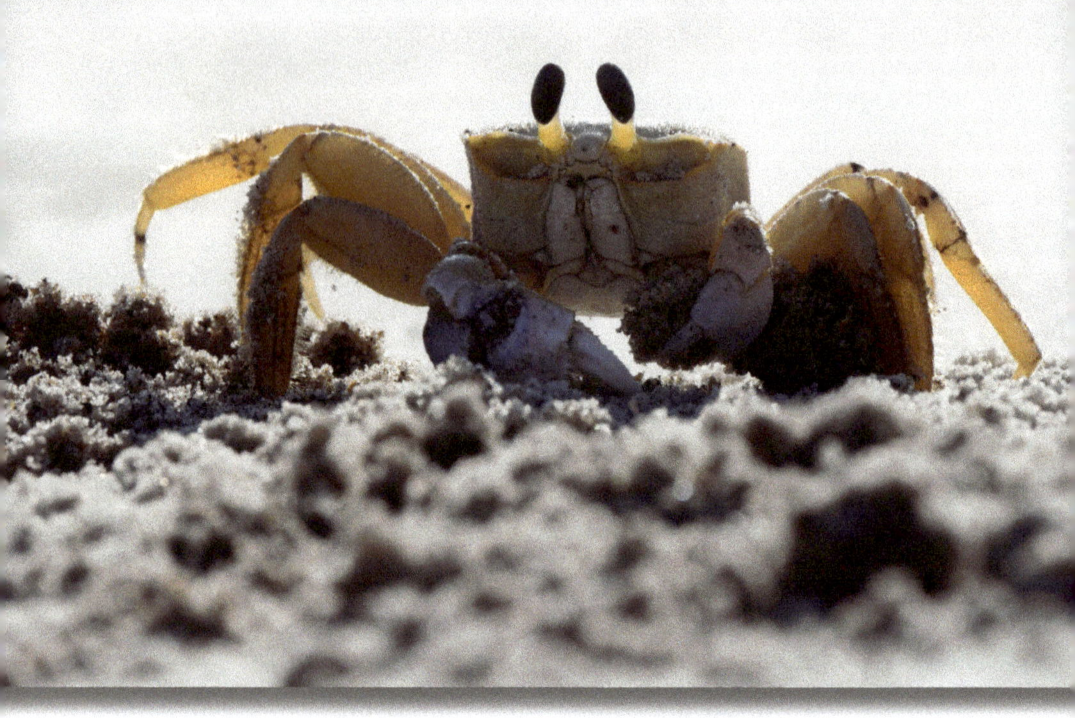

## Focus on: Exposure Compensation

Beach photography very often needs exposure compensation to avoid disappointment. The light-colored sand alone or when coupled with the lighter-skin tones of some beach-goers, white seagulls, or light-colored shells creates what is called a high-key scene. Despite all the technology in the modern-day camera, the computer cannot understand that the average color shade in your picture is whiter than neutral gray. Your camera will underexpose frames dominated by white every time.

Move on down the beach a bit and walk onto the pier. Then, create a photo looking down from the pier or from one of the walkways over the canal or river. Now you have the opposite problem where the camera will set your exposure to be cooked, or blown out. Your photo of the dark waters alone, or coupled with darker-skinned friends, black kayaks, or night herons will always be overexposed.

Exposure compensation is a quick and easy way to fool the camera, so it does not fool you. Usually I am in shutter or aperture priority mode when I use this tool. I'm on the beach and trying to shoot ghost crabs. I immediately press the +/- button and tell the camera to meter, or compensate, to expose at +1 or +2 from a neutral shade, aka 18-percent gray.

I then find myself looking down from the 29th Street walkway at kayakers partaking in Ride the Tide. The water looks black. I instantly know to tell the camera to meter for -2 or -3 from a neutral gray.

The +/- controls the stops-of-light. If you are on aperture priority, setting the exposure compensation to -1 will increase your shutter speed by one full stop increment. If you are in shutter priority, the camera would close your aperture, or f-stop, by one full stop increment.

You are the photographer and the camera is the tool. Exposure compensation is an at-the-ready way to control your camera.

ly oblivious to me pressing the shutter from my supine position on the sand.

Blue crabs, North Carolina's most lucrative seafood catch, are quite common. You will frequently encounter the blue crab along the shore, and even more often on ice, as they wait to be made into a scrumptious meal for a lucky crabber. When you work with sand and water, you get some fine pattern and texture for photography. Those patterns are especially effective when they seem to mirror or accentuate your subject.

The pattern and texture of the cherry-striped porcelain crab combines with the subtler but similar texture of the sand. This jellyfish, shot directly through the water, seems part and parcel to the pattern created as the light bounces off the ripples and sand below.

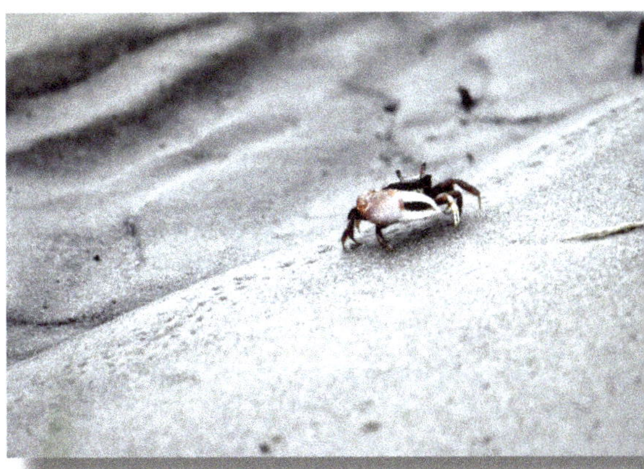

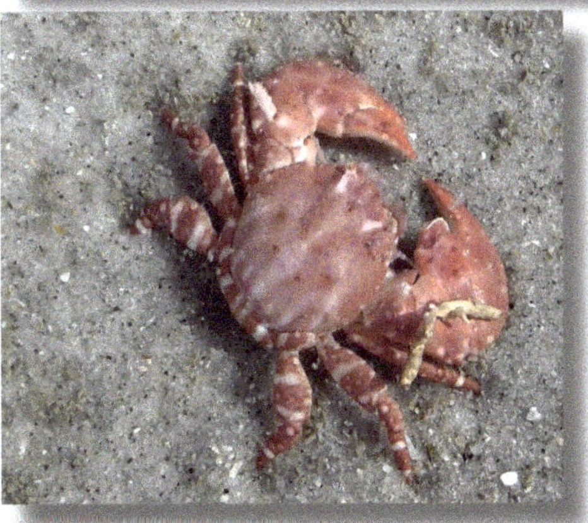

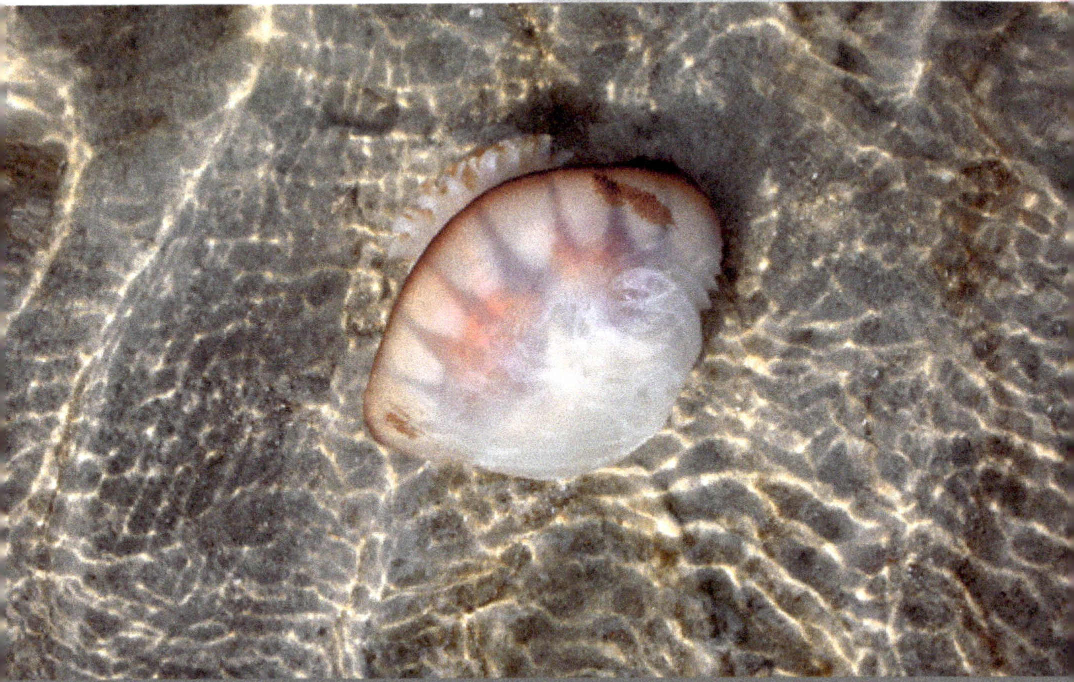

# nearby: brunswick town

Brunswick Town, just 20 miles northeast of Oak Island, is seldom visited by folks coming south to OKI. The site dates to 1726, when Maurice Moore, son of a former South Carolina governor, founded the town, named after the birthplace of George I to whom all North American colonists then owed their allegiance.

ships detained for not having been properly stamped under the Stamp Act of 1766. Eight years before the Boston Tea Party, the North Carolina Sons of Liberty extracted a promise from the British custom officiers, shortly after freeing the merchant ships, that the Stamp Act would not be enforced in North Carolina

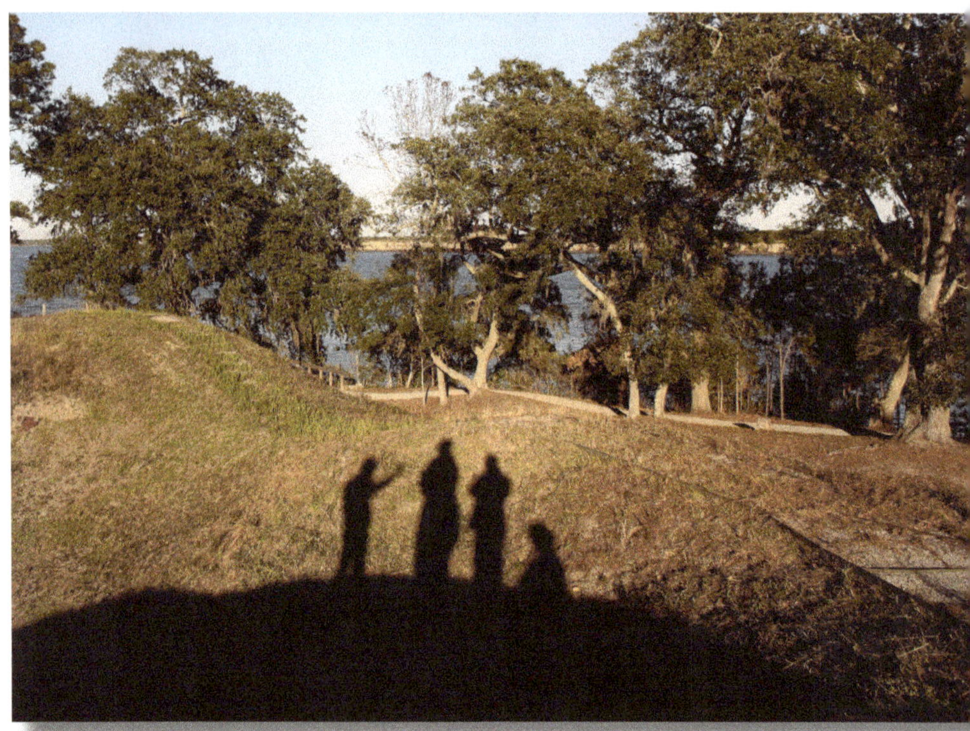

As you stand with a park interpreter looking over the Cape Fear River, you look out to where North Carolina's first deep-water port was built. These banks shipped more naval stores than any other in the British Empire. Picture "seeing" where the Sons of Liberty must have boarded the British Cruiser *Viper*, forcing the release of two merchant

You stand where Brunswick Town once stood. In 1729 it was named the county seat of New Hanover County and from 1758 to 1769 was the seat of North Carolina's colonial government.

Brunswick would soon be no more. The colonial government moved to New Bern in 1770. By 1776, in the early days of the Revolution, few people remained. The British Redcoats came ashore in 1776. Reports indicate that much of the town was burned during the raid, which is surmised to be in retribution for the disloyalty during the days of the Stamp Act—the first known successful armed rebellion against British Authority in America—and for the aiding and abetting of the Patriot forces at the nearby Battle of Moores Creek in February of 1776.

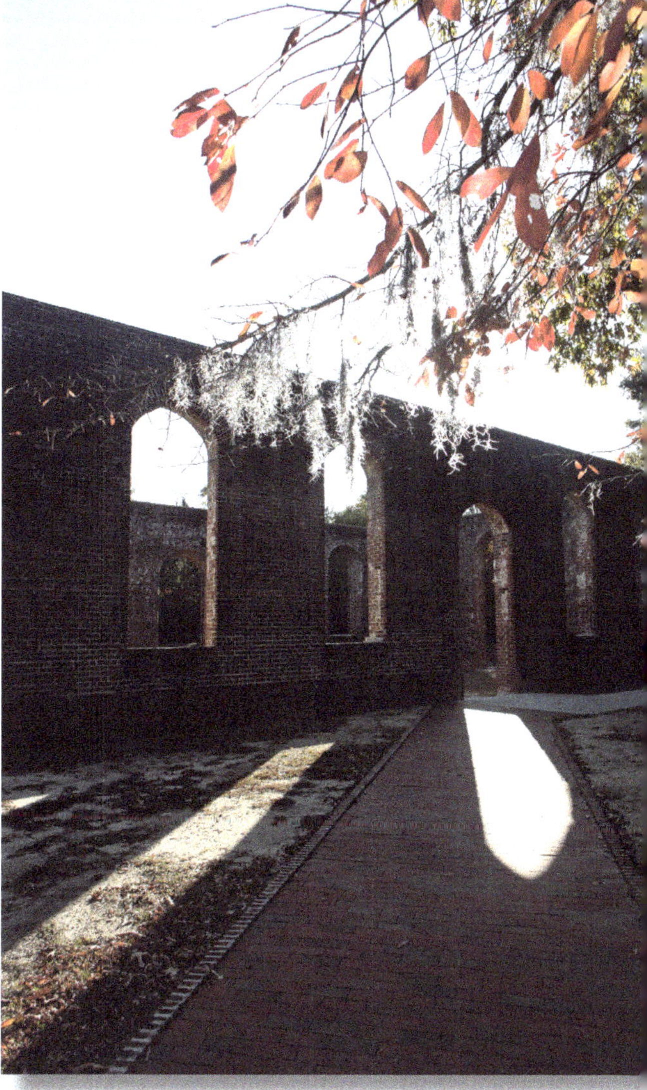

Today very little remains from the Colonial period. The walls of St. Philips are a notable exception. The parish was established in 1740 with the construction of the church commencing in 1754. The initial funding came from goods salvaged from the *La Fortuna*, a Spanish warship sunk in Cape Fear as the colonists reclaimed Brunwick Town from Spanish invaders in 1748.

The church's walls have survived since the church was finished in 1768, Couples were married here as early as Governor Dobbs in 1763, before the church's completion, and as recently as the last bride and groom who used the walls to celebrate their holy matrimony at this popular wedding venue.

While St. Philip's is the most intact of the Colonial era structures, archaeologists have continued to unearth more vestiges of Brunswick's nearly 300 years of thistory as a British settlement. The biggest of the archaeological finds is Russellborough, the residence of two royal governors. It is enormous with a 35' x 45' perimeter.

The archaeologists have been probing, with equal vigilance, the site's Civil War past. Almost a century after the British burned the remnants of Brunswick Town, the Confederacy recognized the site for its logistical and strategic value and built Fort Anderson. The silhouetted interpreter and park visitors pictured are standing on the mounds behind one of the two earthen batteries put in place in 1862.

Battery "A" faces the Cape Fear River. When built there were wooden barricks behind it. Artifacts from the Civil War period continue to be unearthed by teams of archaeologists intent on learning ever more about the life and times of the Tar Heels that were forefathers to today's native North Carolinians.

Each of the two batteries were equipped with five cannons, aimed at the shipping lane to protect the Confederate blockade runners. It is, of course, now, no surprise that Fort Anderson fell to the Union forces.

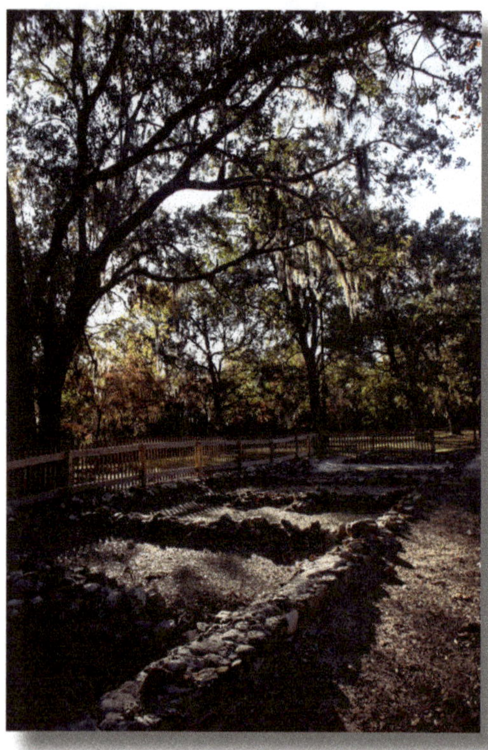

The Union military attacked by both land and sea. After three days the Confederates evacuated the fort under the cover of darkness.

They would get a bit of revenge. Union gunboats fired upon the fort at daybreak, only to shell their own ground troops poised at the walls, ready to attack the fort by daybreak, too.

The staff and volunteers at the visitors' center are ready to provide a whole lot more information about the history of the site, surrounding area, and the most recent archaeological findings. In addition, you will see interesting artifacts including a cannon believed to be from the era of the Spanish invasion. The visitors' center is relatively uncluttered with artifacts that can make nice photos.

If, though, history is not your thing, there are plenty of photo op outdoors. Orton Pond, on your way into the historic site, is picturesque with its bald cypress dripping with moss, made even more captivating than usual, when splattered by fallen autumn leaves. The pond is generally home to alligator.

The site is also a good place to shoot Spanish Moss. It is an even better place to photograph birds. The Cape Fear Audubon Society has quite frequently visited Orton Pond and Brunswick Town for bird watching. In May of 2012, 40 species of birds were spotted. On a visit when history was my intended subject matter, I photographed this Kingfisher because I had my camera-in-hand, and he was irresistible against the vibrantly blue sky. The variety of birds stopping by or making the park home is remarkable. There are wood duck and woodpeckers, bunting and waxwings, hawks and herons, blackbirds and cowbirds, and gnatcatchers and cuckoos. It is a birder's delight.

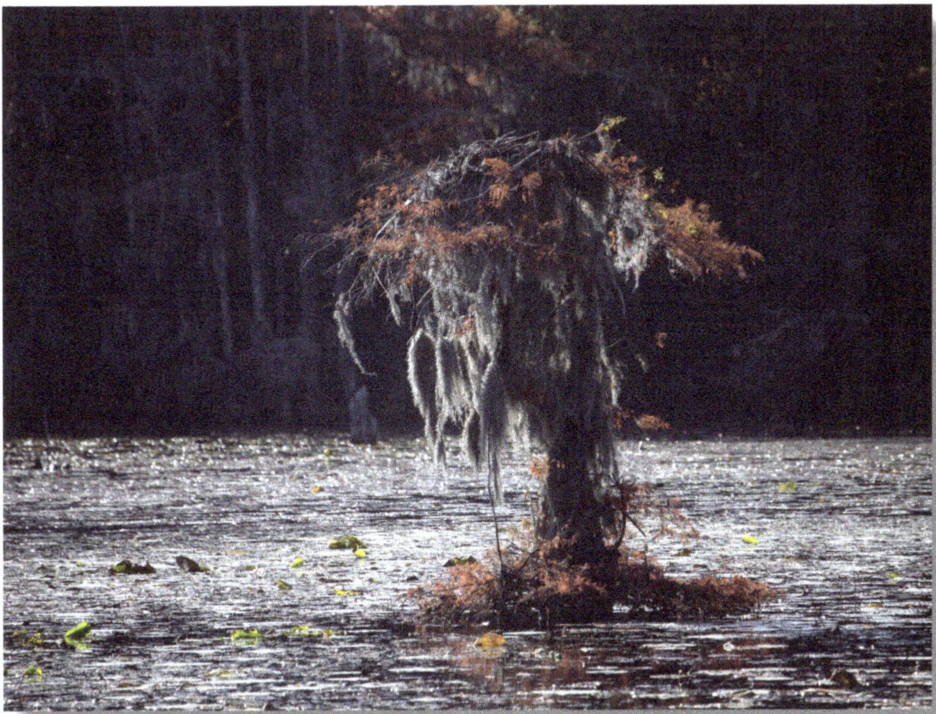

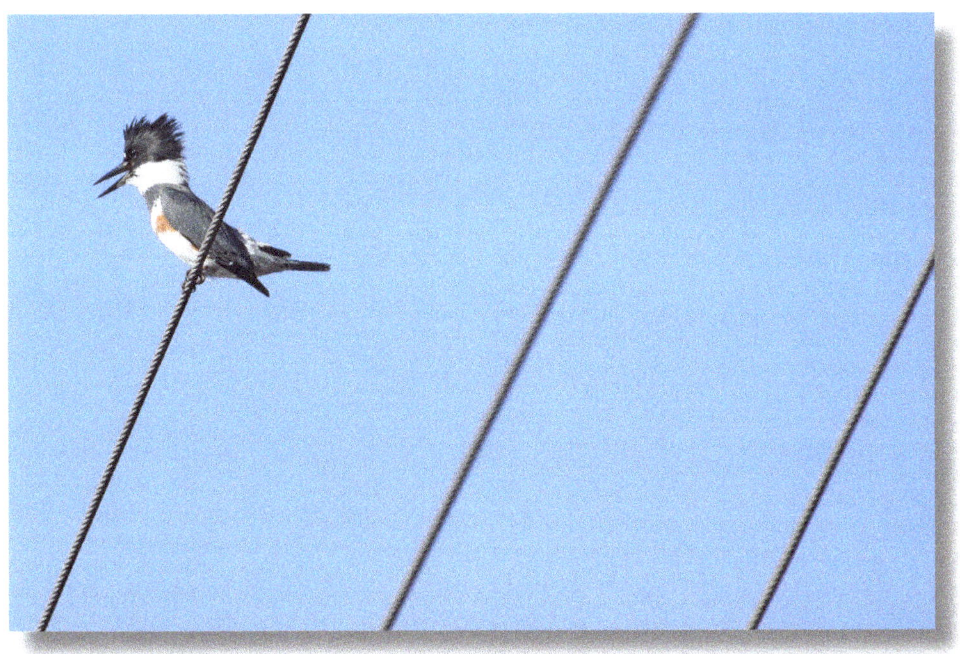

# east beach

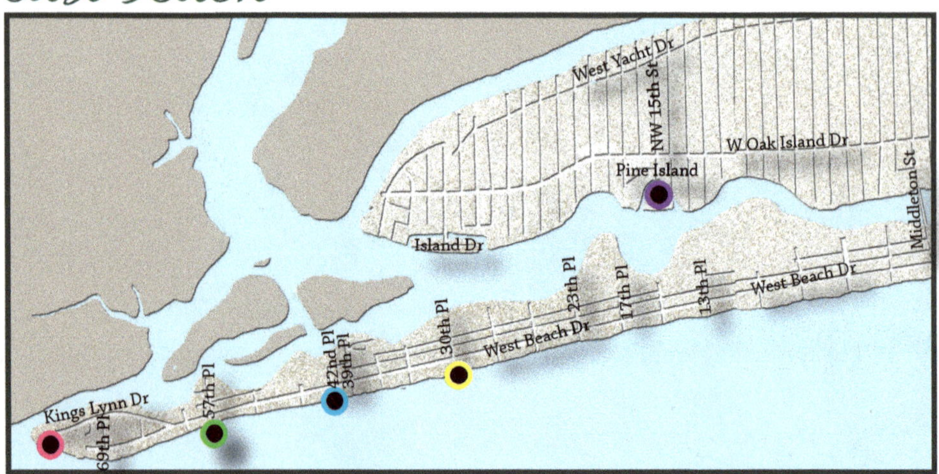


On the featured locations pages, many of the Oak Island places mentioned in the body of the text are mapped. In addition, for some of the photos included, the basic technical properties are given. If you learn best by deduction, these can give you additional insights into the "*hows*" of photographing OKI. If that is not your thing, simply ignore the techie stuff and try and get out to the special places shown. They are sensory delights.

| | | Page * | f-stop | Shutter Speed | ISO | Focal Length | Exp Bias | P ** |
|---|---|---|---|---|---|---|---|---|
| ● (pink) | The Point | 17 BR | f/11 | 1/125 | 200 | 24mm | 0.3 | A |
| | | 34 BL | f/6.3 | 1/1600 | 200 | 400mm | 0.0 | A |
| | | 36 TL | f/8 | 1/500 | 100 | 55mm | 0.0 | O |
| | | 46 TR | f/16 | 1/60 | 200 | 24mm | 0.0 | A |
| | | 46 BL | f/6.3 | 1/500 | 200 | 400mm | 0.0 | A |
| | | 63 TL | f/10 | 1/200 | 200 | 24mm | 0.0 | A |
| ● (green) | Blue Water Point | 20 BL | f/4 | 1/250 | 200 | 73mm | -.3 | A |
| | Marina | 55 BL | f/8 | 1/200 | 64 | 10mm | 0.3 | O |
| | | 83 TR | f/3.5 | 1/160 | 200 | 24mm | 0.0 | A |
| | | 83 BR | f/6.3 | 1/200 | 200 | 24mm | -.3 | A |
| ● (blue) | 42nd Place and Bluff | 123 | | | | | | |
| ● (yellow) | West 30th Canoe Dock | 85 | | | | | | |
| ● (purple) | Pine Island | 37 | | | | | | |
| | | | | | | | | |

* TL=Top Left ML=Mid-Left BL=Bottom Left TR=Top Right MR=Mid-Right BR=Bottom Right ** P=Priority S=Shutter A=Aperture M=Manual O=Point and Shoot Variants

# east beach to east 40th

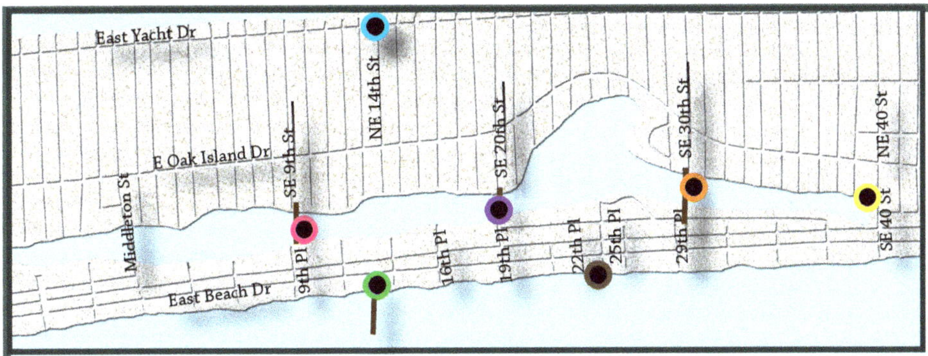

| | | Page * | f-stop | Shutter Speed | ISO | Focal Length | Exp Bias | P ** |
|---|---|---|---|---|---|---|---|---|
| | 9th Street Crossover | 109 | | | | | | |
| | Waterway Park | 21 BL | f/29 | 1/250 | 800 | 400mm | -.7 | S |
| | | 56 TR | f/5 | 1/230 | 100 | 24mm | 0.0 | A |
| | | 89 BL | f/5 | 1/400 | 100 | 24mm | 0.0 | A |
| | | 93 BL | f/5 | 1/320 | 100 | 24mm | 0.0 | A |
| | Ocean Crest Pier | 62 BL | f/7.1 | 1/800 | 200 | 8mm | 0.0 | O |
| | and Motel | 71 TL | f/22 | 1/60 | 100 | 160mm | 0.0 | M |
| | | 71 BL | f/5.6 | 1/1000 | 200 | 400mm | 0.0 | M |
| | | 77 TL | f/4 | 1/2500 | 200 | 200mm | 0.0 | S |
| | | 86 TL | f/5 | 1/6 | 400 | 110mm | -.7 | A |
| | | 87 TL | f/3.2 | 1/400 | 100 | 21mm | 0.3 | S |
| | 19th Street Crossover | 109 | | | | | | |
| | Oak Island Rec | 7 BL | f/8 | 1/800 | 200 | 105mm | 0.0 | M |
| | Center and Kayak | 72 BL | f/5 | 1/500 | 800 | 24mm | 0.0 | M |
| | Canoe Launch | 84 ML | f/11 | 1/640 | 200 | 24mm | 0.0 | M |
| | 22nd Place Access | 30 BL | f/5.6 | 1/1000 | 200 | 120mm | 0.0 | S |
| | | 31 TL | f/9 | 1/2000 | 200 | 35mm | -.3 | A |
| | | 54 TL | f/9 | 1/1000 | 200 | 35mm | -.3 | A |
| | SE 40th Street Beach | 27 TL | f/11 | 1/500 | 150 | 55mm | 0.0 | A |
| | Access and Heron | 51 BL | f/2.8 | 1/400 | 400 | 28mm | 0.1 | A |
| | Lookout Park | 79 BR | f/2.5 | 1/400 | 640 | 24mm | -1.7 | A |
| | | 94 ML | f/1.8 | 1/8 | 800 | 24mm | 0.0 | M |
| | | 95 ML | f/1.8 | 1/8 | 800 | 24mm | 0.0 | M |

# east beach to caswell beach

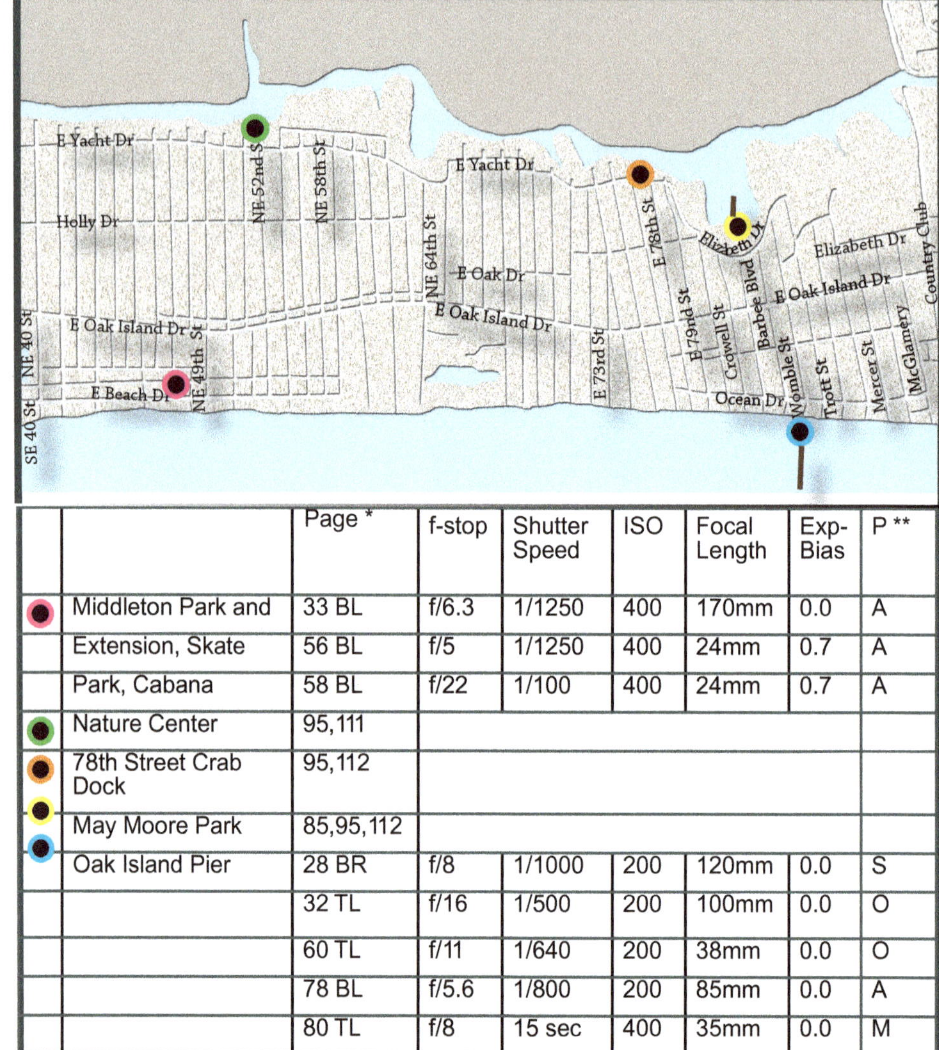


| | | Page * | f-stop | Shutter Speed | ISO | Focal Length | Exp-Bias | P ** |
|---|---|---|---|---|---|---|---|---|
| | Middleton Park and | 33 BL | f/6.3 | 1/1250 | 400 | 170mm | 0.0 | A |
| | Extension, Skate | 56 BL | f/5 | 1/1250 | 400 | 24mm | 0.7 | A |
| | Park, Cabana | 58 BL | f/22 | 1/100 | 400 | 24mm | 0.7 | A |
| | Nature Center | 95,111 | | | | | | |
| | 78th Street Crab Dock | 95,112 | | | | | | |
| | May Moore Park | 85,95,112 | | | | | | |
| | Oak Island Pier | 28 BR | f/8 | 1/1000 | 200 | 120mm | 0.0 | S |
| | | 32 TL | f/16 | 1/500 | 200 | 100mm | 0.0 | O |
| | | 60 TL | f/11 | 1/640 | 200 | 38mm | 0.0 | O |
| | | 78 BL | f/5.6 | 1/800 | 200 | 85mm | 0.0 | A |
| | | 80 TL | f/8 | 15 sec | 400 | 35mm | 0.0 | M |
| | | 81 TL | f/5.6 | 1/640 | 200 | 200mm | 0.0 | A |
| | | 81 BL | f/6.3 | 1/1000 | 200 | 24mm | 0.0 | A |
| | | 88 TL | f/5.6 | 1/250 | 200 | 24mm | -.3 | A |
| | | 92 TL | f/5.6 | 1/1000 | 200 | 110mm | 0.3 | A |

* TL=Top Left ML=Mid-Left BL=Bottom Left TR=Top Right MR=Mid-Right BR=Bottom Right
** P=Priority S=Shutter A=Aperture M=Manual O=Point and Shoot Variants

# caswell beach and off island

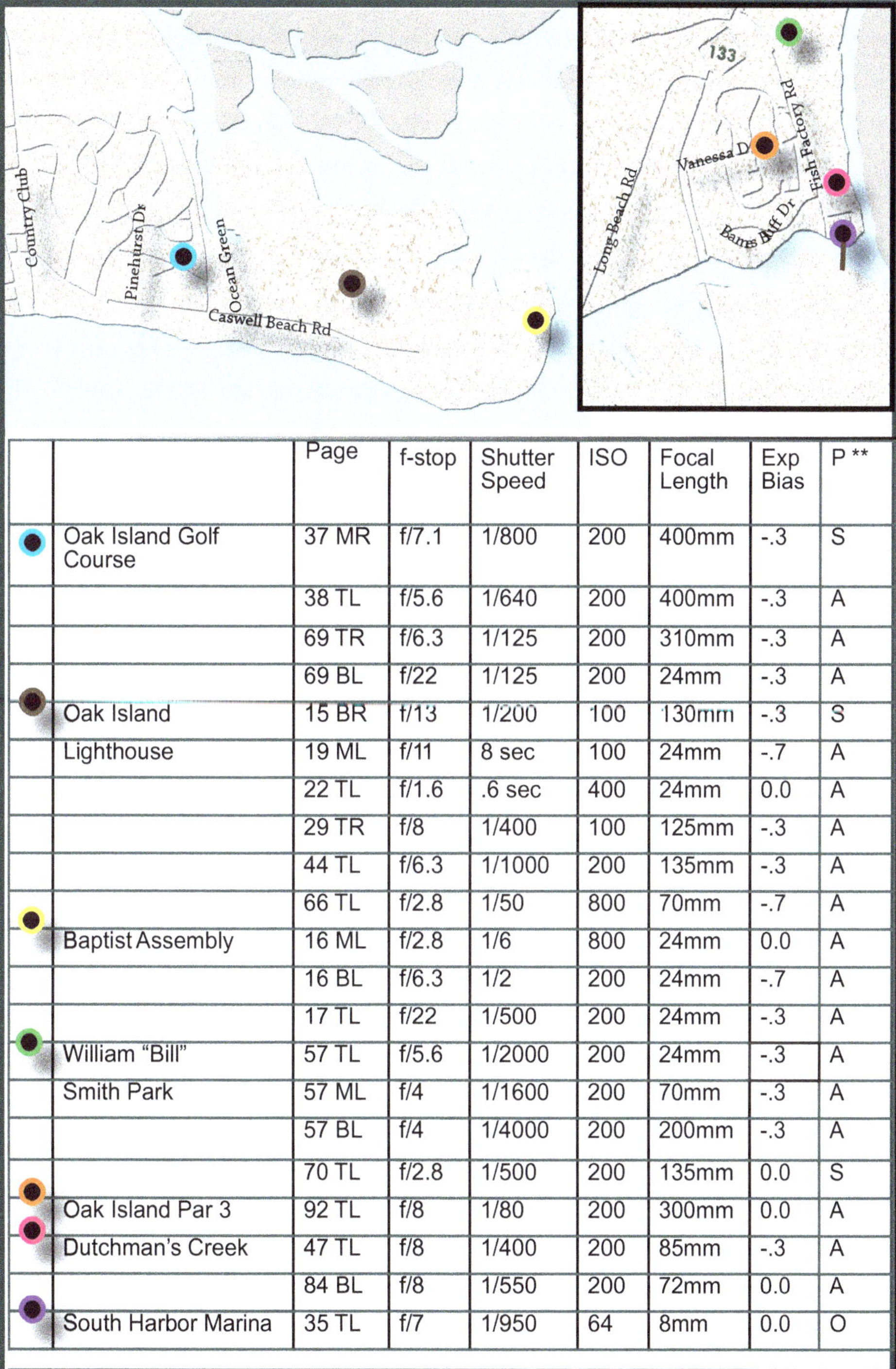


| | | Page | f-stop | Shutter Speed | ISO | Focal Length | Exp Bias | P ** |
|---|---|---|---|---|---|---|---|---|
| | Oak Island Golf Course | 37 MR | f/7.1 | 1/800 | 200 | 400mm | -.3 | S |
| | | 38 TL | f/5.6 | 1/640 | 200 | 400mm | -.3 | A |
| | | 69 TR | f/6.3 | 1/125 | 200 | 310mm | -.3 | A |
| | | 69 BL | f/22 | 1/125 | 200 | 24mm | -.3 | A |
| | Oak Island | 15 BR | f/13 | 1/200 | 100 | 130mm | -.3 | S |
| | Lighthouse | 19 ML | f/11 | 8 sec | 100 | 24mm | -.7 | A |
| | | 22 TL | f/1.6 | .6 sec | 400 | 24mm | 0.0 | A |
| | | 29 TR | f/8 | 1/400 | 100 | 125mm | -.3 | A |
| | | 44 TL | f/6.3 | 1/1000 | 200 | 135mm | -.3 | A |
| | | 66 TL | f/2.8 | 1/50 | 800 | 70mm | -.7 | A |
| | Baptist Assembly | 16 ML | f/2.8 | 1/6 | 800 | 24mm | 0.0 | A |
| | | 16 BL | f/6.3 | 1/2 | 200 | 24mm | -.7 | A |
| | | 17 TL | f/22 | 1/500 | 200 | 24mm | -.3 | A |
| | William "Bill" | 57 TL | f/5.6 | 1/2000 | 200 | 24mm | -.3 | A |
| | Smith Park | 57 ML | f/4 | 1/1600 | 200 | 70mm | -.3 | A |
| | | 57 BL | f/4 | 1/4000 | 200 | 200mm | -.3 | A |
| | | 70 TL | f/2.8 | 1/500 | 200 | 135mm | 0.0 | S |
| | Oak Island Par 3 | 92 TL | f/8 | 1/80 | 200 | 300mm | 0.0 | A |
| | Dutchman's Creek | 47 TL | f/8 | 1/400 | 200 | 85mm | -.3 | A |
| | | 84 BL | f/8 | 1/550 | 200 | 72mm | 0.0 | A |
| | South Harbor Marina | 35 TL | f/7 | 1/950 | 64 | 8mm | 0.0 | O |

# walks and shots

You'll find plenty of places on Oak Island to have a good time. Lots of them are also photogenic. The "Walks and Shots" section describes seven routes clustered with interesting places. Of the photos featured in *Camera-in-Hand,* about half were taken along these seven suggested routes. Six routes are walking loops on the island. They range in length from approximately one mile to three miles. All include a walk on the beach.

The seventh differs in two ways. Unlike the rest, the route starts on the Town of Oak Island mainland <u>and</u> you should move you car at least once. The route includes William "Bill" Smith Park, Dutchman's Creek Park, and the South Harbor Marina. While it is physically possible (though it appears difficult) to walk the entire route along Dutchman's Creek, part of the land includes the local water treatment plant. Trespassing on this land is a Homeland Security concern with wandering photographers likely to be suspect.

# the point

It is a good idea to travel to the far west end of Oak Island early during any Oak Island stay. This proposed loop of The Point is about a mile, not counting any lateral side tripping out to sandbars or similar diversions.

Park at the end of West Beach Drive. From the parking lot you have two good choices. If you are rarin' to get your toes into the ocean, go due south and follow the water's edge west. You can also go southwest on the well-marked path just to the right of the porta potties. This path over a dune is one of the few chances on Oak Island to cross one. Walking through dunes is generally forbidden; it causes beach erosion and disturbs the habitats of Oak Island's native creatures.

As you move along the shore to the west and continue around to the other side, you can expect to see birds in the air, birds on the plants, birds massed on the sand, birds in flocks out on Sheep Island, and birds on most posts.

You will find fishermen, big and small, male and female, along the Atlantic shore, the banks of the Lockwood Folly River and across on the banks of the Intracoastal Waterway. You'll see motorboats and sailboats, jet skis and barges. At low tide, with some luck you'll see starfish. If not, it is a great place for shells and other marine life. The north side at the mouth of the Lockwood Folly River is a regular destination for kayakers and often is a place where dolphins swim alongside the paddlers.

At the end of the accessible beach, walk east along Kings Lynn Drive, turn right onto 69th Place West continuing to West Beach Drive. Turn right and go a short few yards to your car.

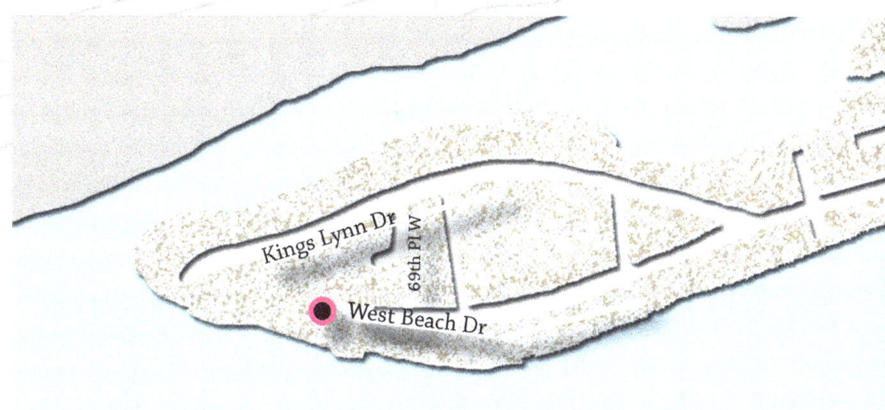

# west beach

On this walk you will be exploring parts of the beach visited by fewer humans than who visit OKI East Beach. There are, though, significantly more turtle visitors on this stretch of beach than on other parts of the island. In 2013 as the island began the fourth of July week, nine sea turtles of the 42 total on Town of Oak Island beaches, had nested along this proposed two and a half mile walking route.

Begin at the 42nd Place West beach access. Walk along the beach to 57th Place. There is very little beach at high tide and a fairly wide swath at low tide. At low tide you will find both children and birds cavorting in the tidal pools left by the receding tides. Go up the 57th Place handicapped beach access. A permanent canopy is part of the access structure. If you are walking with others, it is a nice place on a sunny day to frame a photo with your subjects under the canopy just within the shade barrier.

Cross Beach Drive and visit the Bluewater Point Marina. There is always a lot of boating and fishing activity. It is also a vantage point to check out the birds on the islands in Montgomery Slough, and boats in the Intracoastal Waterway.

Return towards Beach Drive and turn left on Dolphin. At 54th Place turn right and cross Beach Drive. Continue along the beach access to the area just behind the dune. Walk along the backside of the dune to the 48th Place access. Go back up to Beach Drive, and walk past the biggest dune remaining on Oak Island to 42nd Place. (Up on the dune are two of the five structures that survived Hurricane Hazel in 1954.) Use 42nd Place to walk to West Dolphin and glimpses of the Montgomery Slough, as you follow West Dolphin to 39th Place. Turn north to the boat access. Come back on 39th Place to the beach and turn right to your 42nd starting point.

The West 42nd beach access is particularly picturesque. It is both longer and more structured than those typical of the island. It is a good place to get some shots of the interior side of the dune and frames of the large dune across West Beach.

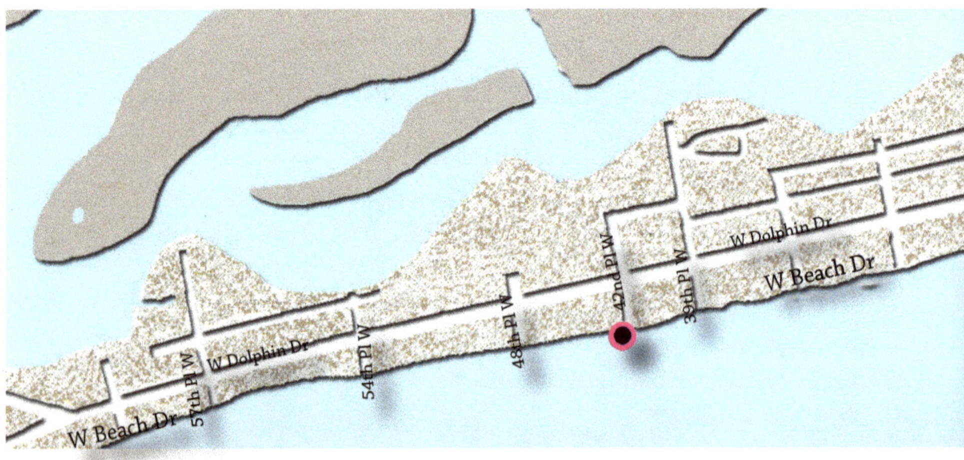

# piers and crossovers

The whole 9th to 20th Street loop is about three miles. If that is too ambitious, you can easily shorten it to one and a half miles. Skip the walk to the waterway from Oak Island Drive.

The photogenic 9th Street beach access is a good starting place. Click the shutter as you pass the colorful bikes usually parked by the dune. Beyond the dune, the beach generally has just enough activity to make it interesting, but never so many people that it feels crowded.

As you look east past the sand builders, kite fliers, cornholers, seagulls and pelicans, you see the Ocean Crest Pier at 14th Street. Built in 1968, the wooden pier juts 893 feet into the Atlantic Ocean. (There is a small charge to walk out on it.) As you walk above the waves, you'll have a pier-level view of surfers to your left, the occasional dolphins traveling by, and lots of folk fishing for flounder, speckled trout, red drum, bluefish, and spots depending on the season. At the pier's end you'll find fisherman after the fisherman's brass ring—a King Mackerel.

Continue to the 19th Street access and cross Beach Drive. Using the walkway to cross Davis Creek, you'll see crabs scurrying in the mudflats, wading birds, kayakers, fishermen on the floating docks, and shadows on the wooden walkway made by railings, people, birds, and vegetation.

Turn left on Oak Island Drive and travel north at 16th Street. Typical of Oak Island residential areas, you'll find there is nothing "cookie-cutter" here.

At the north end of NE 16th Street you will see the Intracoastal Waterway across East Yacht Drive. Waterway Park will be to your left on the Intracoastal. It is a fine place to watch crabbers, families fishing on the platforms, and boats motoring past. There are benches along the water, picnic tables, a gazebo, and vegetation that works nicely to add three-dimensionality to your photographs.

Leave the park, after availing yourself of the porta potty if nature calls. Head west (right) along Yacht Drive to 11th Street. Use it to travel to Oak Island Drive where you will turn right and use the 9th Street walkway to cross Davis Creek. Blue tailed skinks, marsh deer, and an alligator have all been spotted from here. Fiddler crabs, egrets, and marsh hens are common. The benches in the middle of the walkway are setup nicely for a group picture before you end the loop at your car.

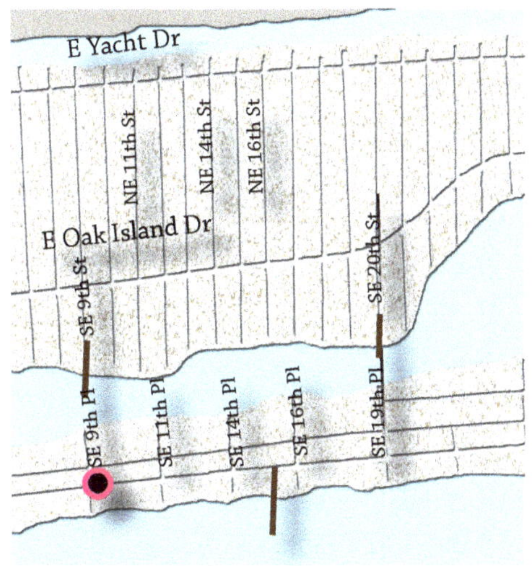

# canal and bluffs

The Canal and Bluffs walk is about two miles. Begin at the OKI Recreation Center between 30th and 31st streets SE. From the parking lot go past the water tower and the kayak dock onto the wooden crossover. It is a good place to get pictures of kayakers or to rent kayaks and incorporate kayaking into this loop. After crossing the Davis Creek, you will turn right and travel along a shady path to the second part of the crossover, which traverses the marsh.

Go across Beach Drive; walk over the beach access and turn left. For about two Oak Island blocks the sand dunes are battered into a bluff with no view of the houses behind them. The bluff makes a clean background for your photos of the whole gamut of beach activity. As you continue east, roofs of houses will peak over the bluff. Continue to the lime green house at 40th Street. Turn left. If you have an urge to shop, you can get an ice cream cone or a cold drink and souvenirs at Sand Beachware; it has plenty to offer.

Continue on the west side of 40th Street to Heron Lookout Park. Folks are almost always crabbing, or castnetting, or using their fishing poles. It is the easiest place on the island to get a good castnetting shot. The background is reliably clean and the fishing enthusiasts are, with rare exception, reliably present. Continue on past high, heavy vegetation to your left. Varieties of herons, egrets, and the occasional ibis are usually in the creek below. You can prepare your camera in what serves as a natural blind and then click away as you come to lower height vegetation closer to Oak Island Drive.

Turn left up Oak Island Drive to SE 38th Street, where you will encounter fine specimens of Spanish Moss draped over the live oaks. If you go down 38th Street to its end, there are two stumps that you can use as foreground elements for pictures of fish jumping, egrets wading, and kayakers passing by, or sit on one and take pictures of crabs underfoot. Then take the path along the reeds to 37th Street and turn north to Oak Island Drive. Idiosyncratic decorative elements abound on the island. The signal light in the front yard at 34th Street is one of only four on the whole island.

Return to the Rec Center. If you still have energy, you can go back down towards the kayak dock and turn right at the path, just before the water tower to explore along the small platforms over the marsh; or go a bit farther towards the kayak dock and turn right to climb the Overlook Tower just a few yards down.

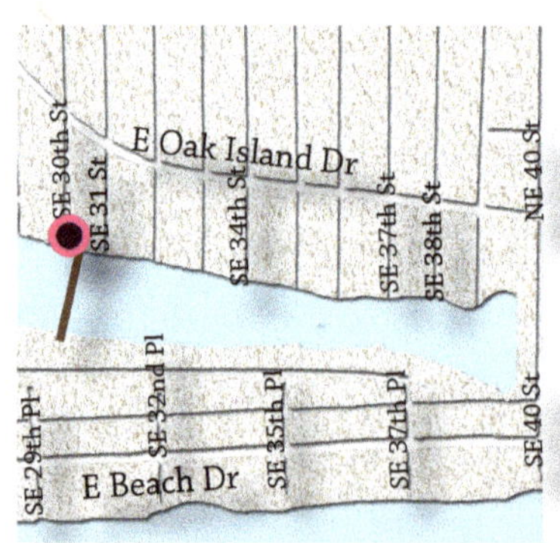


The Rec Center has restrooms, water, and information sheets on upcoming activities and OKI parks and centers. It is staffed by helpful folk who are knowledgeable about all things Oak Island.

# beach to waterway

This is a two and a half mile walk that can be extended to three miles. Start at the 52nd Street beach access and walk to Oak Island Drive; carefully cross and continue on 52nd after a quick right. The residential area you pass is typical of Oak Island mainland's neighborhoods. You'll probably be lulled by the preponderance of unremarkable suburban features, except that houses are on pilings, and then, do a double take at something quite out of the ordinary. Your destination is the Nature Center, with its knowledgeable staff and Malcolm Register Park. It is a shady gem on the Intracoastal, with both a small pier and a short walkway, and a dock out into the marsh. The Nature Center grounds include botanical-garden style signage describing native plant and animal species. It has public restrooms. From the park you will see oyster beds and the picturesque lines of the pier and walkways. There is always something photogenic that you can readily frame, using the park's foliage or featuring the lines of the wooden piers, docks, and benches.

Leave going west along Yacht Drive to 46th Street. Turn right down the street end and check out the waterway. You'll be at one of its narrowest sections, which also has a clean background looking across the Intracoastal. Here, you can take pictures of boats and their goings on with the most basic of cameras. After catching a bit of the action, use 46th Street to return to the beach.

You will be at the Cabana, which has restrooms and foot showers, and a platform with railings that are handy to brace your camera as you frame shots of birds, kites, and beach frolicking. Finish by walking left down the beach.

Or, you can explore some additional Oak Island offerings. Go up the 49th Street beach access and visit the Ocean Education Center, just across Beach Drive. Here you'll learn what is happening with the sea turtles, explore marine life exhibits, and find out what programs are being offered. The interior is remarkably photogenic, perfect for photographing budding child scientists. Just up 49th Street you will come to the Skateboard Park. Continue north; turn left at Dolphin; continue until you see the windsock. Cross the field to the windsock, then the culvert and checkout the Teen/Preteen center under its red roof and the playground to its North. Turn right on Oak Island Drive; right at 48th Street; left at Pelican; right to the beach at 49th; and left along the beach to your car.

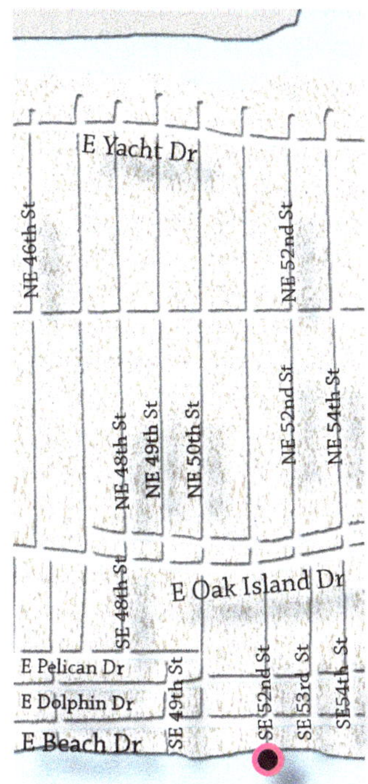

# pier to marshlands

This suggested two and a half mile walk makes a loop from the beach to the Intracoastal and back. Of the "Walks and Shots" you will see the most varied architecture in both style and size on this one. There are two very different octagonal houses, A-Frames, fishermen's cottages, classic Southport-style cottages, clever single wides, and some recently constructed large modern beach homes. Begin at the SE 74th beach access and walk along 74th towards the Intracoastal. At Oak Drive turn right and continue to 75th Street, turn left and take it to Yacht Drive. Turn right, and walk until you come to 78th Street.

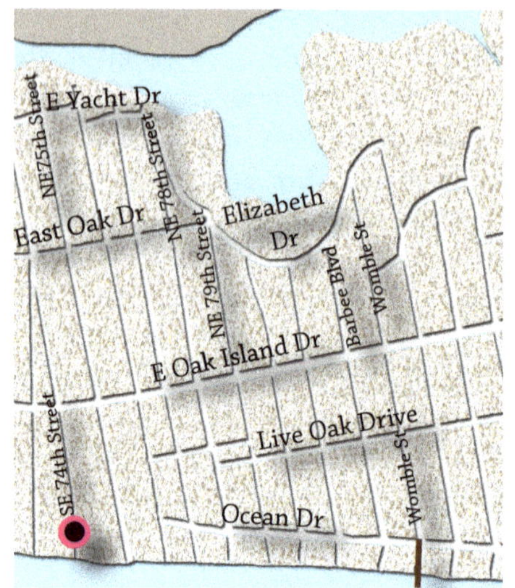


There you will find a little dock and one of the most interesting spots on the island to use a long lens if you have one. The Cape Fear Jetport landing strip is across the marsh, just beyond the Intracoastal. You can photograph a variety of planes, as they take off from or descend onto the landing strip, clearing the trees just above you. Boats of all sorts speed by. They are a good deal farther away than on the west side of the island, but the foreground of the marsh and a clean background make for good photos. To your right you will have a striking panoramic shot of the G.V. Barbee Bridge.

Next, follow Yacht Drive, and then Elizabeth Drive east to Barbee Boulevard. Just a tad beyond Barbee, you will come to May Moore Park on the Elizabeth River. The park is a small shady oasis with picnic tables and bench swings. Use the short fishing pier on the Elizabeth River to get closer to the marsh with its oyster beds and assorted wading birds. Frame the fishermen using rods and reels or cast nets to snag the Elizabeth River bounty. Leave by way of Barbee towards the ocean. Just before Oak Island Drive you will come upon the skeleton of the Mary E. Morris, built in 1884 and sunk in the 1893 hurricane. To your left is Barbee Library, manned by knowledgeable staff that can point you towards a treasure trove of information about Oak Island and answer many questions off the top of their heads.

Continuing on Barbee, turn left at Live Oak Drive, and marvel at the windswept oaks. Make a right turn on Womble and walk upon the Oak Island Pier. You can use the pier to photograph the fishing crowd on the pier, and use it as a vantage point to photograph volleyball games to your left, beach activity below, and to create sweeping panoramic shots of the island.

# parks and their oddities

This suggested walk includes William "Bill" Smith Park, Dutchman's Creek Park, and the South Harbor Village Marina. The first leg begins by traveling across the G.V. Barbee Bridge on Long Beach Road to the OKI mainland by car, turning right at the Fish Factory Road light, then left after less than half a mile into "Bill" Smith Park. Park in the first empty space. If you are interested in birds at all, look up at the field lights; oddly enough, you'll likely see an osprey nest during the summer with the osprey chicks as described in the "Air: Birds" subsection. Walk back towards Fish Factory Road and take the disc golf path to your left that begins just before you get back to Fish Factory. You'll walk by the nine holes of the regulation disc golf course with its opportunities to practice stop action and panning of flying discs. It is in a shady natural oasis undisturbed except for "tee boxes" and "holes," wooden bench swings, colorful metal benches, and a half a dozen signs describing the most common local animals. At the seventh hole walk by the house down to Dutchman's Creek and frame sailboats bobbing in the cove. Complete the slightly more than half mile back to your car.

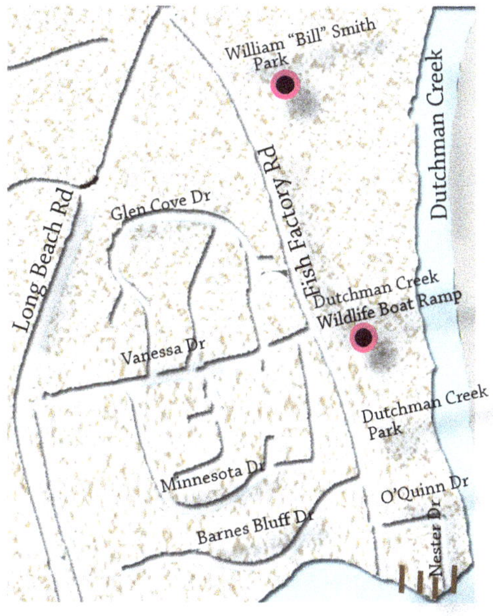


Go back out to Fish Factory Road and turn left; after about half a mile turn left into the Wildlife Boat Ramp. Park at the back right of the lot. Take the path to your right along the beach all the way to the Intracoastal Waterway and then turn right and continue along the beach until you reach the marina. Along the way you will see armies of crabs, boats speeding along Dutchman's Creek, and fishermen in their boats trying to snag some flounder. You will pass a sand bluff colored in the striated colors of the southwest. You will find oysters bedded in the oddest places, most notably at the beach end where they are bedded on the roots of a living live oak tree.

If the tide is fairly low and you don't mind scrambling over a few rocks, you will be at the marina. The grass strip you encounter when you first enter has a wooden horizontal structure that is perfect to stabilize your camera as you take pictures of boats speeding by. Continue passing the boats towards Fish Factory Road. Walk along the road for 100 yards to Dutchman's Creek Park. Enter and walk past the colorful playground on your way to the path above the creek. Turn left and use it to complete this 2 mile loop to your car.

# Ten Shot Thoughts

## *Hold It Steady*

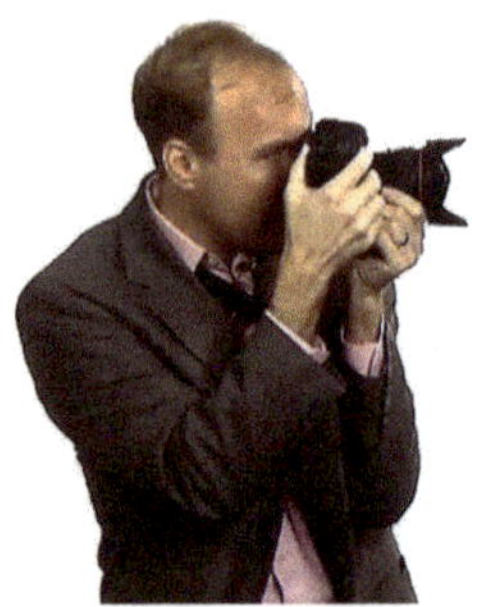

With very few exceptions, good photos are sharp. Unless your camera is steady while the shutter is open, they won't be. As you hold your SLR style camera, keep your right hand steady on the trigger by anchoring your right elbow on your torso. Cradle your lens with your left hand braced, and your arm tight against your body. The principle holds with even the smallest point-and-shoot; your left hand just props the camera's corner instead.

## *Check Your Edges*

One sure way to improve your shots is to use your viewfinder to check the edges of what's in your frame. The picture here is classic. While the brain only saw the billowing pink sunset, the camera faithfully captured the intrusive white architectural element of the beach house. Poles "growing" out of people's heads, thumbs, and flapping camera straps are particularly unfortunate.

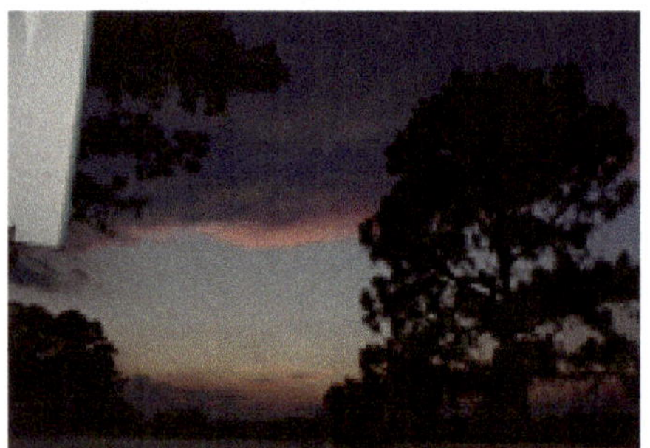

## *Level Your Horizon*

Hold your camera horizontally as if it were a carpenter's level. Sloppiness is not ideal. A little tilt can be corrected with cropping but you will lose a little bit of the image. Using the basic artist rules, including a level horizon, will increase the impact of your photographs. Use the focal point markers in the viewfinder as a visual level.

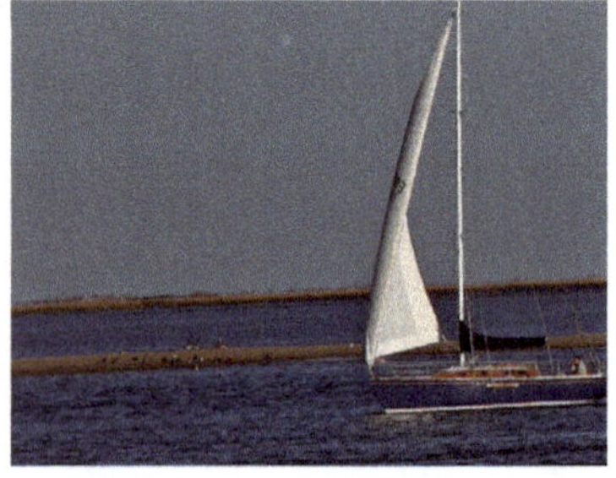

## *Use It or Lose It*

Find a good clean background and use it or "lose" the background you are stuck with. Cluttered backgrounds are a bain of photographers' existences. Oak Island largely spares the photographer that aggravation. The ocean, the dunes, most of the Intracoastal and other inland waters are wonderful backdrops. Use them when you can. Otherwise, set your camera to aperture priority, choose a large aperture (low f-stop of 1/5.6 as a maximum) and keep only your foreground subject in focus. All that matters here, during the Ride the Tide event, is the dog happily being a part of the hoopla, nose to nose with Mayor Betty Wallace, an occurance that begs to be taken using a shallow depth-of-field.

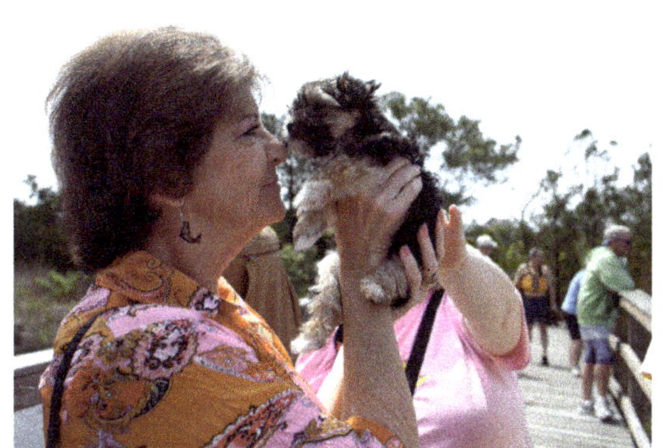

## *Vertical Is Good, Too*

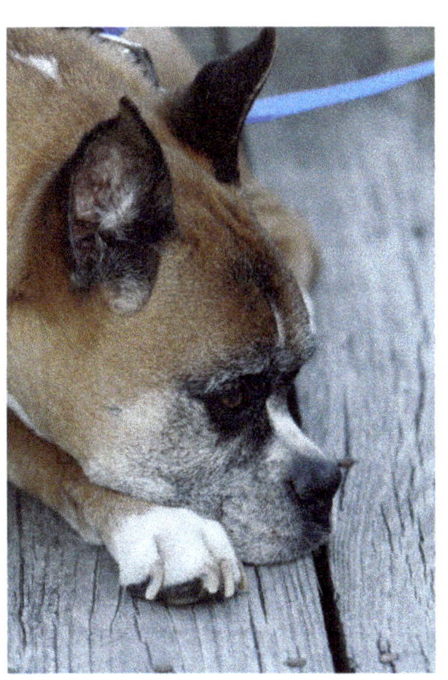

Flip through the pages of a magazine or gaze upon the prints in an art gallery. You will likely find about as many vertical photos as horizontal ones. Casual camera users rarely take a vertical shot, unless in an obvious situation such as in Paris shooting the Eiffel Tower. On OKI the water tower and lighthouse cry for vertical shots. Try taking those as horizontals, instead. Now go out, and take a vertical photo of the pier or a line of pelicans. Portraits are an easy place to start with verticals, but challenge yourself to go vertical and go big.

### *To Flash or Not*

The answer is not. Lots of excellent photography is excellent because of judicious use of artificial light. Essentially, none of it is appropriate for photographing what makes Oak Island special. Artifically-lit nature is the ultimate oxymoron. Figure out how to make your camera *No Flash Complusory.* Ruining a perfectly composed nature shot with unwelcome unnatural light can make you grumpy. Off the island I use artificial light regularly for family and corporate work—just not here or for these pages. There are plenty of sources that describe flash photography if flash dependent events are part of your visit's purpose. If so, read and reactivate.

### *Light*

Getting the right amount of quality light where needed is technically the entirety of photography. The process is straightforward. Choose an ISO appropriate for what you expect. Roughly, set to 100-200 for daylight, 200-400 for gray days and dusk, and 800 plus for after sunset. Use Aperture Priority as your default so you can dial between a small aperture when you want everything in focus and a wide aperture when you want to soft focus the background. Change to shutter priority when you have a really fast-moving subject; think sanderlings if you want to stop action them. For good quality light choose the Golden Hours, dappled clouds, or soft gray skies. That is pretty much all there is to it technically. Everything else that makes a photo good is art.

### *Three-Dimensional*

Rarely is the product of your camera anything but a snapshot unless you apply some technique to make what is a two-dimensional product appear to be of a three-dimensional world. The most common method is to use layers of the grounds--foreground, middle ground, background. Most commonly the subject is framed by the foreground and positioned against a nice background, but the subject can be in any of the three layers. Another possibility is to use line wending towards the top of the photo. Think of footprints in the sand trailing to the horizon. For closeup work, shadows falling towards are often used to create the sense depth you need to add three-dimensionally to the frame.

### *Fill the Frame*

Often less is more. You need no more than these trusting eyes and face to capture the essence of your pet. Discs and only the discs draw the eye in, with their color and the undulating line they form when grouped. They are all that is needed to tell the uninitiated that competitive disc golf is a real sport. Ideally, you fill the frame by focusing your camera on your subject and then move physically towards it, until only essential information is in your viewfinder. Although, sometimes, you will have no choice but to resort to using a long focal length instead.

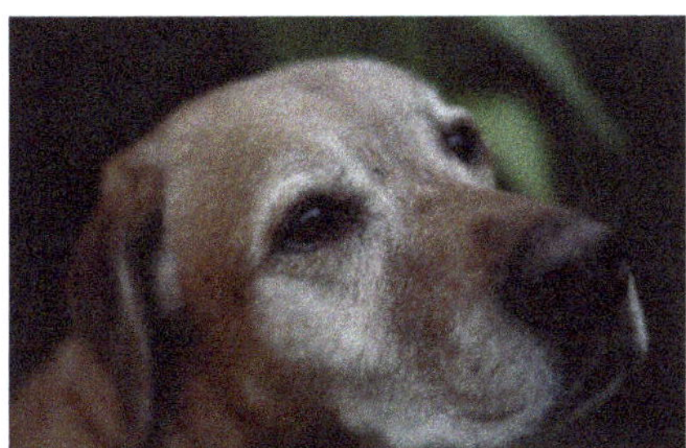

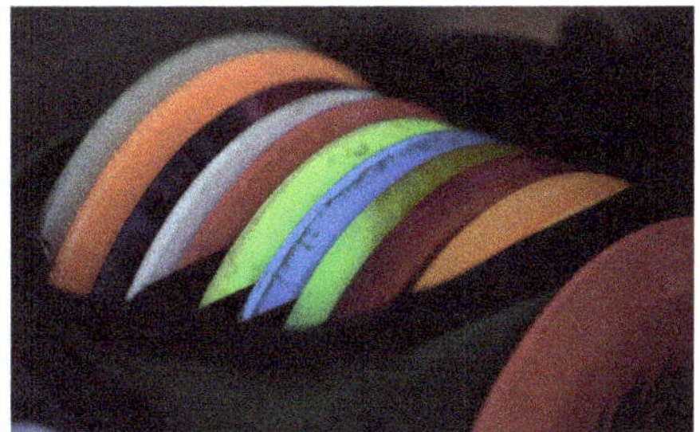

### *Patience and Play*

Good photography requires patience, an adult trait. You will probably have to wait until after a nap to get a smiling, cooperative toddler; you'll sit facing the dune for a good long time before a great line of pelicans flys by; you'll need to wait for low tide to photograph the sand bars. Pushing the limits of patience further, the ibis won't come until late spring, and the baby osprey won't hatch until summer. Then you'll take an inordinate number of frames before, maybe, just maybe, you get one that makes you think "Wow!"

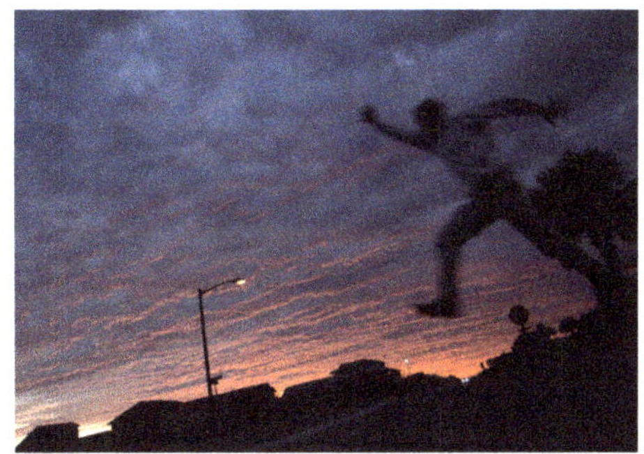

Being a patient adult with your camera can seem like work. Most of us who do photography for a living got hooked in childhood because it was fun. We played with our camera. Play can ignite creativity that is often as important to good photography as technique. Have fun with your camera-in-hand.

# photo fun: scavenger hunts

Photography is a creative outlet. Using your camera to have fun while making art is a way to get exercise, do a family activity and explore this creativity.

Try a photo scavenger hunt! Pick something that is found all over the island such as pelicans, mini versions of the OKI Lighthouse, or the signs of house names. Suggestions for these scavenger hunts are explained in the brown-boxed sidebars of this section.

Consider having a slideshow of the various scavenger hunt images and judge the photos. Base your judging on artistic quality and creativeness and give points for using techniques from the "Focus On" insets. The top 10 images are printed and framed together after your vacation. Now you have a memory and great art you made. For repeat visitors, second-home owners, and residents, you can have the same contest every year and see how you improve from year-to-year.

## Pelicans

Pick a section of 10-20 blocks near where you are staying, and walk around, camera-in-hand. Everytime you come across a pelican—lawn ornament, mailbox decoration, banner flying, mural, fountain, weathervane, house name, stained glass window, or other pelican-themed objects—make a creative photograph. Be mindful of private property.

You can do this as partnerships or individuals and make a points-based game. Every pelican in a photograph gets one point. Limit the number of photographs submitted to say one's best 20 photos. The same pelican only counts once; therefore, if a pelican statue is featured in one photograph and is in the background of another, it only counts once.

Maybe you get three points for each of the different categories of elements you photograph. So, three pelicans as lawn ornaments, six pelicans on various flags, and one stained glass window would be 19 points. Ten points for the number of pelicans and nine points at three points each for the three different categories.

Don't forget about actual, living pelicans!

Each living pelican is worth 10 points. So, a squadron of sex pelicans captured on film would be 60 points. Or maybe you come across a few pilings, each with a pelican on top. A photo with three pelicans would be 30 points.

## Lighthouses

Miniature versions of the OKI Lighthouse are everywhere on the island. Additionally, there are replicas of many different lighthouses and homages to the architectural form of these mighty beacons.

You can make the rules as you see fit. Maybe a copy of the OKI Lighthouse is worth more points than one resembling Old Baldy or the Hatteras Light.

Often, there are multiple mini-lighthouses in one visible stretch. The photographer in you can emerge by practicing layering, depth-of-field, and other "Focus On" tips. I see this leading to a great coffee table book.

You could also go around and take a photo of your children or pet in front of or next to as many lighthouses as you can find. Even try some campy trick photography using perspective to make the kids look like giants.

## House Name Signskrit

Oak Island is laviously speckled with clever house name signs like "1 Salty Sea Dog," "Wishin' I Was Fishin'" and "A Paradise Found." A suggestion for a friends and family vacation activity is to photograph the signs during a walk and then weave them together into a story.

After walking around—absolutely no shooting from your car—to photograph the house signs, take your memory card to a nearby print lab to make 4x6 proofs. Lay the prints out on the carpet or a dining room table. Create a story or just funny phrases. Sometimes you have to use your imagination to fill in the gaps. Don't be afraid to cut out specific words on your print to help with missing verbs. You can read these finished phrases or stories out loud for a chuckle.

If you decide not to make prints, you can use a collage type software or photography editing program to digitally weave the signs' words together. The finished collage can be saved and you can create more. You can order a puzzle of the best collage and piece it together on a rainy day when you are reminiscing about your OKI vacation.

A last signskrit activity is similar to madlibs. One person creates a story, let's say a posterboard leaving blank spaces for the 4x6 prints to go. The other vacationers then use the prints to see if they can figure out the story. Often, a new, bizarre story line will unfold.

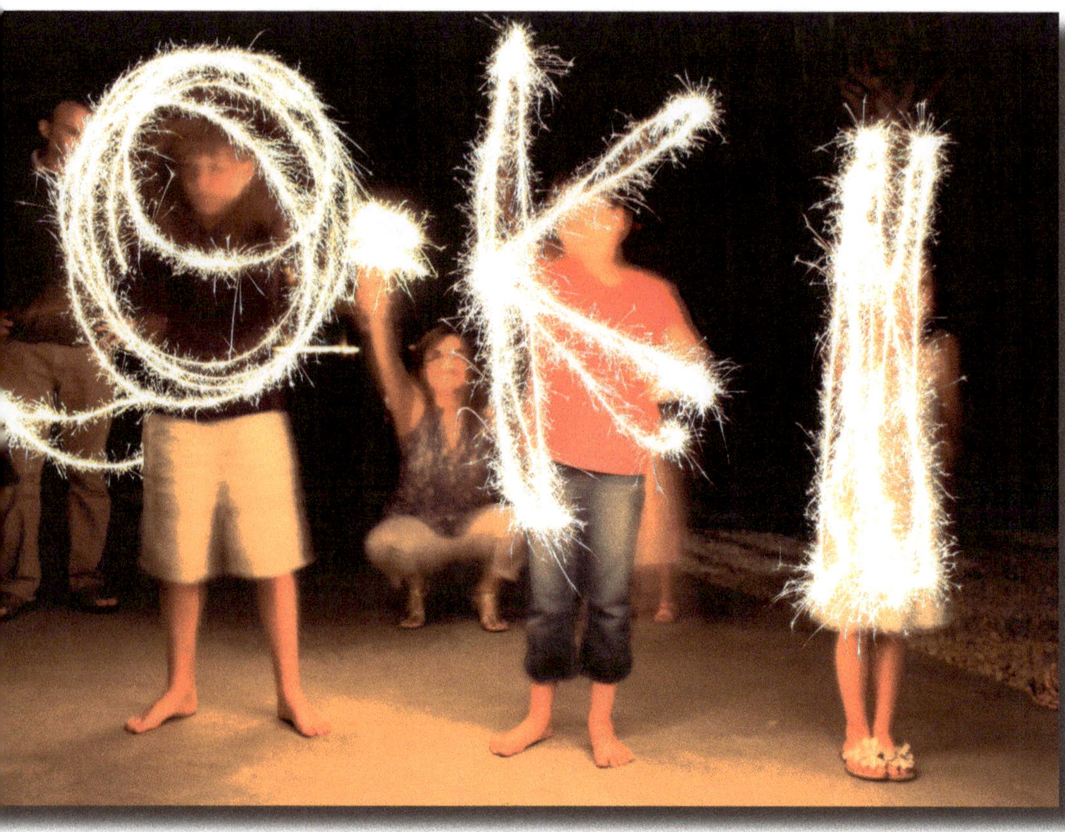

The Fourth of July is a popular time to make a trip to OKI. Aside from shooting the fireworks blasting from the pier, and maybe peeking at the Southport display from across the way, you can safely involve family and friends in painting with light.

Have friends and family "write" in the air with sparklers. Here, children, spell out OKI. The drill for the subjects is: keep the body still except for the arms; "write" your letter with the sparklers in the air. Using a tripod is wise, but you can also prop your camera on a stair, ledge, or even the ground. I use my timer so the camera doesn't have initial shake. The exposure is set to manual, a low ISO like 100 or 200, a long shutter speed of eight to 30 seconds, and an aperture of f/5.6 or f/8.

Prefocus. Get the sparkler lit. While the subjects are getting into place, start the timer. Have the subjects start the motions a second before the shutter is released. Often, the sparklers die before the entire exposure is finished, but it won't really affect your image.

You can use flashlights, glowsticks or candles. Just remember that sparklers are bright, so you might have to set your ISO higher to capture the light if you use glowsticks.

# photo fun: larger than life

Making objects in the foreground look bigger than they are, relative to the background, can create some photo fun. I demostrated this technique with the "giant" white gator that marks the tee box in the golf image on page 69, and then made the fish look like a big catch on page 81.

This technique has lots of imaginative possibilities. The best results will come with an super wide-angle lens just shy of a fisheye. The more depth-of-field you have, the better the trick, too. If everything is sharp, it becomes difficult for the mind to figure out which objects are in the foreground and middle ground. Get as close to filling the frame with the foreground object as possible.

You can also use this effect to create layers and make smaller objects more prominent to tell a story. In the example on this page, my nephew was playing with small plastic dinosaurs on the path between the house and the dunes. It was an interesting scene, with lots of colors and the sun had just set.

The Triceratops, which would fit in the palm of your hand, was about ten feet away from the kids. The low-to-the-ground perpective helps enhance the visual illusion as well. In this case, the shot was made with an iPhone 4s, which has the equivalent of a 35mm focal length.

Aside from the focal length, the distance between the foreground and middle ground elements makes the biggest difference in executing this trick.

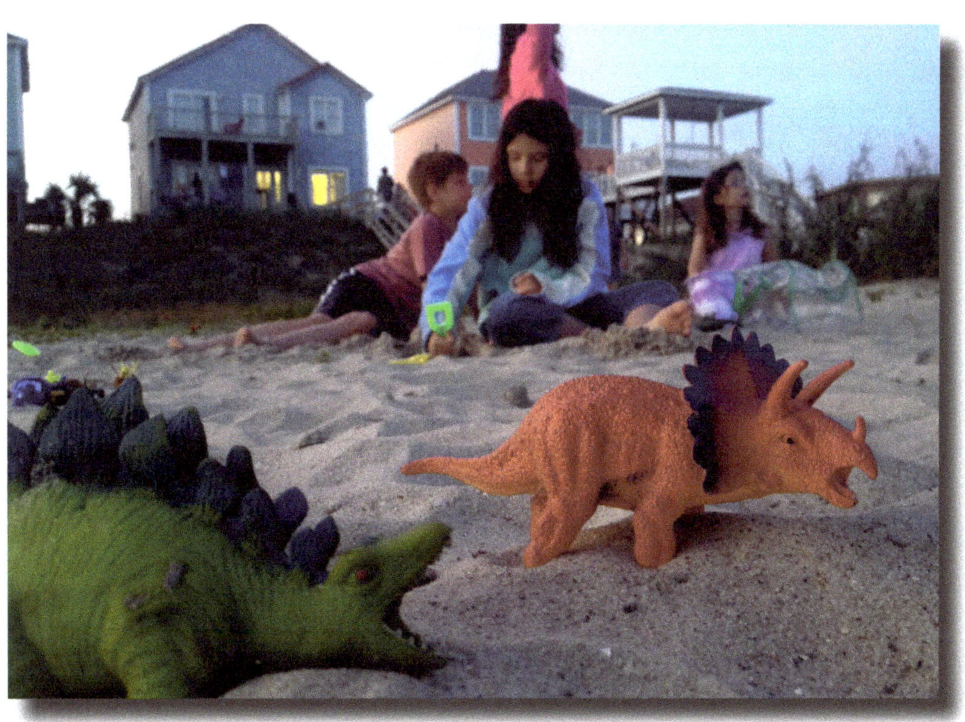

## Fort Caswell

The North Carolina Baptist Assembly at Fort Caswell is located on the site of a fort built originally between 1826-1836. It was in service during the Civil War, largely abandoned until the late 19th century when it was beefed up, and then saw service during WWI and WWII. The Baptist Assembly has been opening it to self-guided tours from the day after Labor Day until the Friday before Memorial Day. The 2013 fee per person was $3.00. Located at the far eastern end of Oak Island, as an historic site, it is impressive.

Leaving aside the history, the location at the mouth of the Elizabeth River, as it flows into Cape Fear, couldn't be better. The views of Bald Head Island, the activity of ships entering Southport, and the birds are impressive.

If you decide to visit, you can call (910) 278-9501 and/or visit www.fortcaswell.com/ to ensure you have the most current info.

## Bubbles

High humidity is the most important ingredient for creating long lasting bubbles. They also need air that is still or moving slowly. Late on a summer day, Oak Island will generally provide both. Shoot with the sun in front of you while having a background in the shade. The sunlight will accentuate the bubble blower, while illuminating the bubbles against the darker background. Longer focal length lenses work best but you can catch the glimmering light off the bubbles with a normal lens as well.

You can buy bubbles at most of OKI's beach or grocery stores and entertain young visitors or the young at heart and make eye-popping photos for a pittance.

## Birds

One or both of two small field guides to birds should suffice for the casual birder. The National Geographic's *Field Guide to Birds: The Carolinas*, edited by Jonathan Alderfer and *Birds of the Carolinas: Field Guide* by Stan Tekiela are excellent. The first is organized by families of birds while the second is organized by coloration.

If you want more, you can use the internet to access the Cornell Lab of Ornithology's website. It has an amazing bird guide that includes bird sounds and videos. It is located at: www.allaboutbirds.org/guide/search

## The Heavens

Photographing planets, stars and celestial objects falls under the category of astrophotography. The same principles apply, but to get great results, there are techniques and equipment that are needed.

True astrophotography is not a genre I am actively exploring. The moon, however, is closer to home.

The moon travels quickly across the sky and is bright. In the case of a full moon at midnight on a clear night, the difference in brightnesss between the moon and objects in the black of night is simply too great to capture without a strobe, modified technique, double exposure, or high dynamic range manipulation.

If you expose for the moon, you cut out all the ambient light on Mother Earth. If you expose for your foreground, the moon becomes blown-out and blurred. You need to be minimally at 1/30 of a second to stop the action of the moon's transit across the sky.

The lit portion of the moon high in the sky, no matter the phase, is a constant exposure equivalent to a noon, clear-day sun on Earth.

One steadfast rule of exposure for high noon is the f/16 rule. The correct exposure at high noon at f/16 is 1/ISO. This rule applies to the lit portion of our moon. If you are photographing a night scene at an ISO 800, the correct exposure for the moon is 1/800 of a second at f/16.

Photographing at times when the light is more balanced such as early twilight, is a possible solution. When the moon is low in the sky, the Earth's atmosphere acts as a filter, cutting out some wavelengths of light such as blue. This means the moon is not as bright and seems red or orange. The Earth's atmosphere acts as a magnifier making the moon appear larger, too.

There is a lot to explain about photographing our heavenly nightscape. If you want to do astrophotography, it is much more difficult, but Oak Island is a good place to try it.

The beach access at 42nd Street West is particularly dark. It is below the highest remaining dune blocking the street light from behind you. During summer turtle season, folks are good about keeping outside beach house lights off to prevent the turtles from becoming confused as they wend their way to the sea; however, the pier lights stay on so boats don't run into them. To the south there is nothing until you get to the Bahamas.

A good place to start for lessons on astrophotography would be the Fayetteville Observer's Backyard Universe by Johnny Horne at: www.fayobserver.com/blogs/features/backyard_universe/

For hands-on learning try the Cape Fear Astronomical Society (CFAS) at: www.capefearastro.org/

Lastly, camera manufacturers such as Canon and Nikon have specific equipment for this market and online resources.

## Group Shots

Large groups of family and friends is often a challenge for even experienced photographers. Oak Island offers an option less prevalent inland. A house built on pilings, as so many are on the island, is a boon to you. Barbecuing is done down below with folks drinking and mingling nearby.

With a minimum of interruption to the ongoing activity, you'll find shooting from above provides an interesting perspective.

Candid shots are often good. If you want to unmistakably document who was there, have everyone face you, and encourage the sage, wit, or poet of the group to offer a toast up toward you.

You should be able to get everyone's face in the picture; height doesn't matter much from above. Eyes looking up are nicely open. In addition, by giving folks something to do with their hands, holding a glass, will make those not knowing what to do look less awkward.

Wedding photographers incorporate this idea as a standard shot. Why? It works.

The elevated house can also provide a shaded canopy of even light at high noon. If you gather your crew and have them under the house, there will not be odd shadows on faces. This light is soft and flattering, too.

## On the Beach

If you find yourself encountering beach phenomenon, such as shown below, that leaves you scratching your head, *How to Read a North Carolina Beach* by Orrin Pilkey of Duke University, William Neal of Grand Valley State University, and Tracy Monegan Rice gives you answers to most of the questions you could imagine asking.

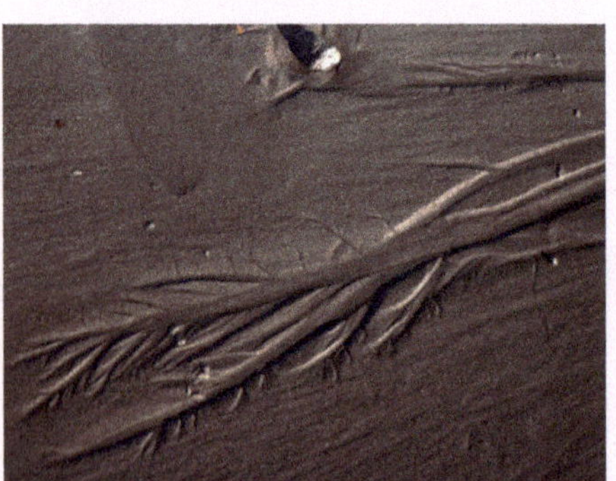

The book's subtitle, *Bubble Holes, Barking Sands, and Rippled Runnels* gives you an inkling of the scope of the material. While it mostly focuses on the earth-science wonders of our North Carolina beaches, it also includes descriptions of the animal life and vegetation that you'll encounter on the dunes, like flotsam washed up from its roots under the sea.

## Events

The State Port Pilot provides the most complete coverage of events on Oak Island. The Pilot is a weekly paper, counted among a dying breed of first-rate privately owned local newspapers. The paper has a long, proud history of keeping the southeastern corner of Brunswick County informed. It is available each Wednesday at local news stands or by subscription.

The Oak Island Recreation Center located on East Oak Island Drive between SE 30th and 31st streets is another excellent source of information. You'll find complete information on the Town of Oak Island managed events, and flyers and handouts available for other local events sponsored by churches, clubs, restaurants, and nonprofits. To learn more visit them or go to: http://www.oakislandnc.com/Departments/Parks-Recreation.aspx

then choose newsletter from the left sidebar.

The Southport Oak Island Chamber of Commerce, which you'll find at 4433 SE Long Beach Rd., is another helpful place to scope out Oak Island events, and to find out about events taking place in nearby towns. Stop by for information on the Southport Oak Island Chamber of Commerce sponsored events and other member interest, or go to:
http://www.southport-oakisland.com

## History

*Long Beach: A North Carolina Town: Its Origin and History* by Wolfgang Furstenau presents a wide sweeping human history of Oak Island from a brief nod to its original Native American population to the book's publication in the mid-90s. At over 300 pages, it's probably not going to be a cover-to-cover beach read; however, it is the most comprehensive guide to the island's history and is replete with interesting tidbits, interspersed with some evocative old photos.

If you want to learn more about the Oak Island Lighthouse, the friends of the lighthouse have a well organized and very informative website. Go to:
www.oakislandlighthouse.org/

Note: If you want to climb the lighthouse, you must give two weeks advance notice to climb the 131 steps to the top platform. These climbs are available year long. Public tours to the first platform offered in the summer months are the only other option.

## Tides

Very often the quality of a Oak Island experience and your photo depend on the tide cycle. You need low tide to jump between the sand bars at The Point. Likewise, oyster beds and wading birds feeding on them are only visible in the inland waters when the tide is low. Conversely, you risk sitting in a kayak, stuck in the sand at low tide in numerous spots on the inland waters.

Fortunately, there are many places on the island to get a tide schedule. The vacation home rental offices, the local bait and tackle shops, and the marinas generally have them.

Note: If you are planning to kayak or fish in the inland waters, the tides will be behind the Oak Island beach schedule by a few minutes to more than an hour depending on the distance the water must travel from the sea. If you have online access, both of the following:
http://www.tides4fishing.com/us/north-carolina/oak-island-atlantic-ocean
and
http://nc.usharbors.com/harbor-guide/oak-island
are good sources with the former providing more complementary information to the tide table but much more, perhaps, than you'll want to absorb on vacation.

## Turtles

Oak Island is a thriving nesting ground for sea turtles, although it has become a popular beach tourist destination. This is largely possible because of the local volunteers who manage the nesting sites. They can only succeed when locals and Oak Island visitors keep distracting lights off during the May through early Fall turtle season, leave the nests undisturbed, and keep refuse off the beaches that can choke the hatchlings.

The basic information about the life cycle of sea turtles and what your responsibilities are to help them can be found at:
http://www.oakislandnc.com/Departments/Parks-Recreation/Sea-Turtle-Program.aspx.

For more detailed information, visit the Ocean Education Center at SE 49th Street in Oak Island during the season.

To see a wonderful video of Oak Island hatchlings that is a real rarity go to You Tube at:
https://www.youtube.com/watch?v=afsBBRbQb_I
(Hatchlings usually emerge after dark making photography impossible without using artificial lighting that can distract the turtles.)

## Fishing

Most people are required to have a North Carolina fishing license to fish in North Carolina's waters. Both the Oak Island ocean waters and the waters within the island were defined as coastal waters when this book went to print. You should only need a coastal waters license and not an inland waters or joint license.

When you fish off the piers, your pier fee also covers the required license. Similarly, boat captains sometimes include the needed fishing license under a group license when you hire a captain and boat or join a fishing outing.

If you are going out otherwise, there are two places on East Oak Island Drive that sell fishing licenses. Island Fishing Center is on the south side at 5721, and Oak Island Sporting Goods is on the north side at 8800.

For information on what kinds of fish are currently biting, Jerry Dilsaver's column in the State Port Pilot or his online info at:

www.captjerry.com/forecast.htm

is the place to most easily get it Oak Island specific information. It comes straight from the pen of an Oak Island resident, who for years spent much of his time as a powerboat captain and now tends toward kayak fishing. He writes the fishing column for the local paper and is a very popular fishing speaker and educator.

A second good source of information is The Fisherman's Post published out of Wilmington. It isn't as Oak Island specific, but does glean information and reports from the Oak Island locals. You can pick up the paper version for free at news stands all over the island or get it online at:

www.fishermanspost.com/category/fishing-reports/southport-oak-island

## Piers

Oak Island has two wooden piers of approximately 900 feet in length. There is a small fee to go out onto each of them, and a charge to fish and rent tackle. You can get the most up to date information about fees, hours, what folks are catching, and check out their webcams from the piers' websites at:

http://www.oakislandpier.com

and

http://www.oceancrestpiernc.com

# authors & acknowledgments

## Author: Kevin Seifert

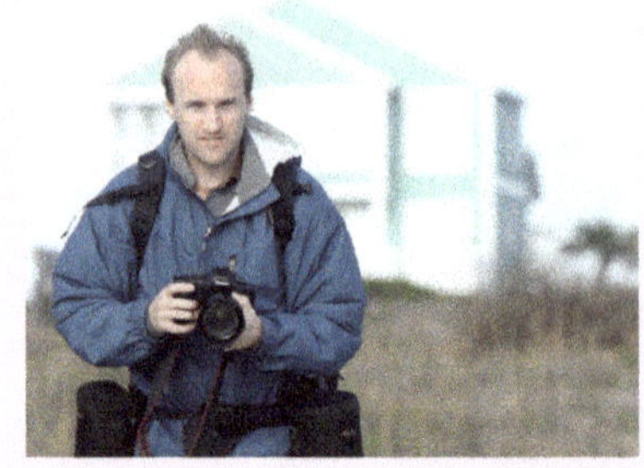

I graduated with honors as a photojournalist from Scripps School of Journalism at Ohio University in 1996, then was a staff photographer at the Kokomo Tribune (Indiana) and The (Durham) Herald-Sun with a focus on sports and event photography.

In 2008, I went full-time as an independent photographer in North Carolina, working mostly in the Triangle and the Southport-Oak Island-Bald Head Island area. I primarily do family, event, and commercial photography as my day job and enjoy it immensely; I do nature photography and artsy stuff, the stuff that motivated me to become a photographer way back in middle school, when I have the chance to get down to Oak Island with my folks. Hence, the collection of photos in this book.

## Author: Linda Seifert

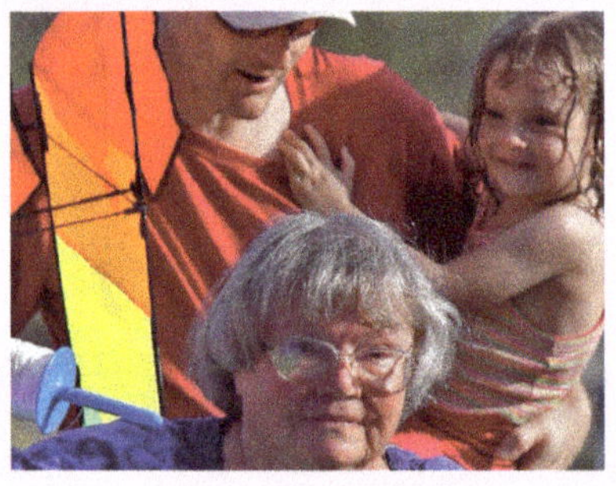

Linda graduated from the University of Wisconsin and was certified to teach English in secondary schools. She took off almost two decades to raise me and my two brothers.

She next spent 20 years working for the National Park Service as a program analyst, with duties that included writing for the Northeast Region website, coordinating and writing the annual accomplishments of the National Park Service's Northeast Region's park and non-park programs, and developing materials used for conference presentations and conference and workshop materials.

Linda is now retired on Oak Island, free to experience its natural and human draws, which were essential to developing the text of this book.

## Photo Credits

The vast majority of the photos you see within these pages are mine. They were taken on Oak Island between 2006 and 2014. With an occasional exception they were taken with either my Canon EOS 5D or with my newer Canon 5D Mark II.

My sister-in-law, Karen Seifert, took two of the photos featured in this book. Karen created the photo of her son, Nick, with the sparkler illuminating his face and the Oak Island teeshirt on page 23. She also framed "Life's A Beach" on page 27. Linda illustrated the text with a handful of photos on what not to do. As examples, there is a what not to do picture of my dad in the salt spray on page 27, and one of my nephew tossing the plastic dragon on page 33. The shots of the Spanish Bayonet in bloom on page 62 and the Mergansers on page 93 are illustrative. In "Ten" Shot Thoughts" you'll find a couple more of her unfortunate examples of what not to do, too.

Of my photos, two notable exceptions are on page 12, the spread was done with my iPhone, and on page 68; Sergio was not on OKI.

## Photo Subjects

I owe special thanks to four young folk who appear in this book. My niece Yzabella, my nephew Nick, and family friends. Emerson and Peyton were cooperative photo subjects. While this book would have been possible without them, it wouldn't have had the "Aaah!" element that only pets and children seem to evoke. Thanks, guys!

I also very much appreciate the unnamed participants in OKI activities who appear in these pages. The enthusiasm shown by them in the photos were a significant part of what made *Discovering Oak Island: Camera-in-Hand* so much fun to photograph and write.

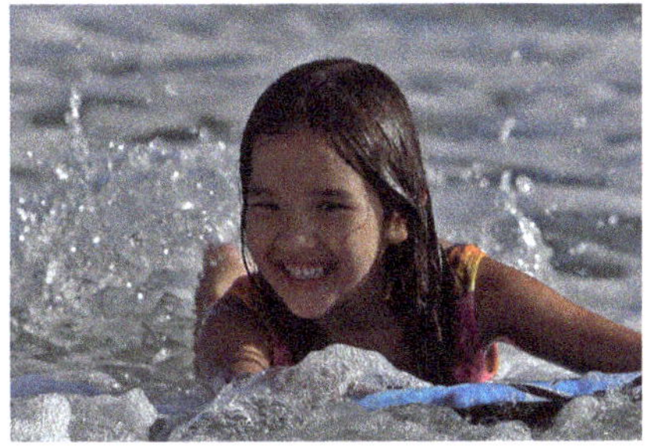

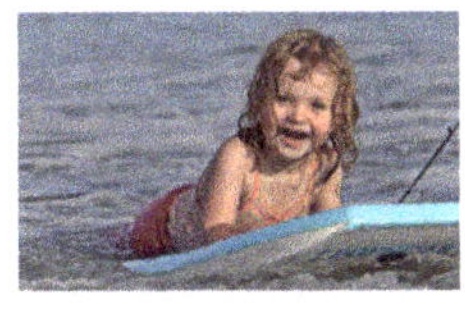

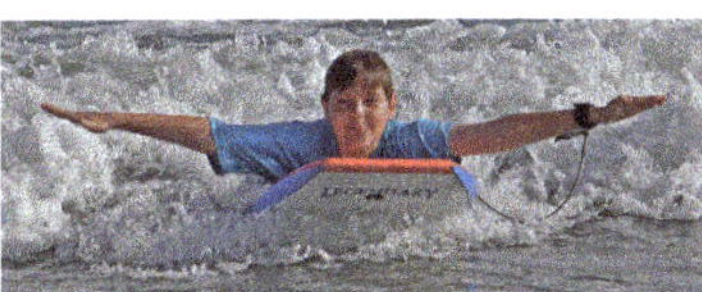

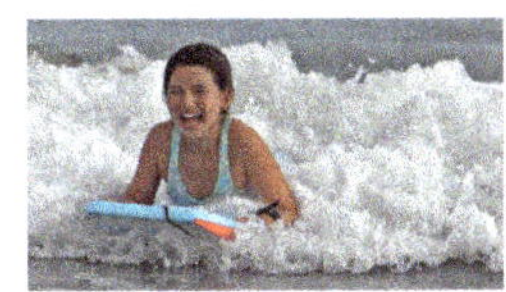

www.ingramcontent.com/pod-product-compliance
Lightning Source LLC
LaVergne TN
LVHW052346100826
845147LV00012B/767

* 9 7 8 1 6 1 1 5 3 1 4 3 5 *